Implementing
Thatcherite
Policies

Public Policy and Management

 Published in association with the
Royal Institute of Public Administration

Series Editor: Professor R.A.W. Rhodes, Department of Politics, University of York.
Series Advisers: Professor Peter Jackson, University of Leicester and Professor Mike Connolly, University of Ulster.

The effectiveness of public policies is a matter of public concern and the efficiency with which policies are put into practice is a continuing problem for governments of all political persuasions. This series contributes to these debates by publishing informed, in-depth and contemporary analyses of public administration, public policy and public management.

The intention is to go beyond the usual textbook approach to the analysis of public policy and management and to encourage authors to move debate about their issue forward. In this sense, each book both describes current thinking and research, and explores future policy directions. Accessibility is a key feature and. as a result, the series will appeal to academics and their students as well as to the informed practitioner.

Current and Forthcoming Titles Include:

Implementing Thatcherite Policies: Audit of an Era
David Marsh and R.A.W. Rhodes (eds)

British Aid and International Trade
O. Morrissey, B. Smith and E. Horesh

Delivering Welfare
T. Butcher

Implementing Thatcherite Policies

Audit of an Era

Edited by
David Marsh and R.A.W. Rhodes

Open University Press
Buckingham · Philadelphia

Open University Press
Celtic Court
22 Ballmoor
Buckingham
MK18 1XW

and
1900 Frost Road, Suite 101
Bristol, PA 19007, USA

First Published 1992

A catalogue record of this book is available from the British Library

Library of Congress Cataloging-in-Publication Data

Implementing Thatcherite policies: audit of an era/edited by David
  Marsh and R.A.W. Rhodes.
       p.   cm. – (Public policy and management series)
  Includes bibliographical references and index.
  ISBN 0-335-15683-5 – ISBN 0-335-15682-7 (pbk.)
  1. Great Britain – Economic policy – 1945- 2. Great Britain – Social
policy – 1979- 3. Great Britain – Politics and government – 1979-
I. Marsh, David, 1946- . II. Rhodes, R.A.W. III. Series.
HC256.6.I45   1992
303.48'4'094109048–dc20   91-44913
                                                                CIP

Typeset by Inforum Typesetting, Portsmouth
Printed in Great Britain by Biddles Ltd, Guildford and King's Lynn

Contents

List of tables and figures

Tables

Figures

Notes on contributors

Jonathan Bradshaw is Professor of Social Policy and Head of the Department of Social Policy and Social Work at the University of York. He was formerly the Director of the Social Policy Research Unit. His main research interests are in poverty, social security policy and living standards. Recent publications include *Child Poverty and Deprivation in the UK* (1990), *Lone Parent Families in the UK* (1991) (with J. Millar). He is currently engaged in research projects on family budgets and a comparative study of child support.

Peter M. Jackson is Professor of Economics and Director of the Public Sector Economics Research at Leicester University; member of the Chartered Institute of Public Finance and Accountancy and Research Director of the Public Finance Foundation. Research interests in public finance, in particular the management, planning and control of public spending. Author of several books and articles including (with C.V. Brown) *Public Sector Economics* (1990).

Peter Kemp is Joseph Rowntree Professor of Housing Policy at the University of York, where he is also Director of the Centre for Housing Policy. His recent publications include *The Future of Private Renting* (1988), *The Private Provision of Rented Housing* (1988) (with T. Crook *et al.*), *The Business Expansion Scheme and Rented Housing* (1991) (with T. Crook *et al.*) and *Housing and Social Policy* (1990) (with D. Chapham and S.J. Smith).

David Marsh is Professor of Government, University of Strathclyde. His recent books include (with M. Read) *Private Member's Bills* (1988) and *The New Politics of British Trade Unions* (1992).

John Peterson is Lecturer in Politics at the University of York and specializes in the politics and policies of the European Community. He has recently published in the *Journal of Common Market Studies, Public Administration,* and *West European Politics.*

R.A.W. Rhodes is Professor of Politics and Head of Department at the University of York. His recent books include *Beyond Westminster and Whitehall* (1988) and (edited with David Marsh) *Policy Networks in British Government* (1992). He is editor of *Public Administration* (the journal of the Royal Institute of Public Administration).

David Samways is a graduate student in the Department of Government at the University of Essex, and is researching on the relationship between scientific knowledge and green political theory.

Martin J. Smith is Lecturer in Politics at the University of Sheffield. His publications include *The Politics of Agricultural Support in Britain* (1990) and *The Changing Labour Party* (co-editor J. Spears, 1992).

Hugh Ward is Senior Lecturer in Government at the University of Essex, and has written widely on rational choice theory, political economy and environmental politics.

Gerald Wistow is Senior Lecturer at the Nuffield Institute, University of Leeds, and Head of the Research and Community Care Units. He has written widely on policy-making, implementation and expenditure issues in the health and personal social services. His current research programme includes studies of the introduction of competition into the supply of health and social care. He is co-author of a large-scale study of the mixed economy of care.

Acknowledgements

This book would not have been possible without the support of The Nuffield Foundation. It funded a workshop held at the University of York, 3–5 January 1991 at which the first drafts of the chapters of this book were discussed. The editors are immensely grateful to the Foundation for its assistance. We are also grateful to Dr Neil Carter (University of York), Professor Andrew Dunsire (University of York), Professor Andrew Gamble (University of Sheffield); Andrew Pendleton (University of Bradford) and Professor Stewart Ransom (University of Birmingham) for their contributions as discussants and chairs. David Marsh would like to thank Hazel Burke for secretarial assistance and Rod Rhodes would like to thank Elspeth Wood for her help in organizing the workshop and preparing the final version of the manuscript; Allison King for compiling the final version of the references, Elizabeth Bomberg for proof reading and compiling the index; and Jeremy Nolan for research assistance. Where appropriate, acknowledgements by the individual authors can be found in their chapters.

1

'Thatcherism': an implementation perspective

R.A.W. Rhodes and David Marsh

Introduction

At one level, Margaret Thatcher's effect on British politics, or at least on British political scientists, is clear; the study of 'Thatcherism' became an academic and journalistic industry. In addition, as Savage and Robins suggest:

> virtually all would agree that the politics and policies which have emerged since 1979 constitute a distinctive phase in the history of post-war British politics. (Savage and Robins 1990: 1)

Unfortunately, in many, if not most, cases such an assessment was not based upon any thorough analysis of the content or effect of 'Thatcherism'.

In an extended review of the literature on Thatcherism we have identified five broad dimensions which observers have concentrated upon when assessing the extent to which British politics has been transformed since 1979: an economic dimension; an electoral dimension; an ideological dimension; a policy style dimension; and a policy agenda dimension (Marsh and Rhodes 1989). Certainly, Thatcherism is variously defined. There is no agreement about the relative importance of the dimensions, or even about which should be included (as no author includes them all). Similarly, there is no agreement on either the content of each dimension or on the relative importance of the varied elements. In sum, Thatcherism is a *diffuse* phenomenon.

It is also clear from our review that a great deal of attention has been given to the electoral, ideological and policy style dimensions. There have been fewer broad analyses of policy and particularly of the extent and effect of policy change.

Some may agree with Marquand's cavalier assertion that the policies are 'small beer' and his view that the paradoxes of policy and the limited degree of change in some policy areas is not very surprising or very interesting (Marquand 1988: 159). However, many others accept the rhetoric of Thatcherism and assume that there have been significant changes in policy without any detailed analysis.

The main aim of this volume is to examine the extent of policy change which occurred in the Thatcher era. There are a number of reasons for this focus. First, as already indicated, this is an area which has received insufficient attention and where previous analyses have been partial or inadequate. Second, it is an important subject. It may be true that 'politics is more fun when it is about people'—(Jenkins 1988: 205) but any competent review of 'Thatcherism' must deal with the content and effect of the Government's policy agenda. Third, policy was important to Mrs Thatcher and her Government, perhaps more important than to some of their predecessors. They claimed to have a distinctive policy agenda and placed a great deal of emphasis on achieving their objectives; the job of government was to govern, to take necessary strong decisive action and force their policies through (see Marsh and Tant 1989). Fourth, it is policies and, in particular, the implementation of policies which affects people, not style. Overall, an emphasis on policy-making and policy outcomes hardly needs justification.

This introduction is divided into three main sections. In the first section we offer a brief review of existing studies of policy in the Thatcher era. The second section introduces the main questions which will be raised in the contributions to this volume and answered in the conclusions. Finally, the third section concentrates upon one of those questions: why was there less change than might have been expected? It highlights a number of implementation problems which face all governments and which, as we shall see, were a major factor in the Thatcher Government's failure to achieve a number of their policy objectives.

The existing literature

The existing literature on the policy agenda has important weaknesses. First, although there is considerable agreement amongst commentators that there is a distinctive policy agenda (see, for example, Kavanagh 1987: ch. 8; Gamble 1988: ch. 4 and 222–36; Jessop et al. 1988: 90–2; and Savage and Robins 1990: 1), there is less agreement about the items on the agenda. For example, Kavanagh (1987: 212) itemizes welfare, privatization, industrial relations, and the economy whereas Gamble (1988: ch. 4) reviews the economy, trade unions, the control of public expenditure, foreign affairs and defence, local government, public order and security.

Second, the coverage of the policy literature is uneven. The first parliament's legislation has been explored in some detail (Bell 1985; and Jackson 1985a). The second parliament's legislation has not been systematically reviewed, except as part of overall assessments of a decade of Thatcherite policy. Coverage of the third parliament's legislation is, as yet, speculative in that policy implementation is in its early stages and commentators focus on the likely, as distinct from actual, effects (see, for example, Stewart and Stoker 1989).

The attempts to evaluate a decade of policy fail because of the brevity and superficiality of the individual case studies. For example, Kavanagh and Seldon (1989) examine changes in both institutions and policies since 1979. Unfortunately, the book has no introduction and no conclusion, so there is no overall assessment of the extent of policy change, or analysis of the reasons for greater policy change in some policy areas than others.

Savage and Robins (1990) do not make the same mistakes but the analysis of policy change is cursory, occupying a mere four pages. The editors offer a three-fold classification of policy areas: areas where there has been radical transformation, areas with some change, and areas marked by policy continuity (p. 245). In doing so, they acknowledge the crucial point that there was more change in some areas than others. However, they make no attempt to explain such variation.

The individual contributions to the Savage and Robins volume provide more or less good summaries of the changes which have occurred in the policy areas since 1979 but none is really good because of the limited space available to contributors. To take one example, David Farnham's chapter on industrial relations is sound on the legislative changes which have occurred. However, it fails to examine the extent to which the legislation has been used by employers and, even more significantly, there is no consideration of the limited extent to which shopfloor industrial relations has actually changed, yet this is the key theme of all the industrial relations literature as distinct from the political science material.

Of course one might say that, in limited space, authors can only cover so much; a fair point but the defence is misguided. The restricted treatment of the policy areas introduces a clear bias into the analysis. There is an unambiguous tendency to overestimate the Thatcher effect because the contributions concentate upon legislative change rather than upon changes in policy outcomes. In effect, both the individual contributions and Savage and Robins' brief overview ignore the major implementation problems experienced by the Government in most policy areas.

Finally, the policy literature is diffuse. A bibliographical search by Rhodes et al. (1992) found a substantial literature, the bulk of which had been written not by political scientists but by specialists in several policy areas. Only a fraction of this literature is known to political scientists. Even more revealing, there are few attempts to compare policy areas.

Inadequate though it may be, the existing literature on the policy agenda suggests three tentative conclusions. First, that there is no constant set of Thatcherite policies. Second, the relative priority accorded to particular policies did not remain the same over the decade. Third, it cannot be assumed that consistent policies were pursued. Both priority and consistency remain matters for investigation, not assumption. Finally, there has been no systematic attempt to explain the variations in policy success/failure during the 1980s. Overall, we would accept that Thatcherite policies were to some extent distinctive and effective. However, the key point is to demonstrate distinctiveness and effectiveness in practice as well as in theory.

The key questions

In order to assess the extent of policy change in the 1980s, it is necessary to answer three key questions.

1 How much change occurred in the Thatcher era?
2 To what extent did this policy change result from a distinct policy agenda and legislative programme which was pursued by the Thatcher Government?
3 Why did more change occur in some policy areas than in others and, in particular, why was there less change than might have been expected?

What do we mean by 'policy change'?

For the electorate, 'policy change' is likely to be the innovative policies contained in the party manifestos. For busy journalists, policy change is the Queen's Speech and the legislation going through parliament that session. However, the hoary old maxim, 'there's many a slip 'twixt cup and lip' is particularly apposite in this context. White papers and statutes are statements of intent. Legislation is not the end of the policy process, merely a step en route. For example, Hogwood (1987: 12) identifies the following stages to the policy process: agenda setting, processing of issues, selection of option, legitimation of option, allocation of resources to policy, implementation, adjudication, impact and its evaluation. Legislation occurs at the stage of legitimation of option or roughly half way through the policy process. The impact of a policy can differ markedly from legislative intent and it is crucial to include the stages of implementation and impact in any assessment of policy change. The case studies in this book are not concerned solely with statements of objectives or the enactment of statutes but with the actual outcomes of such legislation. We explore both intentions *and* outcomes.

Focusing upon outcomes raises a second important distinction: between intended and unintended consequences. A policy may not have the intended outcome, for example new motorways may not remove traffic congestion. In addition it may have a number of unintended outcomes, for instance higher levels of CO_2 emission because of higher traffic volume. It is as important to explore intended and unintended consequences as it is to compare outcomes with intentions.

How much change occurred in the 1980s?

We make no assumptions about the size of policy changes. It is not our intention to characterize policy initiatives in the 1980s as 'incremental'

(Lindblom 1988) with all the attendant problems of distinguishing incremental change (or change at the margin) from major transformations. We employ the Government's own yardstick for the scale and direction of change and we focus on the comparison of policy areas. In addition, and inevitably given the previous discussion, we are concerned about the extent of legislative change and the extent of change in policy outcomes.

The emphasis on comparison is important. Existing policy implementation studies of the 1980s do not systematically compare areas. Such comparison is essential if we are to assess the degree of change because any such assessment will be relative to: prior policy experience; the Government's stated intentions; the actual degree of change compared to both stated intentions and the extent of change in other policy areas. Moreover, the comparison must encompass the whole of the 1980s. Too often the analysis of policy looks at the short-term effects of legislation. However, we know that it takes from five to ten years for the effects of a policy to emerge. Any comparisons must take place over time, therefore, and the decade of the 1980s is a defensible period with one proviso. Several significant policies were enacted after 1987 (e.g. internal markets in the National Health Service). Sufficient time has not yet elapsed for a full evaluation of these policy changes. Necessarily, therefore, the analysis of such policies will be speculative. However, we have concentrated upon policies where the full range of effects have had time to emerge.

Why change?

Even if we assume that there has been a significant degree of change in several policy areas, we still do not know how much of this change can be attributed to Thatcherite policies. Once again, we need to return to the distinction made earlier between legislative change and change in policy outcomes. In the first instance we need to identify the extent to which New Right ideology, party programmes and election manifestos were the key sources of legislation. The existing literature on policy-making in the 1980s suggests that demographic factors, economic factors and political considerations also provided important stimuli to the introduction of legislation. In contrast, the literature on Thatcherism plays down the importance of interest groups; yet in previous administrations such groups played a key role in policy formation. Obviously legislation has an important influence on policy outcomes, but it is not the only influence. Other factors may constrain or prevent the Government's achieving its policy objectives, such as economic and political crises. This volume deals with the relative influence of Thatcherism at *both* stages of the policy process. The aim is to identify the distinctive contribution of Thatcherism to policy change while also offering a better understanding of the process of policy innovation. More specifically, a central hypothesis to be explored throughout the remainder of this book is that, even where there was a significant degree of change, Thatcherite policies were only one of the factors relevant to understanding the change.

Continuity rather than change

The second key hypothesis to be explored in the case studies is that an imple-mentation perspective explains the failure of Thatcherite policy innovations. A brief review of the implementation literature will enable us to restate this hypothesis in a more precise and less provocative form.

The most influential book on implementation in recent times has been Pressman and Wildavsky (1984). They define implementation as: 'a process of interaction between the setting of goals and actions geared to achieving them.' The starting point is a policy. 'Policies imply theories . . . a chain of causation between initial conditions and future consequences. If X then Y.' Conse-quently, implementation is 'the ability to forge subsequent links in the causal chain so as to obtain the desired results.' (All quotations from the expanded third edition, 1984: xxiii.) This approach has been characterized as the top-down model of implementation. As Barrett and Fudge (1981: 10–13) argue, Pressman and Wildavsky see implementation as a process of 'putting policy . . . into effect', a process which involves the following conditions:

1 knowing what you want to do;
2 the availability of the required resources;
3 the ability to marshal and control these resources to achieve the desired end;
4 if others are to carry out the tasks, communicating what is wanted and controlling their performance.

The top–down approach, also known as the rational or systems model of implementation (Elmore 1978), has been criticized on a variety of grounds. First, too much attention is given to the objectives and strategies of central actors and, consequently, the key roles played by other actors in the implemen-tation process are ignored. Second, the conditions necessary for effective im-plementation are unrealistic. For example, there is always a scarcity of resources. Third, discretion is inevitable in all organizations in order to cope with uncertainty. The activities of street-level bureaucrats (e.g. social worker, police) will thus generate 'control deficits' as they develop coping mechanisms to deal with the pressures upon them. Fourth, the top–down model focuses on central objectives and ignores not only the adaptive strategies of street-level bureaucrats but also the unintended consequences of government action. Fifth, some policies do not have, and have never had, explicit objectives. They grow and evolve over considerable periods of time through the interactions of a multiplicity of actors. There is no obvious yardstick with which to assess their outcomes. Finally, the theoretical distinction between policy formulation and policy implementation cannot be sustained in practice because policies are made and remade in the process of implementation. (This list of criticisms has been summarized from: Lipsky 1978; Barrett and Fudge 1981; Elmore 1982; Hjern and Hull 1982; Hogwood and Gunn 1984; and Sabatier 1986a).

The bottom-up model seeks to avoid these problems by treating imple-mentation as a political rather than a managerial problem. For example, the basic unit of analysis in Barrett and Fudge's (1981) account of implementation is a service delivery network, its actors and their interactions. Implementation is seen as a negotiating process in which individual actors pursue their disparate objectives employing multiple strategies. Compliance with central objectives is an inappropriate yardstick of success and failure. They adopt an action perspective, focusing on the perceptions of individual actors, the organizations within which they work and the factors which influence behaviour. The emphasis is placed on the multiplicity and complexity of linkages, the problem of control and co-ordination and the management of conflict and consensus.

Elmore (1978) identifies three variants of the bottom-up model of implementation: *bureaucratic process, organization development* and *conflict and bargaining*. The bureaucratic process model focuses on the interaction within organizations between routines and discretion. Its major propositions are that discretion is an inevitable product of organizational specialization and limits control and that individuals develop coping mechanisms to reduce pressure at the coal face (e.g. Lipsky 1978).

The organization development model focuses on the socio-psychological needs of the individual and the ways in which they conflict with organizational imperatives. Effective implementation requires that work satisfies an individual's need for autonomy and control. Its major propositions are that: decision-making should be devolved, organizational structure should be task oriented and there should be open communication without penalties (e.g. Argyris 1962).

The conflict and bargaining model sees organizations as arenas of conflict in which individuals and groups compete for relative advantage in the exercise of power and the allocation of scarce resources. Implementation is a process; a complex series of bargained decisions reflecting the preferences and resources of the participants (e.g. Bardach 1977).

The bottom-up approach also has its defects. First, it overestimates the discretion of street-level bureaucrats who are subject to legal, financial and organizational constraints. Such constraints may not determine behaviour but they set important parameters upon discretion. Second, the perceptions of actors are identified but not explained. What factors influence, directly and indirectly, individual actors' access to, and their perceptions of the bargaining game. Similarly, it is important to explain the origins of the rules to the bargaining game, the distribution of resources between the participants and the range of strategies available to each participant. Third, as Sabatier (1986a: 35–6) has pointed out, the advocates of the bottom-up model are not primarily concerned with implementation, with whether or not a decision is carried out, but 'with understanding actor interaction in a specific policy sector'. Finally, the criticisms of the top-down model are overstated. Some policies do have clear objectives and it is important to find out whether or not these objectives were realized. The distinction between formulation and implementation is not just a theoretical nicety, because policy decisions are made which do structure the decision-making environment of local actors. The ubiquity of interaction does not invalidate the distinction.

Whilst the dichotomy between top-down and bottom-up approaches is a useful device for summarizing the literature on implementation, like many other dichotomies, it courts the danger of simplifying to the point of inaccuracy. It is more important to select the approach best suited to the problem at hand. The concern in this volume is not with identifying local level implementation structures and understanding the patterns of interaction in a specific policy sector. Rather we want to explain the varying degrees of success and failure in relation to central policy decisions. For this task the rational, or top-down, model of implementation is particularly well suited because it is clear that the Conservative Government of the 1980s adopted the same model. At the outset, Mrs Thatcher intended to operate a 'conviction government'. More specifically, she was determined not to waste time on internal arguments over policy-making; her aim was to set objectives, and to force them through against opposition by holding to her position. This view was well summed-up in the two epithets which characterized the early years of Mrs Thatcher's Prime Ministership: there is no alternative; and the lady's not for turning.

Any number of analyses have pointed to this feature of 'Thatcherism'. Bulpitt (1986: 34) argues that the Conservative Government was searching for an image of 'governing competence, through a reconstruction of . . . traditional central authority'. Similarly, Kavanagh (1987: 9) claims that Mrs Thatcher produced: 'a set of policies designed to produce a strong state and a government strong enough to resist the selfish claims of interest groups'. As a final example, Ivor Crewe (1988: 45) persuasively argues that Mrs Thatcher had 'a warrior style – setting objectives, leading from the front, confronting problems, holding her position'.

The overall picture is unambiguous. The new Government had clear policy objectives, it was a radical, committed Government, consultation in policy-making would at best delay, and at worse defuse, necessary change. So, legislation should be pushed through with limited consultation before, during and after its passage.

In effect, the Government operated with a top-down process model of policy-making in which it could, and should: set the policy agenda and choose the policy options, unencumbered by the constraints provided by interest groups; pass the legislation without amendment, given its majority in Parliament; and control the implementation process to ensure that its objectives were attained (cf. Hogwood: 1987).

The argument can be stated more formally. The rational model of implementation involves the following assumptions (paraphrasing Elmore 1978):

1 organizations act as coordinated units;
2 policy is clearly and precisely expressed;
3 there is a shared understanding of policy;
4 there is hierarchic control of the implementation process.

The analysis of implementation begins, therefore, with a policy decision by the centre and the assumption that there is a stated objective for this decision. Thereafter the following questions need to be posed (see Mazmanian and Sabatier 1986a; and Sabatier 1989):

1 To what extent were the actions of the implementors consistent with the objectives stated by central government?
2 Were the objectives successfully attained? Over what period of time?
3 What factors affected the actual policy outcome?
4 To what extent, and how, was policy reformulated in the light of experience?

Each contributor to this volume has addressed these questions for his policy area.

There are now numerous studies on the 'implementation gap' which have identified the constraints on the top-down model. Indeed, the bottom-up model identifies several possible causes of policy failure. The constraints have been summarized by Sabatier (1986a: 23–4) as follows:

1 ambiguous and inconsistent objectives;
2 inadequate causal theory;
3 failure of the implementation process to win compliance because of:
   (a) inadequate resources
   (b) inappropriate policy instruments;
4 the discretion of street-level bureaucrats and the recalcitrance of the implementing officials;
5 lack of support from the affected interest groups and relevant government agencies; and
6 unstable and uncertain socioeconomic contexts which undermine either political support and/or the causal theory.

It is now possible to reformulate the implementation perspective; policy failure is a product of the foregoing six constraints. Stated in this form, the propositions are too bald. Obviously *all* governments are subject to these constraints and the vast majority of policies fail to some extent. However, the Conservative Government of the 1980s deliberately adopted a top-down model and either failed to recognize, or chose to ignore, the known conditions for effective implementation in its determination to impose its preferred policies. It is legitimate to hypothesize that Conservative policy failure is explained by this *self-inflicted* implementation gap. Implementation problems may be common to all governments but they were uniquely severe for the Conservative Government because it insisted on an inappropriate (and ill-considered) model of implementation.

The implementation perspective suggests an explanation for policy failure in particular policy areas. It also leads to a far more important conclusion. Substantial claims have been made by and for the Thatcher Government: for example, that the 1980s witnessed an 'economic miracle'. It is widely seen as revolutionary, destroying the postwar consensus, turning back the frontiers of the state and initiating a brand new policy agenda. But what was the overall level of success of the Thatcher Government? We will of course return to this question in the final chapter in the light of the case studies. However, the evidence will suggest that, at best, the Government had a mixed record of success and that its achievements fell well below its expectations. The implementation perspective suggests an explanation for this state of affairs: Government policy was undermined by its approach to implementation. The top-down model assumes omnipotent and omnicompetent governments. The 1980s demonstrated, yet again, the fallibility of governments, even those set on returning to the minimalist state.

The case studies

At this juncture we simply introduce the case studies. The final chapter will assess the lessons to be learnt from the policy successes and failures of the 1980s and offer an explanation of the variable incidence of change.

The case studies fall into three broad groupings, following Savage and Robins (1990). Chapters 2–5 cover policy areas characterized by radical change: economic policy, industrial relations, local government and housing. Chapters 6–7 cover policy areas with the potential for radical change: social security, and the national health services. Chapters 8–10 cover policy areas marked by continuity of policy: the environment, agriculture, and the European Community.

This selection also covers the policy areas accorded priority by the Government; for example management of the economy, reform of the welfare state. There is one important exception; we do not cover the privatization programme. Not only has this policy area been intensively studied but Marsh (1991) provides an account which directly parallels the analysis in the following chapters. We have drawn upon this article in the conclusions.

We did not rely on a single criterion for the choice of case studies. To ensure that we had a broad coverage, we selected a policy area from each functional category of public expenditure, with the exception of education, libraries and arts.

No selection of case studies is ever perfect, but the three criteria of degree of change, political priority, and range of coverage do provide a clear rationale for our selection. One other consideration influenced the editors. We wanted the case studies to present in-depth analyses of the policy areas and not skate over complex issues in a few pages. Inevitably, this decision restricted the number of policy areas which could be included.

Finally, in Chapter 11, we review the evidence from the case studies, return to the three questions which have substantially structured this introduction and offer an explanation rooted in implementation theory for the significant degree of policy variation between policy areas.

2

Economic policy

Peter M. Jackson

Many commentators have argued that, as far as the design of UK macro-economic policy was concerned, the election of the Thatcher Government in 1979 represented a break with the past. In this vein, Sir Geoffrey Howe, Margaret Thatcher's first Chancellor of the Exchequer, and his deputy Nigel Lawson, co-ordinated a new macroeconomic strategy, worked out in advance in various Conservative Party think tanks, which was a mixture of financial planning, basic monetarism and supply-side economics (see Howe *et al.* 1977).

Unfortunately, there is a danger that, using hindsight, we can attribute more coherence and consistency to the strategy than in fact existed. Certainly, some observers regard the whole exercise as an experiment. Little was known about the optimal sequence in which the old economic institutions, rules and conventions should be replaced by new ones. As such, ad hocery, incremental-ism and rapid learning and reaction when things went wrong were inevitable. From this perspective, it can be argued, with considerable justification, that the macroeconomic strategy evolved; it did not reflect the implementation of a well-articulated design. Moreover, as time passed, new policies, which did not appear in the original 1979 Manifesto, were tacked on. This was particularly true of the privatization programme which was to become a central feature of the 1983 and 1987 manifestos.

Even authors generally sympathetic to Mrs Thatcher's policies have accepted the absence of a grand strategy. In this vein, David Howell, one of Mrs Thatcher's early speech writers and subsequently a cabinet member, argues:

47

She just knew what she didn't like and that was the Trades Union hegemony and high public spending. She had instincts but no articulation of a clear vision. She was like a housewife wanting to stride into an ill kept, dusty house, determined to clean it up. (*Sunday Telegraph,* 23 April 1984: 14)

Similarly, Professor Patrick Minford has characterized Mrs Thatcher as a 'political entrepreneur', without any grand master design, but with 'finely honed instincts for her trade' (Minford 1988). As a political entrepreneur she sold policies to the electorate. In this she was successful for a while.

The revolution in economic policy

What then was the nature of the Thatcher economic 'revolution' and in what sense was it a break with the past? Was it as some commentators have suggested an end of the postwar Keynesian democratic consensus? The features of the new macroeconomic strategy can be listed as follows:

1 a rejection of Keynesian short-run demand management; a rejection of the idea of being able to fine tune the economy by manipulating policy instruments that affect demand;
2 emphasis upon providing medium-term stability in the private sector's (especially the company's) planning environment;
3 emphasis upon promoting economic growth by introducing supply-side policies that would free up markets, expand choice and increase productivity, by reducing the distorting effects of unnecessary regulations;
4 emphasis upon financial management and control of the money supply (i.e. sound monetary policies) to create a zero rate of inflation and the incentives for investment and growth;
5 a reduction of public expenditure and thus a rolling back of the frontiers of the State, thereby giving individuals greater freedom over their private spending plans through tax reductions; tax reductions were also to contribute to supply-side management by creating incentives that would increase work effort, job search, savings and risk taking (i.e. promoting entrepreneurship and the enterprise culture) and therefore generally contributing to productivity improvements;
6 abandonment of price controls and incomes policies.

Underpinning the package outlined above was the general belief that the primary target of economic policy had to be the combating of inflation. This theme ran consistently through many of Mrs Thatcher's early speeches. In a lecture at Roosevelt University in Chicago, in 1975, she said:

Inflation is a pernicious evil capable of destroying any society . . . when money can no longer be counted on to act as a store of value, savings and investment are undermined, the basis of contracts is distorted. (Cooke 1989: 1)

36

At the Conservative Summer School, in 1979, she said:

> We see it as a first duty of responsible government to re-establish sound
> money and to squeeze inflation out of the system . . . One of the great
> curses of inflation is that the whole nation spends more of its time
> wrestling with the changing value of money, and arguing about the
> distributions of income and wealth than it devotes to productive effort
> and creative management . . . There is no sound foundation for steady
> expansion unless the country is winning the fight against inflation.
> (Cooke 1989: 91)

In 1980 she repeated:

> Our prime economic objective – the defeat of inflation. Inflation de-
> stroys nations and societies as surely as invading armies do. Inflation is the
> parent of unemployment. It is the unseen robber of those who have
> saved. (Cooke 1989: 113)

To place the combating of inflation as the *primary* objective of economic
policy was to depart from the postwar Keynesian consensus for which the fight
against unemployment had been the principal policy objective. Economists
have long argued there is a trade-off between inflation and unemployment;
Mrs Thatcher, however, shifted the terms of that trade-off. Keynesians generally regarded the social and private costs of unemployment to be considerably
greater than those costs associated with inflation. They weighted, therefore,
their policies more heavily towards reducing unemployment whilst accepting a
tolerable rate of inflation. Part of the Thatcher 'revolution' was to turn this on
its head. The pain and cost of unemployment were regarded as a reasonable
price to pay for bringing down the rate of inflation – but, of course, it was to be
an unequally distributed pain, those who were at greatest risk from the pain of
unemployment were often the least advantaged in society.

The reduction of unemployment by direct intervention in the economy
was not seen by the 1979 Conservative Government to be the business of
government. The advocates of this view-point asserted that all a government
can do is to create the climate for enterprise, for job creation and for economic
growth. This was to be achieved by: reducing inflation through sound monetary policies; creating incentives through lower taxation and less interference
by government; and implementing supply-side policies that would, amongst
other things, reduce government regulations.

All of this adds up to a firm belief in the power of the market economy to
increase social welfare. The lineage of this view is readily found in the works of
Hayek (1944) and Friedman (1969). The adoption of this kind of thinking,
which has its foundations in the long-standing libertarian tradition, was itself a
revolution because it required 'Thatcherism' to turn its back on much of the
Conservative Party's own thinking, teaching, and long-established beliefs. A
tension grew up between the libertarian Thatcherite approach and the more
traditional Conservative approach.

Monetary
policy
Vs
Fiscal
policy

The economic policy revolution also reversed the relationship between fiscal and monetary policies giving primary importance to the latter. The postwar practice by which fiscal policy (spending and taxation decisions) was set first and monetary policy (especially interest rates) then accommodated it was reversed with money-supply targets established first and fiscal policy (especially the public sector borrowing requirement – PSBR) adjusted to help fulfil those targets.

The philosophy of the medium-term financial strategy (MTFS) was set out in the Financial Statement and Budget Report 1980/81:

QUOTE.
(4)

> It is not the intention to achieve this reduction in monetary growth by excessive reliance on interest rates. The consequences of the high level of public sector borrowing has been high nominal interest rates and greater financing problems for the private sector. If interest rates are to be brought down to acceptable levels the PSBR must be substantially reduced as a proportion of GDP over the next few years.   69

Control of the PSBR was, therefore, not only necessary if the Government was to achieve its money supply targets, it was also required to bring down interest rates which, commentators such as Bacon and Eltis (1978) and Minford (1980) have argued, crowd out private investment – this view has been challenged by, amongst others, Jackson (1990a).

Full details of the MTFS are found in Chancellor Nigel Lawson's 1984 Mais lecture (see *Economic Trends* 1985). The following gives a flavour of the thinking behind the MTFS:

> Our first priority was the reduction of inflation. That is the first duty of government in the economic sphere and can be achieved only by creating and sustaining sound financial conditions. That does not mean holding the economy back. It means guaranteeing that there is sufficient growth in the money supply to sustain the economy's natural growth potential while not pumping more cash into the economy than the natural growth rate justifies. (Lawson 1985)

Another departure from the past was that the MTFS emphasized the importance of the *medium* term. Major decisions, buying a house, setting wages and investing in physical capital are sensitive to decision makers' expectations of what will happen to inflation over the next few years (the medium term). Thus, by announcing money supply targets over the next five years the Government was signalling to private sector decision-makers its commitment to a reduction in inflation rates. This is the basis of the famous no 'U' turn and 'there is no alternative' (TINA) epithets. A government essentially enters into a social contract with the private sector which guarantees that no matter what happens to the economy it will not falter from its resolve to bring down the rate of inflation. Thus, private sector decison-makers, when, for example, setting wages, cannot expect that if they settle at too high a rate and unemployment rises then the Government will, at the eleventh hour, reverse its policies and bail them out. Announcing in advance that there will be no 'U' turns, that there are no alternatives, is a signal to the private sector to discipline its decisions and to get their decision-making right. This was important if the Government policy over the medium term was to be 'credible'.

The MTFS was strengthened by policies which were designed to reduce the power of trades unions, to make the labour market more competitive and more flexible, which would moderate wage demands and thereby set the conditions for full employment. Successive legislation was introduced in 1980, 1982 and 1984 which was aimed at weakening the closed shop, curtailing trade union immunities by narrowing the definition of a trade dispute and restricting the use of secondary picketing (see Chapter 3 for more details).

The Thatcher administration of the 1980s thus made a number of substantial changes to the conduct of macroeconomic policy. The objectives of policy became the elimination of inflation rather than unemployment; the instruments of policy were financial and monetary management over the medium term coupled with supply side changes, rather than fine tuning using fiscal policies aimed at demand management over the short term. Thatcherism replaced the neo-corporatism of the 1970s, and its emphasis upon incomes policies, with a set of policies aimed at liberating market processes.

Assessing economic performance

Before considering the impact of the Thatcher Government's macroeconomic strategies upon the performance of the UK economy it is worthwhile considering how the performance of an economy might best be assessed.

The purpose of any policy intervention must be to improve the welfare of the citizens of an economy compared to the state which would otherwise exist. Both unemployment and inflation have costs associated with them. They contribue to the 'economic pain index'. However, should performance be judged in terms of the minimization of pain in the short run or the long run? It is often argued that reductions in the short-run costs of increasing unemployment levels are achieved at the expense of even greater reductions in pain in the longer run which could be obtained from reductions in inflation. Economists are, however, not agreed on their estimatee of the relative size of the welfare costs of inflation and unemployment over the short and medium terms.

Another dimension to the measurement of economic performance is the distribution of the benefits and costs of economic and structural adjustments. Who benefits from the policy changes and what is the impact of the policies upon the distribution of welfare?

Conflict is the substance of politics and the political economy of the 1980s has involved disagreement over the appropriate trade-offs between the short- and long-term costs of Thatcherite policies and the distribution of the net benefits of these policies across individuals.

Finally, the performance of an economic strategy can be assessed relative to the performance of alternative strategies. Thus, for example, it can be asked how did the UK economy perform relative to those other OECD economies during the 1980s?

In the following sections the performance of the UK economy during the 1980s will be assessed:

1 over the short run (one to two years);
2 by examining changes in the long-run trend in productivity;
3 by looking at the changes in income distribution;
4 by comparison with other economies.

The short run

The 1980/81 recession

The first budget of the 1979 Thatcher Government, which was introduced by Geoffrey Howe, provided a substantial shock to an economy that was already entering into a recession. The increase in world oil prices in 1978/79 rocked the world economy. At the same time, the production of North Sea oil and the movement of the UK towards self-sufficiency in oil had caused an appreciation in the Sterling exchange rate. Exports became less competitive whilst imports became cheaper. The revenue benefits of North Sea oil were off-set by the deindustrialization caused by the appreciation of the exchange rate.

Howe's first budget introduced tight monetary and fiscal policies and floated the exchange rate. Tight fiscal policy and the overriding of the auto-matic stabilizers reduced demand in the economy, whilst the tight monetary policy caused nominal interest rates to rise, which dampened consumer and investment spending, caused a further appreciation in the exchange rate and pushed the economy further into deindustrialization. Whilst firms were fight-ing for survival they needed to borrow short-term from the banks but at much higher rates of interest. Many firms simply ceased trading over this period and the UK lost a significant part of its manufacturing base and its productive potential.

The 1980/81 recession has been studied at great length (see Buiter and Miller 1981 and 1983; Jackson 1981 and 1985; Bachelor 1983; Alt 1985; Walters 1986; Burns 1988; Maynard 1988; Layard and Nickell 1989). The economy experienced negative growth during 1980 and 1981 and a rapid rise in unemployment. The impact on UK manufacturing was worse than during the Great Depression of the 1930s. Between June 1979 and January 1981 manufacturing output fell by 19.6 per cent – about 22 per cent of the manufac-turing sector's capital and equipment was destroyed and 1.7 million jobs or 23 per cent of the 1979 manufacturing labour force were lost.

There is a dispute about how much the tight fiscal and monetary policies of the 1979 and 1980 budgets contributed to the recession. The majority of studies argue that policy was a major contributing factor but Matthews and Minford (1987) conclude that it was tight external and supply side shocks that caused the recession. They argue that the recession was caused by the appreciation of Sterling following the production of North Sea oil, although they do attribute some of the rise in unemployment to the tightening of monetary policy. Between 1979 and 1980 (fourth quarter) the money supply growth (MO) was reduced from 12 per cent per annum to 5.7 per cent. The Liverpool model estimates that this caused unemployment to rise by 800,000 between 1980 and 1985. Between 1979 (first quarter) and 1980 (fourth quarter) the Sterling exchange rate rose by 25 per cent.

In contrast Bean's (1987) analysis could only attribute about 8 per cent–12 per cent of the appreciation in Sterling to North Sea oil and the increase in the world price of oil. He argued that the remaining 13 per cent–17 per cent was due to the monetary squeeze of the MTFS which caused UK interest rates to rise relative to world rates and hence the Sterling exchange rate to appreciate (for a similar view see Dornbush *et al.* 1986; Bean and Symons 1989). More specifically, Bean and Gavosto (1989) and Newell and Symons (1987) attribute 3.5 percentage points of the rise in unemployment from the late 1970s to the early 1980s to demand shocks, so that most of the unemployment is explained by tight monetary and fiscal policy (see also Layard and Nickell 1986).

The Howe 1979 budget also scored a major own goal by increasing the rate of value added tax. This change in tax structure helped the Government to meet its objective of not raising direct tax rates on incomes but it upset the Government's chances of bringing down inflationary expectations in the short run. The increase in Value Added Tax (VAT) added about 4 per cent to the rate of inflation and reduced real incomes, which in turn took demand out of the economy and contributed to the increase in unemployment.

An experiment in practical monetarism

Over the period 1980/83 the first Thatcher Government implemented its monetarist experiment. This was a time during which much was learned about the limitations of practical monetarism. After 1983 there was a gradual abandonment of the use of monetary targets and a relaxation of monetary policy. What went wrong and what was learned?

The objective of monetary policy and the MTFS was to wring inflationary expectations out of the UK economy by providing a relatively stable medium-term financial planning environment. It would also enable the Government to bring down interest rates because public sector deficits would be consistent with the money supply targets. This view of the world was, however, seriously flawed. It was based upon inappropriate theoretical foundations, which, even if they had been correct, could not have been implemented. Most would now agree that:

1 short-term intererst rates are sensitive to external events which influence exchange rates;

2 the supply of assets, such as public debt, have little or no impact upon interest rates (see Buiter and Tobin 1980; Cairncross 1980; Kaldor 1980; Frankel 1985; and Jackson 1990);
3 linkages between the PSBR and the money supply have been found to be weak (see Kaldor 1980; and Jackson 1990).

These empirical studies cast doubt on the role of public sector deficits in the MTFS and their role in the Government's fight against inflation. Indeed, a closer examination of the Conservative Government's theory of inflation suggests that it is more appropriate to an economy in a developing country rather than an advanced capitalist country such as the UK, which has a highly sophisticated set of money and capital markets.

One particular weakness in the thinking which lay behind the MTFS was that it had paid little attention to the importance and relevance of UK monetary and financial institutional detail for the successful implementation of the new monetary policy (see Goodhart 1984 and Jackson 1985). The Treasury and the Bank of England have a variety of definitions of the money supply from which to choose for control purposes. Each definition differs from the others with respect to the coverage of liquid assets that are included in the definition. For the purposes of the MTFS, the Treasury chose to control sterling M3 (£M3), a reasonably broad-based definition of money which is not closely related to the general public's transactions demand and which is sensitive to the rate of interest.

It was soon discovered that £M3 was very difficult to control and was not relevant for controlling inflation since it is the narrow money supplied for transaction purposes which should be rationed if inflation is to be reduced. Because £M3 is sensitive to interest rates a paradox emerged. Increases in interest rates, which were in part a consequence of tight monetary control, meant increased savings held in bank deposits which were counted as part of £M3. Thus, tight monetary control caused a subsequent expansion in £M3 and the money supply targets were breached.

The reaction was a further round of monetary controls, a further rise in interest rates and an expansion in £M3. Furthermore, the Government's scrapping of the 'corset' (a set of controls over bank lending introduced in the 1970s) and its liberalization of the financial services industry, which allowed banks and building societies to compete for the same business, promoted a rapid expansion in credit and an increase in £M3 well beyond its targets.

The Government's tight monetary and fiscal policies also had a perverse impact upon £M3. Companies whose order books had been cut back partly as a result of oil price rises and government policy, sought finance to bail them out. They turned to the banks for short-term finance rather than borrowing long term because expectations of higher inflation made long-term borrowing unfavourable. This short-run borrowing from the banking system resulted in an increase in £M3, since such borrowings are part of this definition of the

Table 2.1 Target and actual monetary growth in the MTFS

	Monetary aggregate				Growth rates (%)			
	£M3		M1		PSL2		MO	
MTFS	Target	Actual	Target	Actual	Target	Actual	Target	Actual
1980	7–11	19.50						
1981	6–10	12.75						
1983	8–12	11.25	8–12	12.25	8–12	11.50		
1984	6–10	12.00					4–8	5.50
1985	5–9	16.50					3–7	3.50
1986	11–15	14.50					2–6	4.00
1987							2–6	5.75
1988							1–5	6.50
1989							1–5	6.00
1990							1–5	

Source: Financial Statement and Budget Report, various issues.

money supply. Again this was not appreciated by the architects of the MTFS who had been obsessed by the PSBR and monetization.

Finally, high short-term interest rates in the UK, relative to short-term rates in other countries, caused speculative balances to flow rapidly into the UK banking system, thereby causing a further expansion in £M3.

The Government found that £M3 was uncontrollable. As Table 2.1 illustrates, the money supply targets were breached. So, in the mid-1980s the money supply targets of the MTFS were gradually dropped. Other monetary measures such as M1 and PSL2 were used for a short time to supplement the £M3 indicator and, from 1986, the narrow definition of money, MO, was targeted.

After 1986 the exchange rate dominated the formation of monetary policy. A view emerged from the Treasury that in order to control inflation it was necessary to control the exchange rate. Interest rates were to be used to adjust the exchange rate. However, it is impossible to use a single instrument of policy to target two objectives. Either interest rates are used to control the money supply or they are used to control exchange rates. They cannot be used for both. Having chosen to manage exchange rates in the fight against inflation the Government effectively gave up its control of the money supply.

During this period Nigel Lawson, then Chancellor of the Exchequer, was likened to a single-club golfer – he had reduced his macroeconomic instruments to one, interest rate controls for the purpose of exchange rate management and the achievement of inflation targets.

Between 1986 and 1988 (April) the exchange rate policy adopted was to track the German mark. The UK was, at that time, outside the European exchange rate mechanism (ERM) and a substantial volume of UK trade was with Germany and the rest of Europe rather than with the USA. As such, it was thought that stabilizing the £/DM exchange rate would have beneficial trade effects whilst at the same time securing some of the advantages of ERM membership. In particular, German monetary policies, used to control German inflation rates, would, it was thought, spillover into the UK (see Vines 1989 for details of the policy).

This policy was abandoned in 1988 and there then emerged a protracted and public disagreement between Mrs Thatcher and her Chancellor Nigel Lawson. At the technical level the debate was between Sir Alan Walters, Mrs Thatcher's personal economic adviser, and the Treasury.

The Treasury wanted to keep the £ below DM3. This, however, posed a threat to the Government's anti-inflation policy. It sustained the consumption boom whilst at the same time sucked in imports which worsened the balance of payments. Mrs Thatcher, on the other hand, wanted to raise interest rates and to allow the exchange rate to appreciate. The danger of this policy was that it would depress investment and cause a deterioration in the current account of the balance of payments. The balance of payments, it was argued, would be relatively worse under the Thatcher policy than under the Lawson approach. The division between Thatcher and Lawson revolved around inflation vs investment. Lawson wanted to keep the boom going long enough (and risk inflation) in order to boost investment for long-run take off.

In the event the situation worsened. Consumption continued to rise rapidly. The foreign exchange markets became nervous because they expected a rise in interest rates to curb the consumption boom. Also, the foreign exchange markets became worried about the worsening balance of payments – they feared a devaluation of Sterling. To keep the exchange markets happy required the maintenance of high interest rates which further depressed investment.

An alternative policy would have been to take the heat out of the consumption boom by raising taxes – especially income taxes. That, however, was ruled out. Such a policy would have had the advantage that interest rates need not have been increased. By the end of 1988 interest rates were 13 per cent compared to 7.5 per cent in mid-1988.

When John Major took over as Chancellor of the Exchequer in 1989 the Treasury strategy was to keep interest rates high and hope that the recession would not be too severe (hope for a soft landing). Recession set in to the property and construction sectors, especially in the South East of England, early in 1989. The manufacturing sector was hit during 1989/90 by a high £ and high interest rates. Consumption began to slow down; the Bank of England was being asked increasingly to prop up failing companies; company profits began to fall.

In 1990 the UK joined the ERM. Most commentators including Sir Alan Walters, Professor John Williamson and the Confederation of British Industry (CBI) argue that the UK joined on the wrong terms. In choosing to join at DM3 Sterling was over-valued by at least 10 per cent, perhaps even 16 per cent. If this is true then the UK faces painful adjustment problems during the early years of the 1990s. That is how the UK entered the 1980s – *plus ça change!*

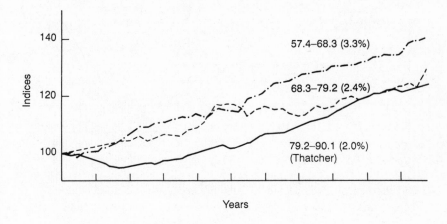

Figure 2.1   Trends in total output

A key question remains. Did anything of substance change in the economy over the period 1980/90 to make it stronger and more able to adjust to the more demanding conditions of ERM membership?

Indicators of economic performance

Controlling inflation, adjusting supply-side incentives and providing a stable planning environment were supposed to unleash economic forces that would result in a growth of output and rising living standards. What was the actual outcome? Figure 2.1 shows the trends in total output in the economy over a number of time periods including the Thatcher years 1979(2) and 1990(1). It is readily seen that annual growth over the Thatcher period was 2 per cent per annum, which is slower than in the previous periods of similar length. In fact, immediately after the 1979 Government was elected, there was a period of two years during which growth was negative. This was the period in which deindustrialization set in.

This pattern is confirmed in Figure 2.2 which shows what happened to manufacturing output growth. Between 1979(2) and 1980(4) manufacturing output fell by 17 per cent. Manufacturing output growth did recover towards the end of the period giving an overall growth in manufacturing output of 1 per cent per annum. This compares favourably with the period 1955/73.

Some commentators have measured growth during the Thatcher years using the fourth quarter of 1980 as the base. This results in a growth rate of about 4 per cent per annum, which is well in excess of anything that has been experienced over the postwar period. Such an approach is not, however, legitimate. Trend measures must be taken from peak to peak or trough to trough over the cycle. Using 1980(4) as the base is to measure trough to peak which is wholly inappropriate.

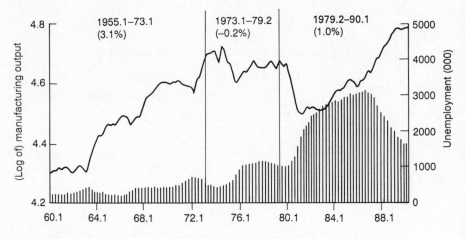

Figure 2.2 Three stages of growth and unemployment

Data on unemployment are also shown in Figure 2.2. It can be seen that unemployment grew dramatically post-1979 – leaving aside the numerous changes that have been made to the official definition of unemployment – and peaked at 11.1 per cent in 1986. Unemployment was not only caused by a destruction of the number of jobs on offer. Demographic factors, such as an increase in the number of young people seeking employment and an increase in the participation rate of women in the work force, increased the demand for jobs. Coutts *et al.* (1990) point out that the long-term annual rate of growth of output has to be in the range of 2.5 per cent–3.5 per cent to keep unemployment constant. Growth rates, as shown above, were below this during the Thatcher years.

Some of the rise in unemployment was undoubtedly a result of labour hoarding during the 1970s which subsequently proved too costly. But much of the apparent recovery in unemployment post-1986 was due to manipulation of the unemployment statistics and the introduction of policies which made it more difficult to claim unemployment benefits.

The erosion of the UK's manufacturing base, and the expansion of consumption in the second half of the 1980s, caused the economy to hit its capacity constraint. This resulted in an increase in the volume of imports and a deterioration of the balance of payments. In 1982 the UK imported more manufactured goods than it exported; this was the first time in 200 years that it experienced a manufacturing deficit. Figure 2.3 shows the UK's visible trade balance and the rapidly deteriorating position of the non-oil balance since 1981. The Conservative Government's policies probably did more to increase employment in Germany and Japan than in the UK.

The balance of manufactured goods (i.e. exports less imports) has deteriorated over a number of years, from a surplus of 9 per cent of Gross Domestic Product (GDP) in the mid-1950s to a deficit of more than 3 per cent in 1988/89. Whilst the recession of 1979/81 speeded up the decline, the process

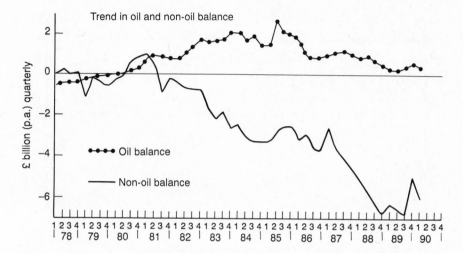

Figure 2.3   Visible trade balance

of import penetration has been a feature of the UK economy for many years. The problem lies at the heart of the fundamentals of the UK economy and has more to do with non-price factors, such as the quality of UK exports, delivery times, after sales service, and so on. This means that whilst the exchange rate can give a temporary respite it is insufficient to correct the problem at the root.

Whilst the volume of exports has continued to rise throughout the 1980s, exports as a percentage of GDP have shown very little change (see Figure 2.4). This has been taken by some commentators to be a clear indication that supply-side policies have had no fundamental impact upon the strength of the UK's external trading position. However, John Odling-Smee (1989) argues that it is too early to make such a strong judgement. The UK's share of the world trade fell from 40 per cent in 1880 to 8 per cent in 1980 but has stabilized since then. His argument is that the end of the decline is an indication of the strengthening of the UK economy in world markets during the 1980s. Whether or not this levelling off in the process of decline can be sustained into and beyond the 1990s remains to be seen. (See Wells 1989 for a more detailed analysis.)

Supply-side policies promised a revolution in which entrepreneurial energies would be unleashed, investment would boom, profits would rise and new enterprises would multiply. What happened? The 1989 Financial Statement and Budget Report compares investment during the 1980s and the 1970s. These figures are, however, misleading. They include purchases by the private sector of public sector assets (i.e. resulting from the privatization programme) and public sector housing sales. In addition, some public sector investment is now being classified as private sector investment as a result of privatization. These book-keeping problems distort the picture. If a more disaggregated approach is used, as in Figure 2.5, then it can be seen that real expenditure (at 1985 prices) on manufacturing investment was only marginally

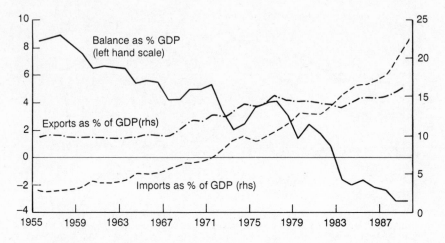

Figure 2.4   Trade in manufactures: various indicators

higher in 1989 than in 1979. The growth in investment has come mainly from the services sector (distribution and banking). Manufacturing investment as a percentage of GDP fell from 3.1 per cent in 1979 to 2.8 per cent in 1989, having reached a low of 2.2 per cent in 1982. These data, however, can be re-interpreted if we examine what has happened to *net* investment. Over the period between 1980 and 1988 total net manufacturing investment fell by 30 per cent and this has had a significant effect on the capital base. It is doubtful whether all of this involved simply scrapping redundant capital. Rather, it suggests that the capacity of the manufacturing sector has been reduced, which is reflected in increasing import volumes.

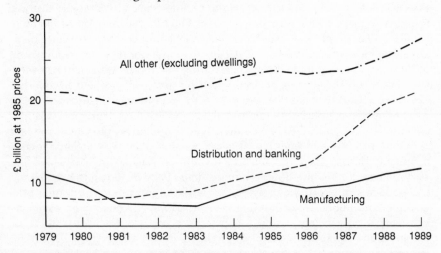

Figure 2.5   Gross domestic fixed capital formation

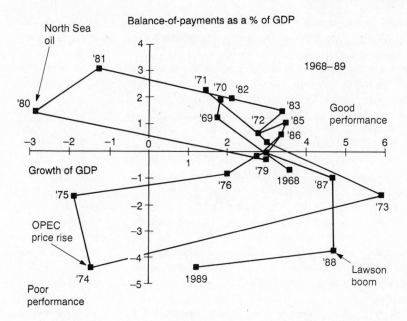

Figure 2.6 Growth and balance-of-payments trade-off, 1968–87

During the 1980s personal sector savings fell from about 15 per cent of personal disposable incomes during the 1970s to an average of 5 per cent in the 1980s (they reached a low of 3 per cent in 1988). This had important consequences. First, an important source of funds for financing investment disappeared, though this was in part balanced by an increase in retained profits. Second, the fall in savings contributed to the consumption boom of the late 1980s, which was also fuelled by income tax reductions and cheap credit. The Lawson consumption boom placed upward pressures on prices and sucked in imports.

The primary objective of the Government's policy was to bring down the rate of inflation. When the Conservative Government came to power inflation was running at 10.4 per cent. It rose sharply during 1980/81 and then fell to 3 per cent during 1986 due in part to a fall in import prices (see Figure 2.6). Since then it has increased, fuelled in part by the consumer boom, house price rises, increases in mortgage interest rates, the introduction of the community charge and higher money wages. During most of the 1980s average earnings rose by about 8 per cent per annum. This was well in excess of productivity growth and gives a clear indication that the labour market was not behaving as the Government wished it would.

Productivity trends and long-run analysis

Between 1985/89 the economy grew at 3 per cent per annum, that is faster than during the period 1968/84 but slower than between 1957/68. This enhancement of growth was heralded in a variety of ways; the 'supply-side miracle' or 'the Thatcher factor'. It was thought that the short-run pain of the policies introduced in the early 1980s had been justified by long-run benefits. If supply was expanding whilst demand was also expanding then there would be no fear of inflationary pressures arising on the demand side. In addition, balance-of-payments deficits would be a thing of the past.

Events, however, have proved this view to be wrong. Whilst supply increased, demand grew faster, resulting in the consumption-led boom of the 1980s, the rise in inflation and a worsening balance of payments. This repeated the pattern of 1960, 1964, 1968, 1973 and 1979. The problem is that it is difficult to plan demand without an accurate analysis of the supply side of the economy. This means that a key question is: what happened to the supply-side improvements (productivity) in the 1980s and is this change sustainable into the 1990s?

Much controversy surrounds the interpretation of the supply-side data. However, the dominant view is that the UK productivity improvements during the 1980s were better than those of other countries, better than those during the 1973/79 cycle but worse than those between 1960/73. Godley (1989) shows that from 1980 to 1988 the growth in manufacturing output was 0.8 per cent per annum which was similar to that between 1969(4) and 1979(2) of 0.9 per cent per annum but well below that of 1960(2) to 1969(4), which was 3.1 per cent per annum.

There are three components to productivity changes: (a) a cyclical element; measured productivity will rise on the up-swing of a cycle and fall on the down-swing; (b) there is that change in productivity which arises from factor input substitution, i.e. less labour and more capital; and (c) the long-run trend in productivity arising from technical progress. If we are considering a supply-side miracle it is the long-term trend that is of interest. The other two elements need to be separated out since they tend to be short-run phenomena.

If we compare productivity changes in the 1970s and the 1980s then the cyclical element plays an important role. Productivity did fall on the downside of the cycle during the 1970s and rose again on the upside of the 1980 cycle, but that does not constitute a supply-side miracle.

In an intensive study of the rise in productivity during the 1980s, Muellbauer (1986) concludes that about 40 per cent of the increase was due to labour-shedding and the upturn in the cycle. The remainder of the increase in productivity is accounted for by the long-term underlying trend in productivity. This suggests that supply-side policies had no perceptible impact on the trend of productivity. This empirical result is confirmed by studies by Wren-Lewis (1989), Crafts (1988) and Bean and Symons (1989).

In contrast, other commentators, such as Spencer (1989) and Odling-Smee (1989), believe that it is too early to judge whether or not a supply-side effect has taken place. They argue that the change in the general cultural climate of the country, with its emphasis upon enterprise, and the change in industrial relations (see Metcalf 1989) will have lasting effects and will, in the fullness of time, raise the trend growth in productivity.

Table 2.2 Changes in GDP and its components, 1979–89

	1979	% change* 1989	1979/89
Gross Domestic Product	92.8	116.2	25.2
of which			
Manufacturing	106.0	119.2	12.5
Energy and water	82.5	89.8	8.8
Construction	95.1	125.7	32.2
Services	89.3	119.3	33.6
of which			
Banking, finance, etc.	71.0	144.0	102.8
Distribution	93.0	112.5	31.7
Transport	98.2	122.9	25.2
Communications	80.2	130.1	61.0
Education and health	94.0	108.0	14.9
Other services	82.0	123.0	50.0
Consumer Expenditure	89.7	124.7	39.0
of which			
Durable goods	79.8	144.8	81.5
Fixed Investment	93.5	134.2	43.5

Note: *1985 = 100.
Source: CSO Blue Book (1990: tables 1.7, 2.4, 4.6, 13.7).

To date, however, there is little evidence to support the claim that a supply-side miracle took place in the UK during the 1980s. Improvements in productivity simply brought the economy back to its long run postwar trend. Moreover, any improvement in the *relative position* of the UK's productivity compared to that of other economies is explained by the slowing down of these economies during the 1980s rather than by a speeding up in the UK.

The period 1979/89 is summarized in Table 2.2. It is readily seen that the boom in the economy was concentrated in the construction and services sector and that, within the services sector, financial services played an important role. Over the whole period, annual growth in GDP was, on average, 2.5 per cent, which is no greater than the postwar average. The end of the Thatcher decade was also characterized by an acceleration in the number of business failures (see Table 2.3). In 1990, business failures reached their highest level during the past 50 years. Many small businessess simply could not survive the high interest rates and accelerating inflation.

Another summary view of the decade is given in Figure 2.6. In this figure the trade-off between economic growth and the balance of payments is shown. Good performance combines a strong balance of payments and rapid growth. In 1979 the economy, after the 'stagflation' years of the mid-1970s caused by the OPEC price shock, was on the verge of entering the good performance quadrant of Figure 2.6. The shock of the Howe budget and the production of

Table 2.3   Business failures: England and Wales, 1980–90

	Liquidations	Bankruptcies	Total failures
1980	6814	3814	10651
1981	8227	4976	13203
1982	11131	5436	16567
1983	12466	6821	19287
1984	13647	8035	21682
1985	14363	6580	20943
1986	13689	6991	20680
1987	10644	6761	17405
1988	9276	7286	16652
1989	10197	7966	18163
1990	1361	10831	24442

Source: Surveys by Dun and Bradstreet.

North Sea oil took the economy off in a new direction. During the mid–1980s, there were a few years of good performance but then the economy fell into decline with lower growth and a deterioration in the balance of payments.

Distributional performance

How have the gains from the improvement in economic performance been distributed? A number of studies show that both pre-tax and post-tax income distributions have widened in the UK during the period 1980/89. The degree of inequality has also increased within occupations.

Some have argued that an 'underclass' was created during the 1980s; that is a group who do not enjoy the benefits of economic prosperity. They have no access to the enterprise culture but instead rely upon some of the benefits of enterprise to trickle down to them. To the extent that it is useful to think in terms of an underclass this was not created in the 1980s, it has always been there. However, it probably became more pronounced as the Thatcher Governments attempted to break the expectations associated with the dependency culture.

Many studies have reported upon the widening divides in British society during the 1980s. The Church of England's publication 'Faith in the City' focused upon innner city deprivation whilst a number of others examined the growing feminization of poverty (see Cockburn 1983 and 1985; Martin and Roberts 1984; Beechey and Perkins 1987; Dex 1987; Glendinning and Miller 1987; and Joshi 1989). More generally, a recent study by the Institute for Fiscal Studies (1989) shows that the trickle down effect is small and the process is very long.

Why did incomes become more unequal during the 1980s? Between 1979 and 1986 £8 billion of tax cuts were made in successive budgets. The benefits of these tax cuts, however, were distributed to the top 2 per cent of income earners. The rise in house prices meant that mortgage tax relief increased for the rich – between 1978/79 and 1986/87 mortgage tax relief increased by £2.4 billion (see Chapter 5). Thus, the fiscal system contributed to the growth in inequality.

The distribution of incomes during the 1980s was influenced by the distribution of productivity increases. Non-manual workers such as finance specialists, accountants and managers gained relative to manual workers. The unemployed (outsiders) did relatively worse compared to those inside the labour market. The increase in the number of unemployed and the erosion of the relative value of unemployment benefits, due mainly to statutory changes, meant that the incomes of the unemployed became relatively worse.

Other policy changes have had an impact on income inequality. In 1988 the introduction of the Social Fund replaced individual grants for essential items; the real value of child benefit fell by 7 per cent between 1979/89 (CPAG 1988); the take up rate for family credits is only 36 per cent; and the community charge has had significant distributional effects (Jackson 1990; and Chapter 6 below).

Finally, the quality of many jobs changed. There are a growing number of people who could be regarded as 'just inside' the labour market and no more. These are individuals in low-paid casual and part-time jobs. Such jobs, which are taken up by second-income earners in low-income households, are insecure.

The relative performance of the UK

All international comparisons are subject to data problems. The data presented in Table 2.4 are drawn from the OECD and are based on a common set of conventions. The general picture which emerges from Table 2.4 is that the

Table 2.4 UK relative economic performance, 1980–89

	USA	Canada	Japan	France	Germany	Italy	UK	OECD
Average annual growth rate (%)	2.9	3.3	4.4	2.2	1.9	2.3	2.8	2.9
Average unemployment rate (%)	7.1	9.3	2.6	9.0	6.0	9.8	10.0	7.3
Average inflation rate (%)	5.0	7.0	1.9	7.7	2.6	13.6	7.2	6.4
Average short-term interest rates (%)	9.9	11.0	6.2	11.0	6.8	15.8	11.0	–
Import index*	148	136	114	119	123	119	131	–
Growth in average earnings, 1980/89 (%)	59	81	49	97	30	–	111	–

Note: *Volume of imports relative to domestic demand in 1989, with 1980 = 100.
Source: Unpublished Data Set National Institute for Social and Economic Research.

performance of the UK economy, relative to other European and OECD economies, was not spectacular.

The UK's average annual growth rate was good compared to those other European countries but not above average when compared to other OECD countries. Unemployment in the UK was persistently higher in the UK during 1980/89 and was well above the OECD average.

Inflation rates in the UK were also relatively high. The growth in average earnings in the UK over the period 1980/89 may seem to be spectacular but it also indicates a weakness, namely that the UK was paying itself too much in wages. The high growth in output was based on the back of a consumer boom and was not investment or export led, thus making it fragile. Finally, the import penetration index shows clearly that UK final demand had a high import content when compared to other European countries.

Conclusions

Thatcherism was an ideology of the minority. Few actually believed in it and this made it difficult to implement. The market dream is not generally accepted by the working class or by the educated who have different values.

Despite Thatcherism, the boom/bust cycle remains a dominant feature of the UK economic landscape. Inflation has not been tamed; unemployment remains well above the levels of the 1960s and 1970s; and income inequality is worse. There have, however, been changes. Attitudes towards enterprise, competition, the unions and the public sector have changed. Incentives are now probably better related to growth and productivity improvements. But there has been no cultural revolution nor an economic renaissance or miracle. At best, the economy has returned to its long run path of productivity improvements. Whether this would have happened without Thatcherism is an open question.

This was a decade of lost opportunities given the resources of North Sea oil and privatization. But not all was negative. Thatcherism did produce some benefits. The Thatcher experiment forced others to carry out a detailed analysis of its underlying claims. As a result of this, high quality academic research has deepened our understanding of the fundamentals of the UK economy. The Thatcher experiment acted as a catalyst and, in that sense, there was an external benefit. Managerial attitudes changed for the better and a strong argument could be advanced that suggests that industrial relations in Britain are now better than they have been (Metcalf 1989; and Chapter 3 below).

Because Thatcherism was based upon intellectual quicksands any economic policies built upon it were doomed to eventual failure. Hahn (1988), one of Britain's leading economic theorists and a strong critic of Thatcherite economic policies, argued:

Thatcherism as represented by Mrs Thatcher herself is intellectually without interest. It consists of homilies on the virtues of hard work and ambition and on providing the carrot and stick to elicit those virtues. Her macro-economic views are so incoherent as to make them undiscussable. (p. 123)

The failure of Thatcherism was that despite the rhetoric of supply side economics it took a very narrow view of what constituted supply-side policy. It ignored the vital role played by education and training, and investment in fundamental research and development. These are areas where markets are not efficient and do fail, where government needs to take a lead and where other governments have shown the way. The UK economy has changed, but only at the margin. It has probably not changed at the core. 'Hand bagging' institutions results in resistance rather than change – to change institutions requires an approach to leadership that proceeds through negotiation – a concept that had no place in the Thatcher portfolio.

3

Industrial relations

David Marsh

It is widely believed in academic circles that union power has been significantly reduced since 1979. Indeed, Savage and Robins identify industrial relations as one of four areas in which there was serious and even radical transformation during the Thatcher years (Savage and Robins 1990: 245. See also Holmes 1985: 214; Crouch 1986: 131; Kavanagh 1987: 243; Gamble 1988: 126–7; King 1988: 62; Minford 1988: 99; Roberts 1989: 78).

Of course, not everyone accepts this view. In particular, many authors in the industrial relations literature argue that little has altered on the shopfloor (Kelly 1987: 8, 12, 14, 16–17; McInnes 1987: 6; McIlroy 1988: 233), and that those changes which have occurred resulted more from the transformation of the occupational structure and the macro-economy than from Government policy and legislation (Wedderburn 1985: 33; Kelly 1987: 17; McInnes 1987; McIlroy 1988).

One aim of this chapter will be to examine these competing views on the two key questions raised in the literature. How much has changed since 1979? Why has this change occurred?

The other main aim of the chapter is separate but clearly related. The Conservatives had clear objectives in relation to industrial relations policy when they came to power. One of the key intentions of this chapter and indeed the volume is to establish both the extent to which policy objectives have been achieved and the reasons for policy 'success' and policy 'failure'. However, before we can deal with this question we need to establish the Thatcher Government's objectives. In fact, the Conservatives had both detailed policy commitments which were included in their manifesto and a

limited number of broader aims. It is important to make this distinction because the detailed commitments have proved easier to achieve than the broader
aims.

The structure of this chapter reflects its aims. It has three substantive
sections. The first section deals with the Conservatives' detailed policy commitments while the second section examines their broader aims. In both cases I
shall identify the objectives and assess the extent to which they have been
achieved. The final substantive section then attempts to establish the extent to
which those changes in industrial relations which have occurred result from a
'Thatcher effect'.

The detailed commitments: a legislative onslaught

As Table 3.1 indicates, the Government fulfilled the vast majority of its manifesto commitments. Only the promises in the 1983 manifesto to replace 'contracting out' with 'contracting in' for the political levy and to introduce
legislation to curtail strikes in essential services were not honoured. However,
the Conservatives introduced reforms which were not in the manifestos. In
particular, the 1982 Employment Act removed the blanket immunity enjoyed
by unions and the 1990 Employment Act requires unions to repudiate or adopt
unofficial strikes and allows the selective dismissal of unofficial strikers.

Five major pieces of trade union legislation were passed between 1979
and 1990. These five Acts – the 1980 Employment Act, the 1982 Employment
Act, the 1984 Trade Union Act, the 1988 Employment Act and the 1990
Employment Act – significantly changed the legal position of unions.

The legislation has seven major elements: the blanket immunity enjoyed
by unions, as distinct from unionists, was removed by the Employment Act
1982; the definition of a legitimate trade dispute has been successively narrowed so as to reduce the immunities enjoyed by unionists (and now unions);
the legal basis of the closed shop was initially restricted by the 1980 and 1982
Employment Acts and subsequently removed in the Employment Acts of 1988
and 1990; under the Trade Union Act of 1984 unions are required to hold
secret ballots for the election of officers; this legislation also requires unions to
conduct political fund ballots; the Employment Act of 1988 gives individual
unionists a series of rights *vis-à-vis* their unions; and the 1990 Employment Act
makes unions responsible for their members' unofficial action, unless the
unions repudiate the strike, or make it official, after a ballot.

The first two are the most important elements. The removal of blanket
immunity, which unions had enjoyed since the 1906 Trade Dispute Act, made
unions liable for civil actions in tort and, as such, claims for damages for losses
incurred in 'an illegitimate strike' could be pursued against the funds of the
unions. As we shall see later, once the 1982 Employment Act came into force,
employers overwhelmingly took out injunctions against trade unions rather
than unionists. Nevertheless, it is the removal of the immunities, which gave
unionists, and now unions, protection against civil actions in tort, which was

Table 3.1 Conservative manifesto commitments and legislative action on trade union reform, 1979–90

1979 Manifesto commitments	Enacted?	1983 Manifesto commitments	Enacted?	1987 Manifesto commitments	Enacted?
1. Removal of immunities in relation to picketing	1. Immunity for secondary picketing removed in 1980 Employment Act	1. Removal of immunity if no secret ballot before strike	1. Secret ballots before strikes required in 1984 Trade Union Act	1. Empower individual members to stop unions from calling them out on strike without holding a secret ballot	1. Enacted in 1988 Employment Act
2. Restrictions on closed shop	2. Yes. Restrictions in both 1980 and 1982 Employment Acts	2. Require secret ballots for the election of union executives	2. Required in 1984 Trade Union Act	2. Protect trade union members from union disciplinary action if refuse to join strike	2. Enacted in 1988 Employment Act
3. Encouragement of wider use of secret ballots by unions	3. Public funds allocated for union secret ballots in 1980 Employment Act	3. Require periodical political fund ballots	3. Required in 1984 Trade Union Act	3. Require secret ballots for elections for all members of union governing body	3. Enacted in 1988 Employment Act
4. Restriction on benefits for strikers	4. Reduced benefits in 1980 Social Security Act	4. Introduce contracting in to political levy	4. Dropped – the one Trade Union victory	4. Further limit to closed shop	4. Abolished in 1988 and 1990 Employment Acts
		5. Curb the use of strikes within the public sector	Not proceeded with	5. Establish new Trade Union Commissioner	5. Established in 1988 Employment Act

the crucial development. In particular, unions and unionists now no longer enjoy any protection for industrial action: involving secondary action; on which there has not been a prior secret ballot; or involving support for workers selectively dismissed.

The 1980s legislation differs from the 1971 Industrial Relations Act and the 'In Place of Strife' proposals of 1968/69 in four ways. First, and most obviously, the changes in the 1980s have been cumulative, involving five stages rather than one. Second, the 1971 legislation included some positive gains for unions; greater employment protection, disclosure of information by employers to unions and the encouragement of collective bargaining. The current legislation contains no such provisions. Third, the 1980s legislation has a different structure from, and omits certain provisions which were included in, the 1971 Act. All the legislation has involved amending existing laws, the Government has not proposed an entirely new system of law, rather it has altered the existing rules. No separate judicial system has been established, there is no equivalent of the National Industrial Relations Court, rather the amended laws are operated by the existing legal structure, the industrial tribunals and the courts. The Secretary of State is not involved at all in the legal process, everything is left to the affected parties and to the courts so that the Government plays no direct role in the operation of the legislation. There has been no attempt to make collective agreements between employers and unions legally binding. Fourth, the 1980s legislation has also included restrictions on unions not included in the Industrial Relations Act and, to that extent, is much more radical. In particular, the current laws: remove more of the immunities unions and unionists enjoyed; intervene much more in the internal affairs of the union, requiring ballots on the election of all officers and the unions' political funds; place more restrictions on picketing; constrain all secondary action rather than just some; give union members more rights in relation to their unions; and outlaw labour-only clauses in contracts and tenders.

Many of these differences result from conscious decisions by the Conservative Government based upon the experience of the Heath Government. However, we must be cautious before suggesting that a deliberate step-by-step policy has been pursued. It all depends upon what 'step-by-step' is taken to mean. Certainly, the Conservatives' approach has been cautious, largely because of the perceived problems of compliance. At the same time, each piece of legislation has, in important senses, built upon previous legislation. So, for example, the outlawing of the closed shop has occurred in four distinct stages. Similarly, the immunity enjoyed where secondary action was involved was removed in two steps.

Undoubtedly then, the process has been a cumulative one. However, in 1978 Moran, and most other observers, were unsure of the shape of future legislation (Moran 1979) and even in 1980 it was far from certain how things would develop. Certainly, it would appear mistaken to see the legislative approach of the Conservatives as a coherent approach developed in opposition and followed through in power. Rather the Conservative party wanted to curb the unions, and Margaret Thatcher loathed them, but was unsure how to proceed, particularly given the problem of compliance. However, once it became increasingly clear after 1981 that compliance was not a major problem, Mrs Thatcher's ideological aversion to unions coincided with her pragmatic political judgement. Unions could be successfully curbed and this simple fact, in her terms, removed a crucial constraint upon the operation of the market. In addition, the curbing of union power could be portrayed as evidence of the Conservatives' governing competence while, at the same time, proving electorally popular (see Marsh 1992: ch. 3).

The Conservatives' broader aims

However, Kavanagh and others are not merely concerned with the Thatcher Government's fulfilment of their manifesto commitments. The argument is that the Government also had a limited number of broader aims which it achieved. Overall, it wanted to weaken the unions' position in relation to both Government and employers; to restrict what many observers saw as their excessive power. More specifically, it wished to: end the corporatist embrace and remove the unions' role in the policy-making process; assert its authority, and therefore its image of governing competence, by standing up to the unions; stiffen the resolve of employers and make them more willing to use the new legislation; change the attitudes and strategies of unions instilling a 'new realism'; and alter the balance on the shopfloor in favour of management. How successful was the Government in achieving these aims?

The end of corporatism and the reduction of the unions' political role

The Conservatives came to power determined to reduce consultation generally, and the role of the unions specifically in the policy-making process. There were three clear reasons for this strategy. First, the Conservatives were committed to market, rather than corporatist, solutions to economic problems. No attempt at a corporatist solution is feasible without union involvement because such a strategy is based upon supply-side management and Government intervention in the relationship between capital and labour. In contrast, while market solutions may involve some less direct Government legislation, for example, by establishing cash limits in the public sector which effect wages, such intervention is not negotiated with unions – there is no exchange involved – but rather imposed upon them.

Second, the Conservatives were strongly influenced by the government-overload thesis, which suggested that one of the major reasons for Britain's economic decline was the proliferation of demands placed upon Government resources. For many observers this was a consequence of incorporating interest groups into the policy-making process (see King 1975). It was implicit in much of the literature on Government-overload, but explicit in Conservative rhetoric, that foremost among these powerful groups was the trade unions.

Third, and in many ways most importantly, much of the policy of the incoming government, and even more of its rhetoric, was a conscious response to the failures of Mr Heath (see Marsh 1992: ch. 3). If Mr Heath became the spectre at the feast, the trade unions remained the devil, to be invoked and held responsible for the failure of both Mr Heath and the Labour Government. As such, to negotiate with the unions would have been to sup with the devil.

After 1979, meaningful consultation between the unions almost ceased. As Mitchell (1987) shows the number of contacts between the Government and the unions did not decrease but the pattern and quality of those contacts changed significantly. In particular, after 1979 there were fewer meetings than before (10 per cent as opposed to 27 per cent); so less personal contact. In addition, fewer of the contacts were initiated by the Government after 1979 than previously (8 per cent as opposed to 18 per cent). What is more, the number of contacts initiated by the Government fell from 15 in the first year of the Conservative Government to six in both 1983 and 1984.

Certainly, the unions had virtually no effect on any of the Conservative legislation (for figures see Mitchell 1987). The only exception was their success in preventing the inclusion of a provision to require unionists to 'contract in' to, rather than 'contract out' from, the union's political funds in the 1984 Trade Union Act. This concession occurred as a result of a series of judgements made by the Government about the political, and, in particular, the electoral consequences of pursuing the proposal. The Government was well aware that any extended legislative battle on 'contracting in' would have focused attention on the methods by which the Conservative Party was financed (Taylor 1987: 216). Although trade union contributions to the Labour Party are greater than company contributions to the Conservatives, and make up a much greater proportion of the Labour Party's income, nevertheless company contributions are a significant element in Conservative finance.

At the same time, and more importantly, the Government was conscious of its image of governing competence and responsiveness to public opinion on the industrial relations issue. It wished to ensure that the legislation was not only passed but also accepted and complied with in order to preserve its reputation for governing competence. In addition, it was aware that, with the Trades Union Congress (TUC) embracing new realism and expressing a willingness to talk, any confrontation over contracting in might result in the Government losing the battle for the hearts and minds of the electorate and, particularly, of unionists.

On this one issue then, the Government made a significant concession to the unions. However, this 'success', was qualitatively different from that achieved in relation to 'In Place of Strife' or the 1971 Industrial Relations Act.

Asserting the Government's authority

There is no doubt that the Conservative Government successfully reasserted the authority of Government in relation to trade unions. Not only have unions had little effect on policy but, in addition, the legislation once passed has been, to a large extent, complied with by the unions. The problem of compliance, which turned the 1971 Industrial Relations Act into a virtual dead letter by the time it was repealed, has not proved crucial, despite the fact that the Conservative legislation is very radical.

At the same time, the Government's commitment to strong decisive action was also reflected in their attitude to a series of strikes in the public sector. The failure of the steel strike in 1980 and the collapse of the miners strike of 1984/85 showed the Government was resolved not to intervene and offer money to nationalized industries to 'buy-off' striking workers. In both cases the Government's stance clearly reinforced an image of governing competence (see Bulpitt 1986) which Crewe argues has been a key reason for the Conservatives' electoral successes (Crewe 1988).

However, even here it is important to be circumspect. The teachers' strike of 1985/86 resulted in what was generally perceived as a victory for the unions. Certainly, they succeeded in preventing, or at least delaying, any move away from central bargaining (see Seifert 1989). Similarly, the railway workers action in 1989, despite the fact that it inconvenienced a large section of the public, resulted in a wage settlement significantly above the Government's unofficial norm and British Rail's initial offer. So, unions are not inevitably defeated by a management backed by the Government, even in the public sector.

Stiffening the resolve of the employers: using the legislation

One of the major reasons for the failure of the 1971 Industrial Relations Act was the reluctance of employers, especially large employers, to use the legislations (Weekes *et al.* 1975). The Conservative Government clearly hoped that this reluctance would disappear in the 1980s. In fact, less has changed than they hoped.

There has been a marked increase in the number of legal actions brought by employers against unions or union members since 1979. The vast majority of these cases which were brought under legislation introduced by the Conservative Government involved application for injunctions. In fact, Labour Research calculated that of the 46 cases they identified which were brought between January 1983 and July 1985, 38 (83 per cent) involved such applications (*Labour Research* October 1985; also see Marsh 1992). For this reason the major emphasis in this section will be on the use of injunctions.

I have reviewed the evidence on the use of legislation elsewhere (Marsh 1992: ch. 4). The two main conclusions of this analysis of the use of the law are: it is relatively rarely used; and it is used mainly in those industries with a history of bad industrial relations. More specifically, three other points are clear. First, over 90 per cent of the injunctions requested by employers between 1980 and 1988 were granted. Second, in most cases unions comply with any injunction and suspend their industrial action. Third, although employers do usually initiate proceedings for contempt of court if a union fails to comply with an injunction, they rarely proceed with an action to a full trial or pursue damages if the injunction is granted.

It is clear then that the Government legislation did not result in a substantial increase in employers' use of litigation. However, after 1979, employers' support for the legislation grew, not because most large employers expected to use it, but because they were well aware that it restricted the unions' room for manoeuvre in relation to industrial action and, thus, bargaining. Indeed, the indirect effect of the legislation may be more important than the direct effect. Certainly, union leaders were circumspect in their preparations for industrial action because they knew that, if they did not take the steps required by the law, they were likely to be served with an injunction. The Transport and General Workers Union's (TGWU's) manoeuvring in relation to the dispute over the abolition of the National Dock Labour Scheme (NDLS) in 1989 amply illustrated this point.

Once the Government had decided to abolish the NDLS, it was virtually impossible, given their Parliamentary majority and antipathy to trade unions, that any industrial action would have led them to reconsider. However, if the legislation of the 1980s had not been passed, the TGWU would have had a much freer hand to use a variety of tactics in support of its attempts to persuade the port employers to accept a new national agreement to replace the scheme. If they had been able to pursue more decisive action earlier without any fear of legal consequences, then it is quite possible that they could have achieved this aim. As it was, they were forced to delay industrial action in order to stay within the new laws. Such delay clearly significantly weakened the TGWU's bargaining position with employers. In the end, they emerged from the strike in a much weaker position.

The development of 'new realism'

'New realism' is a catch-all concept. Bassett (1987: ch. 4) and McIlroy (1988: 54–6) emphasize the changed attitudes and strategies of the TUC and individual unions after the 1983 election defeat. The argument put forward by Len Murray, then TUC General Secretary, and others was that unions had to be prepared to take a conciliatory, rather than confrontational, approach and talk to Mrs Thatcher. However, this initiative quickly received two body blows. In January 1984 the Government banned trade unions in the Government Communications Headquarters and then the miners' strike further damaged relations between the unions and the Government. Subsequently, the TUC has been most concerned to present a united front with the Labour Party and their contacts with the Conservative Government have not improved (see Marsh 1992: ch. 6).

Of course, a number of observers identify 'new realism' with a new system of industrial relations associated with the Electrical, Electronic, Telecommunication and Plumbing Union (EETPU) and characterized by single union agreements and strike free deals (see Bassett 1987: esp. ch. 5). However, as we shall see later, these developments are hardly an important feature of contemporary industrial relations. Single union agreements and strike-free deals are almost exclusively confined to green-field sites.

In fact, it is difficult to see 'new realism' as a key aspect of industrial relations except in a very minimalist sense of the term. Of course, there is more 'realism' in unions' attitude to government, and in their relations with employers, because they are faced with a harsher economic, political and legal climate. However, three points need emphasizing. First, unions have always been more realistic in hard times. Second, as we shall see in the next section, many of the institutions and practices of shopfloor industrial relations remain the same despite this increased 'realism'. Third, if the situation changes, then so will the strategies and tactics adopted by unions.

Changes on the shopfloor

How much has changed on the shopfloor? Has more changed in the public sector or the private sector? I shall answer these questions by reference to a number of aspects of shopfloor relations: the level of unionization, the extent of union recognition; the coverage of collective bargaining; the coverage of the closed shop; the number of strikes; picketing; and wage levels.

The level of unionization
Total union density dropped from 58.9 per cent in 1978 to 46.5 per cent in 1988 while the density of unions affiliated to the TUC fell from 54.5 per cent to 38.7 per cent in the same period. In this way, TUC affiliated unions suffered more than other unions and it was only in the public sector that membership density held up. Bassett claims that non-unionism is now dominant in Britain (Bassett 1988: 45). This is clearly an exaggerated claim, but there has been a considerable fall in union density, particularly in the private sector.

Derecognition
Millward and Stevens (1986) emphasize how rare derecognition of unions has been. Of the 181 companies they studied in both 1980 and 1984, only three withdrew union recognition, while nine granted it for the first time. In their sample 68 per cent of the companies recognized unions in 1984 as compared with 66 per cent in 1980. However, there is some evidence that derecognition may have increased since 1984. Claydon (1989) identified 49 cases of derecognition in 1987/88. This figure is much larger than that reported by Labour Research, although they also found that derecognition grew from nine cases in 1986 to 15 cases in 1987. They concluded, 'the tendency towards derecognition seems to have been increasing since the GCHQ episode' (Labour Research, April 1988: 133).

In the private sector, the majority of cases of derecognition have occurred in two industries with a history of industrial relations; newspaper and book publishing and coastal shipping (see Claydon 1989: 215). Claydon makes the key point:

> The extent to which employers feel that it is desirable and possible to terminate collective bargaining will depend partly on their experience of trade union activity and their relations with the workforce shop stewards and full-time officials. (Claydon 1989: 219)

Overall, the conclusion of the Labour Research study, which confirms Millward and Stevens' findings, is probably accurate:

> In general, however, outside specific sectors like publishing, the unions report that recognition is not yet a major threat although a new and growing phenomenon. (*Labour Research*, April 1988: 13)

Clearly, it is the history and current status of industrial relations in a given company which has most effect on a firm's decision to derecognize.

Collective bargaining

Millward and Stevens emphasize that there was little change in collective bargaining arrangements in either the private or the public sector (Millward and Stevens 1986: ch. 9; see also Ingram and Cahill 1989: 281). However, this does not mean that there were no attempts by employers to change bargaining structures. As an example, in July 1989 British Telecom moved from a negotiated pay structure to one based upon personal contracts, but only for their 3,000 most senior staff from a workforce of 40,000 (*Labour Research*, December 1989).

Millward and Stevens identify three other developments in collective bargaining which others have confirmed. First, collective bargaining is becoming more exclusively focused on pay; other issues such as levels of employment are now more rarely discussed (Millward and Stevens 1986: 248–53). Second, managements have increasingly demanded productivity or flexibility deals in return for higher wages (Millward and Stevens 1986: 246–9; McIlroy 1988: 206). Third, there has been a move away from national level multi-employer negotiations and a growth in single employer bargaining at company level (Millward and Stevens 1986: 231–3; Ingram and Cahill 1989).

The closed shop

The scope of the closed shop was significantly reduced between 1980 and 1984 as Millward and Stevens' evidence indicates. Since this time, the closed shop has been made illegal by provisions in the 1988 and 1990 Employment Acts. However, two additional points need to be made. As Dunn and Gennard show, the closed shop was in jeopardy well before the Conservative legislation came into operation (Dunn and Gennard 1984). The growth of pre-entry closed shop occurred almost entirely in a past era. They were not widespread and by 1979 they covered some 800,000 people; about 4 per cent of the total workforce. The two main industries in which such shops existed were printing and shipping.

In contrast, by the early 1960s 12 per cent of the British workforce, some three million people, were covered by post-entry closed shops; the major concentration being in the engineering and coalmining industries. However, there was a major growth in these agreements in the late 1960s and 1970s; so that by 1979 4.5 million people were covered in a wide variety of different industries in both the private and the public sector. This growth was, to a large extent, encouraged by employers who saw the closed shop as a means by which to secure greater order on the shopfloor. However, by mid-1982, before the Conservatives' legislation took effect, the closed shop population had declined fairly rapidly; it fell by 13 per cent between 1979 and 1982 to approximately 4.5 million (see Dunn and Gennard 1984: 96).

In essence, the legislative changes in the mid-1980s accelerated the closed shop decline but that decline was already under way, largely because of changes in the economic structure, particularly the decline of the manufacturing sector, associated with technological change and managerial opportunism.

It is also worth emphasizing that although pre-entry and post-entry closed shops are now illegal, they may well continue in practice. The point here is simple. Certain employers, particularly large employers, do not in fact oppose closed shops because they can be a means of increasing discipline among the workforce. For that reason, many employers initially opposed the early closed-shop reforms and many may tacitly accept, and even encourage, unions' efforts to impose a de facto closed shop.

Strikes

The Department of Employment figures clearly indicate that strikes have de-clined significantly since 1979 and authors like Finer (1987) and Biddiss (1987) see this decline as a major achievement of the Conservative Government's legislation. However, we must be a little wary about so bold a conclusion. Millward and Stevens' thorough analysis indicates that the number of strikes in companies has not significantly reduced. The problem is that the Department of Employment does not record any stoppages which last less than three days; yet Millward and Stevens show that such stoppages and other forms of indus-trial action short of a strike – working-to-rule, go-slows or overtime bans – have increased. This is not to suggest that industrial conflict has remained at the level it was before 1979; indeed, the switch to shorter actions is itself a reflec-tion of this change. In addition, it must be acknowledged that public sector unions like the miners and private sector unions, like the print unions, have suffered damaging defeats. However, the tendency of some authors to be dazzled by the Department of Employment statistics does lead them to neglect the fact that unions and workers have adapted their strategies to changed circumstances.

Overall, there is little doubt that the incidence of industrial action has fallen significantly. Certainly, it is difficult to accept McInnes' view that, 'Thatcherism has not ushered in an era of industrial peace where there was previously strife. As with so much else, little has changed' (McInnes 1987:

108). Unions still strike and they increasingly use 'cut-price' industrial action short of striking. However, they strike less often and, as we will see later, they picket more circumspectly, and both these trends are most evident among manual workers in the manufacturing sector. All is not as it was, but neither is the situation transformed.

Picketing

Obviously, given the number of strikes has fallen, so has the extent of picketing. Millward and Stevens found that the amount of picketing halved between 1980 and 1984 (Millward and Stevens 1986: 283–4). In the light of this, it is perhaps not surprising that between 1984 and 1989 only 12 per cent of the injunctions applied for by employers against unions and unionists were on the grounds of illegal picketing.

East, Power and Thomas claim that the age of mass picketing is past (East *et al.* 1985). This conclusion may be a trifle too sweeping, as the Wapping confrontation occurred after they wrote. However, union leaders will clearly be circumspect before taking such action. Auerbach makes the key point:

> The *Stockport Messenger*, miners' and News International disputes have demonstrated that the possibility of incurring crippling fines or sequestration must be taken very seriously by any union contemplating the use of picketing as a central tactic in a major dispute. (Auerbach 1987: 227)

Wages

As many authors indicate real wages have risen fairly consistently since 1979 (see McInnes 1987: 80–4; Longstreth 1988: 421–2; McIlroy 1988: 206–11; Brown and Wadhwani 1990: 65). Indeed Longstreth argues that they rose more in real terms in the Thatcher years than in any comparable earlier period (Longstreth 1988: 421).

A time-series analysis carried out of wage changes since 1963 in 14 different industry gro pings suggests that there has been a significant and important 'Thatcher effect' on wages (Marsh 1992: ch. 8). This effect persists even when they control for the rate of inflation and levels of productivity and profitability. What is more, none of the three union variables used, level of trade union membership, number of strikes or number of days lost through strikes, had any effect on wages outside the mining industry. However, the 'Thatcher effect' disappeared when they included a dummy variable to take acount of the existence, or otherwise, of incomes policy. It appears that wages have increased since 1979 in large part because of the absence of incomes policy.

There is little evidence then from aggregate level or sectoral level analysis of wages of any major decline in the bargaining position of unions. In contrast, firm level studies indicate the 'insider' factors, profitability and productivity in a particular firm, are more important than 'outsider' factors, the aggregate level of employment and inflation, in determining wage levels in that firm.

Gregory *et al.* (1985), use the CBI Databank which has questionnaire material on 1,200 manufacturing establishments. Their material reports firms' perceptions of the relative importance of various factors influencing pay negotiations and is particularly interesting. They found that the two key factors seen as exerting *upward* pressure on the level of pay settlements were inflation (stressed by 60 per cent of respondents in 1979/80 and 40 per cent in 1983/84) and the level of establishment/company profits (11 per cent in 1979/80, 21 per cent in 1983/84). Three factors were seen as exerting *downward* pressure on pay settlements, the level of establishment company profits (45 per cent in both years), the level of profitability (38 per cent in 1979/80 and 51 per cent in 1983/84) and the risk of redundancy (20 per cent in 1979/80 and 21 per cent in 1983/84). Generally, 'insider' factors rather than 'outsider' factors had more influence on wage settlements (see Gregory *et al.* 1985: 350–2, and also Gregory *et al.* 1987).

Nickell and Wadhwani (1990) use data based upon the published accounts of 219 UK quoted manufacturing companies over the period 1972–82. They found that 'insider' forces, particularly the firms' own prices and productivity levels had a major effect on the level of wages. The top 20 per cent of companies raised the real wages of their employees by some 18 per cent more than the bottom 20 per cent 'solely because of their superior average revenue product growth and financial performance' (Nickell and Wadhwani 1990: 507).

Overall, the firm-based findings are fairly convincing and support a key conclusion of this chapter. It is the state of industrial relations and the specific economic circumstances within individual companies which affect the level of wages and strikes. Of course, government can have little direct influence on these factors. 'Outsider' factors are not unimportant; certainly inflation plays a key role. However, in most cases these factors appear less important. At the same time, what we need is a longer-run time series data set, of the type used by Nickell and Wadhwani, which would allow us to discover if the 'Thatcher effect', or perhaps more accurately 'the income policy effect', highlighted here holds when firm-level data, on profitability and productivity particularly, is used.

Comparing changes in the public and the private sectors

I have inevitably concentrated upon shopfloor changes in the private sector because much less attention has been paid in the industrial relations literature to changes in the public sector. The Workplace Industrial Relations Survey (WIRS) study of the 1980–84 period suggests that less has changed in the public sector than in the private sector. Certainly, there has been no move to derecognition and no significant decline in collective bargaining. However, studies of individual sections of the public sector reveal more change. In particular, the Government has placed many more constraints on the autonomy of national management through its control of the purse strings and its ability directly to change the rules of the game within which public sector managers are operating. As such, there is little doubt that the consultation and agreement which often marked public sector industrial relations has been replaced by a more adversarial style (see Marsh 1992: ch. 9).

At the local level, while the institutions of industrial relations were largely intact, practice appears to have changed more. Certainly, Edwards and Heery's (1989) study of Freightliners found that the operation of the local institutions of industrial relations were more or less unchanged, although the management style was more aggressive and some changes in working practices had occurred. Similarly, Pendleton (1991) emphasizes that while the basic structural features on the shopfloor in British Rail remain the same, the approach of local managements had changed. In particular, there was less consultation and less commitment by management to agreements. In consequence only 30 per cent of the train drivers' representatives Pendleton surveyed in 1989 believed that local industrial relations were good, while 28 per cent believed they were bad; in contrast, in 1980 70 per cent of respondents in a similar survey responded positively and only 6 per cent negatively.

Overall, a clear pattern emerges. The institutions of shopfloor industrial relations have not changed but the atmosphere and, to an extent, the practices have altered. Unions in both the public and the private sector and at the national and the local level clearly occupy a much more defensive role than before 1979.

Explaining change: the influence of the Conservative legislation

Many people suggest that structural economic changes have had more effect on the decline of the position of unions than has the Government's legislation (see, for example, Brown and Wadhwani 1990). In contrast, others stress the importance of the legislation (see, for example, Metcalf 1990a). Of course, it is difficult to disentangle the impact of the changes in law from that of the deep recession at the beginning of the 1980s and the subsequent economic structuring (on the economic changes see Marsh 1992: ch. 7). However, there have been a number of attempts in the literature to do so. In particular, we have analyses which assess the relative effect of the law and the recession upon: the decline in union membership; the use of strikes; and productivity.

Union density

As we saw earlier, there has been a major decline in union membership which results in part from a combination of the rise in unemployment and economic restructuring. However, if the rise in unemployment was the sole reason for the decline in union membership then one would have expected union density to remain constant but it has also fallen markedly. Historically, union strength has been concentrated among male, full-time manual workers employed in large plants in the manufacturing sector in the North, the Midlands and London. This pattern has persisted. As the 1989 Labour Force Survey indicates, union density is still greatest for: those in full-time (43 per cent) rather than part-time employment (22 per cent); employees in large rather than small plants; manual (43 per cent) rather than non-manual employees (35 per cent); the middle-aged rather than the young and old; public sector employees rather than private sector employees; and in the North (52 per cent) rather than the South East (30 per cent) (see *Employment Gazette*, August 1990: 403–13; see also Beaumont 1987: 192).

It is noticeable that those unions who represent workers in the declining industries have experienced the largest falls in membership. Union membership grew generally in the 1970s, as the Labour Government encouraged union recognition and membership, although the major expansion was in the public sector. In the 1980s, in contrast, union membership has fallen, particularly for unions whose strength was in the manufacturing sector; between 1979 and 1989 the TGWU membership declined by 39 per cent, the Amalgamated Union of Engineering Workers (AUEW) by 39 per cent and Union of Construction, Allied Trades and Technicians (UCATT) by 26 per cent.

There has been a heated controversy among industrial relations specialists as to the cause of the decline in union density. Three main factors are emphasized in the literature; the changing composition of the workforce; the macro-economic changes which have occurred (particularly rising unemployment and inflation); and the Conservative Government's employment legislation.

Freeman and Pelletier (1990) argue that the decrease in manufacturing employment, while it may have hurt unions, cannot have been a major cause of this decline because: density declined in most sectors of the economy, not just in heavy manufacturing; it did not decline in Ireland where the changes in the industrial mix of employment were similar; and the decrease in manufacturing employment was almost as great in the 1970s when union density rose. Similarly, they suggest that the rise in female, part-time and white collar employment has had a limited effect on density. Their calculations indicate that the increase in female employment may explain 0.6 per cent of the decline in density, while the increase in the non-manual workforce can explain at most 1.3 per cent of this fall. They conclude:

> Our calculations imply that 3.1 per cent points of the 1980–86 drop in density are due to changes in (structural factors) – leaving 5.5 per cent or nearly two-thirds of the observed change attributable to other factors. (Freeman and Pelletier 1990: 145)

Freeman and Pelletier are equally convinced that changes in the level of British economic performance had little influence on union density. In particular, they emphasize that the upturn in economic performance in the second half of the 1980s was not matched by an increase in density (ibid. 145). In addition, they cite Booth (1989) who argues that during the 1980s a business cycle model over-predicted a level of density, such that by 1986 actual density was 7 per cent lower than the model predicted.

Freeman and Pelletier are adamant: 'the vast bulk of the observed 1980s decline in union density in the UK is due to the changed legal environment for industrial relations' (1990: 156).

This conclusion is based upon an econometric analysis of levels of union density from 1945 to 1986. The analysis revealed that increases in the manufacturing sector's share of employment, inflation and unemployment raise density. However, an index which quantified the favourableness or unfavourableness of British industrial relations laws to unions had a greater effect on density. Indeed, Freeman and Pelletier suggest a 1 point increase in the legal index, which results from a legal change in unions' favour, induces a significant 1.3 per cent increase in density (p. 153).

These results have not gone unquestioned. In particular, Disney points out that it is difficult to separate out cause and effect (Disney 1990: 170–1). It is plausible to suggest that the Government legislation is a response to the weakening of union power and union density. Certainly, I have argued elsewhere that the Thatcher legislation built upon, rather than transformed, public opinion on unions and that it proceeded, using a step-by-step approach, as a response to union reaction (Marsh 1990). This would suggest that as union density fell the Government became more confident and introduced more radical legislation.

In fact, although Disney concedes that changes in the composition of the workforce have had little effect on density, he argues that macro-economic factors are most important. He suggests that most critiques of business–cycle models rest upon the fact that while unemployment has decreased in the recent period, density has fallen. However, he argues that unemployment has much less impact on density than does inflation and shows that, if a business cycle model is more accurately specified to take account of the greater importance of inflation, then it has more explanatory power (Disney 1990: 168–9). He asserts:

> the explanation of the decline in trade union membership in the 1980s in Britain is straightforward: a period of rising unemployment, high real-wage growth and a Conservative Government is sufficient to explain the decline in density. (p. 168)

This debate remains unresolved. Metcalf's position appears most sound. He argues that the decline in membership was the result of a complex interaction of five factors: the macroeconomic climate; the composition of jobs and the workforce; the policy of the state; the attitudes and conduct of employers; and the stance taken by unions themselves (Metcalf 1990c: 32). Certainly, all factors have played some role and it would be wrong to rely on mono-causal explanations which stress either the role of the legislation or the effect of macroeconomic factors.

Strikes and picketing

There has been a major decline in the number of strikes, as defined by the Department of Employment figures, and in the extent of picketing. However, these changes do not result in any simple way from the impact of Thatcherism.

The number of days lost from strikes declined throughout the world during the period between 1983–87 as compared with the previous period, 1978–82 (Department of Employment *Gazette*, June 1989). Most significantly, Britain ranked seventh out of 20 industrialized countries in the strike table in both periods. Nevertheless, McConnell and Takla (1990) using Department of Employment figures, conclude that the Conservative legislation has had an important effect on the number of strikes and the days lost through strikes, after controlling for the effect of macroeconomic variables. In contrast, it had no effect on the number of workers involved in strikes. This analysis would suggest that the legislation has, as the WIRS implied, reduced the length of strikes.

Productivity

There is no doubt that productivity, measured in terms of output per operative hour in manufacturing, improved significantly in the 1980s (see Metcalf 1990c). There are, however, competing explanations of this improvement. Metcalf argues strongly that it results from increased labour productivity; more efficient use of labour by employers. In contrast, the work of Smith-Garvine and Bennett (1990) suggests that it is increased technological productivity, the installation and more efficient use of technology, which is crucial.

It appears best to conclude that to the extent that labour productivity, rather than technological productivity, had increased, this owes something to the effect of technological productivity, and this does appear to be an important, if not the key, determinant of overall productivity.

Clearly, both the legislation and the changes which have occurred in the macro-economy have affected the position of unions. However, the econometric evidence certainly does not allow us clearly to identify one of these factors as more important than the other.

Conclusion

Much has changed since 1979. Indeed, more has changed than many academics specializing in industrial relations admit. At the same time, less has changed than the Government or some notable political scientists have claimed. To what extent did the Thatcher Government achieve their aims?

Certainly, the Conservatives had no difficulty in fulfilling their detailed commitments. Almost all of their manifesto commitments on industrial relations were enacted. Their legislative proposals were passed without significant amendment by Parliament. The proposal to replace 'contracting out' to the political fund by 'contracting in' was the only significant concession made by the Government to the unions.

In contrast, the Thatcher Government was less successful in achieving its broader aims; although here the pattern is more complex. Certainly, shopfloor industrial relations has changed less than the Government hoped or expected. The unions have been excluded from the policy-making process: beer and sandwiches at Downing Street are definitely a thing of the past. At the same time, the Government's firmness in the face of key public sector strikes did contribute to an image of governing competence which had apparent electoral benefits. However, the attitudes and behaviour of unions and management have not been transformed. 'New realism' reflects a realistic assessment by unions of the changes in their bargaining position rather than a permanent transformation in union attitudes or a new style of industrial relations. Similarly, employers have not rushed to use the new legislation. Indeed, its use is largely confined to the industries in which the history of industrial relations is marked by conflict, particularly to the printing and shipping industries.

Much less has changed on the shopfloor. In particular there is little evidence of a major move to derecognize unions or to restrict collective bargaining. Nevertheless, one must beware of claiming that all is the same. The coverage of collective bargaining may have remained fairly constant but its content and scope have changed. Similarly, while industrial conflict is still not a thing of the past, the number of strikes and the amount of picketing has significantly reduced.

It is very difficult to assess whether Government legislation or macro-economic developments have had more influence on the trade unions. The econometric material dealing with union density, strikes and productivity is inconclusive. However, it does seem clear that there has been greater change in those industries marked by a history of poor industrial relations; in such cases employers are more likely to use legislation and more likely to derecognize trade unions.

This evidence, together with the fact that company-level studies suggest that wages are strongly affected by the levels of profitability and productivity in individual companies, indicates that it is the history and current state of relations between capital and labour within a given company which has most effect on the institutions and outcomes of industrial relations in that company. In the private sector at least, the Government can only influence the legal framework and the ideological context within which industrial relations occur; this influence is important but it is indirect.

4

Local government finance

R.A.W. Rhodes

Introduction

During the 1980s there were some 40 Acts affecting local government in general and local government finance in particular. The scale of activity was daunting and its consequences were manifold and unintended. This chapter provides a survey of developments and answers the questions 'What changed, by how much and why?'

For many commentators there is an obvious answer to the question: the 1980s witnessed the demise of local government and an unprecedented degree of centralization (Burgess and Travers 1980; Jones and Stewart 1983; Stewart and Stoker 1989b). This chapter explores the gap between the rhetoric and reality in the Government's policy on local government finance, arguing that the centre's relations with local government were characterized more by unintended consequences than by revolutionary change. There was centralization, but the most important consequence was the creation of a policy mess (Rhodes 1984) in which neither level of government achieved its objectives.

The first section of the chapter describes the stated objectives of the policy drawn from official government statements (e.g. white papers, green papers, bills/Acts and the speeches of Ministers). The second section tells briefly the story of local government finance from 1979 to the decision to abolish the community charge in 1991. The third section explores the outcomes of the Government's policy, and the final section offers an explanation of the 'implementation gap' in local government finance.

The plot of this particular story is well known; the Government sought to reduce local current expenditure and failed. The reasons for this failure are more interesting than Conservative diatribes against recalcitrant Labour controlled authorities. I will argue that the policy failed for a complexity of reasons including an inadequate causal theory, inappropriate policy instruments, and the politicization and recalcitrance of local authorities and professions.

The objectives

There were two explicit and one implicit objectives running through the Government's policy on local government finance during the 1980s:

1. The first objective was to control local expenditure as part of its broader strategy of reducing public expenditure.
2. The second objective was to strengthen local accountability by introducing a clear link between the provision of services, paying for them and voting in local elections.
3. The third and implicit objective was 'to bury socialism'.

The Conservative Manifesto 1979 illustrates the initial disinterest of the party in local government for it contains precious little worthy of comment other than the threat to cut public, and therefore local, expenditure. The Chancellor's budget speech on 12 June 1979 gave an altogether clearer indication of what was to come:

> The need for substantial economies applies equally to local authorities, where the Government's contribution is made through the rate support grant. We shall take account of pay settlements in calculating the increase orders for the rate support grant, *but we shall make significant across-the-board reductions from the total so calculated.* (cited in Meadows 1981: 45, emphasis added)

This theme of spending reductions was taken up vigorously by the Secretary of State for the Environment, Michael Heseltine:

> So far as overspending is concerned, while a majority of local authorities have shown a willingness to keep in step with the Government's guidelines on public expenditure, a minority of authorities persist in maintaining levels of expenditure which the present economic circumstances simply do not justify. (cited in Travers 1986: 83)

The key concept had become 'the problem of the overspenders', a synonym for recalcitrant and profligate Labour-controlled councils.

The second objective of accountability has its roots in the Conservative manifesto of 1974 and the promise to abolish the rates. In a qualified form, this promise was repeated in the 1979 manifesto which stated that: 'cutting income tax must take priority for the time being over the abolition of the domestic rating system' (p. 14). The promise was taken up in the Green Paper *Alternatives to the Domestic Rates* (HMSO 1981). In the Government's view, any new system of local taxation had to be not only practical, fair and cost effective but it must also encourage local accountability:

Public authorities should be accountable to their electorates for what they spend and for the revenue they raise. To encourage efficiency and safeguard against extravagance by local authorities, local electors need to be aware of decisions about expenditure and revenue and the effects of those decisions on the level of local taxes that they pay.

To foster local accountability a local tax should:

(a) be clearly perceptible to local electors and taxpayers, who should be aware of how much tax they are paying, which authority they are paying it to and what services it provides; and

(b) as far as possible be paid directly by as many as possible of those who benefit from the services provided by the local authorities. (HMSO 1981: 6)

The objective of accountability was enshrined in the Green Paper, *Paying for Local Government* (HMSO 1986) and the proposal to introduce the community charge. The clarion call is on the first page: '*Effective local accountability must be the cornerstone of successful local government*' (p. viii, emphasis added). Thus the community charge aimed to make local authorities more accountable to their electors by ensuring that 'the local electors know what the costs of their local services are, so that armed with this knowledge they can influence the spending decisions through the ballot box' (p. vii). There was to be a clear relationship between paying for, and the receipt of, local services; between paying for services and voting in elections. The argument was cogently stated by the Secretary of State for the Environment, Nicholas Ridley:

The community charge will be a flat rate charge for local services. It has to be a flat rate charge because crucial to the change is the concept that there should be a 'price' for local government services. Like the price for goods in the shops, the community charge 'price' can only work properly if it is roughly the same for everyone. (Nicholas Ridley, cited in Esam and Oppenheim 1989: 37; see also Foster 1986; and Gibson 1990: ch. 12)

The third objective of burying socialism was implicit but it occurred in the innumerable references to overspending councils, profligate Labour authorities and waste by the Metropolitan County Councils (MCCs) and the Greater London Council (GLC) (all Labour controlled):

It was her [Thatcher's] purpose to bury socialism which she saw as chief perpetrator of the decline which she was pledged to arrest and reverse . . . She aimed her attack at the bastions of Labour power – the trade unions, the council estates, the Socialist local authorities, and the nationalised industries. (Jenkins 1988: 168)

The point was made in his own inimicable way by Norman Tebbit who cut through all the verbiage about streamlining the cities and baldly stated that the GLC was being abolished because it was 'Labour dominated, high spending and at odds with the government's view of the world' (cited in James 1990: 493–4).

It is against these three objectives that the Government's success in implementing its policies must be evaluated. Within each of these objectives, there were a number of more or less explicit sub-objectives but I have not analysed them in detail, primarily because of lack of space. Where important, the Government's record will be noted.

The legislation

Consultation was the 'normal' style in central–local fiscal relations for the bulk of the postwar period. For example, between 1967 and 1973, forecasts of local authority current expenditure were the basis of meetings between the then Ministry of Housing and Local Government and officials of the local authority associations. These 'informal' negotiations preceded the statutory meeting between the Minister and elected representatives from the associations. Although decisions were substantially influenced by the Treasury's view of the economic situation, there was room for manoeuvre at the margin. For example, the 1970 grant negotiations saw agreed local expenditure growth rates of three per cent for 1969/70 and 5 per cent for 1970/71, in each case one per cent above the Government's initial offer (Rhodes 1986: 102–7). Such marginal shifts do not seem great, and undoubtedly the balance of negotiating advantage lay with the Government, but the sums of money involved were considerable. For all the disappointment expressed by the associations, the grant negotiating process exemplifies incremental budgeting. With the benefit of hindsight's rose-coloured spectacles, these seem like halcyon days.

With the onset of the oil crisis, world recession, Britain's relative economic decline and the International Monetary Fund's (IMF's) stringent economic conditions, the party was over. The Labour Government's response to the economic crisis was to incorporate the local authority associations into a 'social contract' on local authority expenditure. For the first time, Whitehall had a forum in which to discuss the long-run future of local spending with the local authority associations. This body, called the Consultative Council on Local Government Finance, was noteworthy because it brought the Treasury and local authority elected representatives together for the first time to discuss the future of local expenditure. The Government, by involving the associations in policy-making affecting local government, hoped to persuade them of the 'realities' of the economic situation, and thus enlist them as allies in the battle against inflation. The Consultative Council was successful in getting the local authority associations to persuade their members to behave with restraint. Of course, there were other pressures in the same direction: e.g. cash limits on central grants to local authorities. However, what ever else it accomplished the Consultative Council helped to shift influence within local government away from service oriented councillors and officers towards local politicians and finance directors more concerned with increased efficiency and financial soundness and, in so doing, it reinforced local government's 'responsibility ethic' or willingness to defer to central government's responsibility for, and its stated views on, the management of the economy (Bramley and Stewart 1981: 60).

The justification for this brief historical excursion is to make the point that there are marked continuities after 1979, in particular the use of cash limits and the cuts in local expenditure. Of course, there were marked discontinuities: for example, the Conservative Government had little faith in consultative devices. In reality, the Government tended to accelerate pre-existing trends rather than introduce radical new policies. The Local Government, Planning and Land Act, 1980 is one such example.

The key proposal at the heart of this Act was the introduction of block grant which had been anticipated in the Layfield Committee Report (HMSO 1976: 231–3) and the Labour Government's Green Paper, *Local Government Finance* (HMSO 1977: para. 3.7 and appendix 1). The block grant system brought together the resources and needs elements of rate support grant. The needs element sought to equalize the need to spend between local authorities, by, for example, compensating an authority for having a high proportion of elderly. The resources element sought to equalize rateable values. The distribution of the grant required an assessment of an authority's spending needs – known as the grant related expenditure assessment (GREA) – and its rateable value per head. In theory an authority's grant entitlement was the difference between its GREA and its rate income. In practice, if actual expenditure exceeded a threshold of 10 per cent above national average GREA per head, then an authority lost grant at a punitive rate. In short, the centre sought to exercise downward pressure on local government expenditure and to make local authorities pay for any increases in expenditure significantly above GREA.

Unfortunately, from the Government's point of view, the new grant system did not deliver *immediate* reductions in local expenditure. Targets and penalties were introduced to effect these cuts. In brief, local authorities had to reduce expenditure by 5.6 per cent taking their out-turn expenditure for 1978–79 as the base. If any local authority exceeded its target, it would also lose grant through a system of grant 'holdbacks', a term which means exactly what it says. Unfortunately, the Government did not have the legal power to so penalize local authorities. Further legislation was required.

The original Local Government Finance Bill gave the Government power to fix the maximum rate of an authority and required any local authority spending above that level to seek approval in a local referendum. These proposals were dropped under a barrage of criticism from Conservative backbenchers. The revised Bill gave the Government power to hold back grant, abolish supplementary rates and set up an Audit Commission to promote value for money in local government. In total, the period 1979–83 saw seven major changes to the grant system in England and Wales (Jones and Stewart 1983: 55–6; see also Travers 1986: tables 8.4 and 8.8, 126–8).

We had entered an era of repetitive legislation wherein laws were made and remade throughout the term of office because of the high degree of uncertainty surrounding their viability. The objective of this cycle of frenetic activity was the control of not only local current expenditure but also local income and the means was direct control through budgetary ceilings imposed on every individual local authority.

As the General Election drew nigh, the Conservatives faced a choice. They could intensify the search for direct control or search for a more conciliatory mix of strategies. The then Secretary of State for the Environment, Tom King, seemed to be extending an olive branch by talking of abolishing volume targets. A process of consultation was underway on the Green Paper on *Alternatives to the Domestic Rates* (HMSO 1981). Department of the Environment civil servants cautioned against both the detailed control of local finance and the dismantling of the GLC and the MCCs. But it was all in vain. The Prime Minister wanted to 'do something' about local government (Forrester *et al.* 1985: 64–6 from which the following is paraphrased – see also Flynn *et al.* 1985; O'Leary 1987; and Rhodes 1991). No matter that a Cabinet committee, MISC 79 with William Whitelaw in the chair, had concluded that there was no viable alternative to the rates. Somewhat tentatively, it had suggested the abolition of the 'overspending' GLC and MCCs but Tom King was known to doubt the wisdom of such a move. Margaret Thatcher was dissatisfied and established a sub-committee of the Economic Committee of the Cabinet, which endorsed the abolition proposal and, once again, reviewed the rates. Enter the Treasury in the guise of the Chief Secretary, Leon Brittan, with a proposal to limit rate increases. Again no matter that the proposal had already been rejected by the Cabinet. There was a gap to be filled and Mrs Thatcher disregarded all known opposition within the Government and the party and inserted rate-capping and abolition into the manifesto. The Government then issued two White Papers, *Rates* (HMSO 1983a) and *Streamlining the Cities* (HMSO 1983b) and proceeded to expend vast amounts of parliamentary time putting its proposals on the statute book.

The Rates Act 1984 took away the power of local authorities to determine their own rate level. For this purpose, local authorities fell into two groups; those subject to the selective limitation scheme and the rest, subject to a general limitation scheme to be activated should the need arise. Under the selective limitation scheme, the Secretary of State for the Environment chose the local authorities to be ratecapped. He had to specify the criteria for selection; that is, they had to be high spending authorities with total expenditure in excess of £10 million and above their GREA. The Secretary of State then stipulated a notional level of expenditure for each selected authority. The authority could appeal against the total; i.e. seek a derogation. When the total grant available to local authorities was known, the expenditure limit was translated into a maximum rate, taking into account the financial reserves of the authority. If the two sides agreed on this rate level, it became the legal limit. Assuming that the local authority did not agree with the rate level, and that it was not able to renegotiate it with the Secretary of State, the latter either laid an order before the House of Commons setting the maximum rate or imposed without parliamentary approval an interim maximum rate. The local authority could not levy a rate in excess of this maximum.

For 1985–86, the Government capped 18 local authorities, of which one was Conservative controlled. A phoney war broke out with the Labour councils threatening not to set a rate. However, this opposition slowly crumbled as the legal implications of non–compliance became all too clear. By 31 May, 15 councils had set a rate. Only Lambeth and Liverpool challenged the district auditor in the courts and their councillors were duly surcharged and disqualified from standing for the council. The political drama was muted in subsequent years (for a more detailed résumé see Travers 1986: 164–76).

During the early years of the 1980s, the Conservative Government avoided structural reform. It made an exception for the GLC and the MCCs. The local authorities fought a highly effective rearguard campaign in which they were assisted by the Government's maladroit management of the legislative process: for example, the attempt to cancel the London elections of May 1985 was defeated by the House of Lords.

None the less, the Government had its way and the councils were abolished. To be brief, functions were reallocated to private companies, central departments, non–departmental public bodies, district/borough councils, indirectly elected London/county–wide bodies and indirectly elected bodies which cover only part of the county/London. The most visible features are the new joint bodies (some voluntary, some statutory) for waste disposal, consumer protection/trading standards, planning and highways and traffic (for a more detailed summary see Leach and Davis 1990; and Hebbert and Travers 1988). The significance of this summary is that the fragmentation of sub–central government in the conurbations makes it difficult to assess the financial effects of the change. At long last, the Government produced its figures on the likely savings from abolition. Cautiously, it claimed a saving in the order of £100 million annually. Few were able to determine how this figure had been derived at the time. The Government has provided no figures on *actual* savings subsequently. In fact, the abolition of the GLC and the MCCs led to no reduction in local expenditure. Skelcher and Leach (1990: 40–1) estimate that rate and grant borne expenditure for the transferred services increased by 4 per cent between 1984/85 and 1987/88.

Nor did rate capping have the intended effect. As Travers (1986: 172 and 176) reports capping only slowed down the rate of increase in expenditure in the capped authorities from the average of 4.2 per cent in England as a whole to 2.9 per cent. In addition, the capped authorities increased their expenditure within the rate limits. To further compound the Government's problems, the uncertainty generated by the new system caused local authorities to adopt risk avoidance strategies. For example, local authorities increased the rates not to maintain or improve services but to accumulate reserves to counter such uncertainties as the threat of rate capping and cuts in block grant. Even the most rudimentary consultation with local authority treasurers would have revealed the likelihood of such action by local authorities.

Other aspects of the Government's policy were also under attack, this time from unimpeachable sources. The Committee of Public Accounts (1985) joined the Audit Commission (1984) in producing a report which criticized the existing block grant arrangements. As a result, targets and penalties were abandoned. It might seem that some respite for both the Government and local authorities was in order. The Scottish rating revaluation put paid to that idle dream. The political outcry in Scotland – coupled with the determination of the Scottish Secretary, George Younger, supported by Mrs Thatcher – forced a reluctant Cabinet to consider the issue yet again. Abolition of the domestic rate was now high on the political agenda.

The future was unveiled in the Green Paper, *Paying for Local Government* (HMSO 1986) which contained the major proposals that: the domestic rates be abolished and replaced by the community charge, otherwise known as the poll tax; the non-domestic rate be vested in central government; and block grant be abolished and the grant system simplified. In its place there would be a needs grant, corresponding to an authority's GREA, which would compensate for cost differences in providing a standard level of service; and a standard grant which would be a contribution per adult.

The Green Paper had little or no immediate impact. The Government was waiting for a third term of office before mounting its next attack on the 'problem' of local government finance. There was a stand-off. Not only were targets and penalties abolished but the grant settlements were more favourable to local government. This local government stand-off is one instance of drift in Government policy (Young 1989: 500). It was the lull before the storm.

After the 1987 election, the narrow fixation on local expenditure gave way to a broader set of themes designed to restructure local government. The pro-gramme has been described as revolutionary (Stewart and Stoker 1989a: 1). The Government abandoned direct control in favour of a market-oriented strategy designed to return control to citizens, now redesignated as consumers. The emphasis fell on accountability to the local electorate, responsiveness to clients, competition and contracting out to the private sector, greater efficiency and better management (for further details see Rhodes 1991). The centre-piece of this revolution was the community charge. But it was to herald no revolution, only catastrophe. Starting with demonstrations and backbench disquiet, it led to defeat in both by-elections and local elections. Its widespread unpopularity was there for all to see. It contributed not only to the Government's poor showing in the opinion polls but also to the downfall of the Prime Minister. Mrs Thatcher was closely identified with the community charge. She had forced it upon a reluctant Cabinet (*Sunday Times*, 1 April 1991). It provided Michael Heseltine with a golden opportunity to garner support amongst backbench MPs nervous about its possible effect on their re-election. (On the relationship between the poll tax and the Conservative Party's marginal seats see Gibson 1990: 257–9.) But the lack of political support was only one of the Government's problems with the tax (see pp. 62–4). With John Major as Prime Minister and Michael Heseltine back at the Department of the Environment, the next problem was to persuade a reluctant Cabinet that community charge should be abolished. There were fears that its abolition would open up a split within the party and a sceptical Treasury had to be convinced about the validity of any replacement tax. For example, the income tax implications of transferring all or part of education to the centre were seen as unacceptable. With a general election looming, and further by-election losses, the fate of the community charge was sealed. It was abolished and after some wavering its replacement was announced. Lo and behold, policy turned full circle. The new council tax is to be a revamped property tax, known colloquially to us all as the rates.

The consequences

This section provides a broad overview of the expenditure, accountability and political consequences of the Government's policy on local government finance. Additional consequences will emerge from the review of implementation problems in the next section.

The record on local expenditure for the 1980s is shown in Table 4.1. There is one inescapable conclusion. At the aggregate level, there was no cut in local expenditure. Whatever qualifications are introduced, and several will be noted in a moment, this oft-stated and brutally simple policy objective was not attained. Between 1979 and 1988 local current expenditure rose at 1980 prices by 15 per cent in real terms, representing 10.4 per cent of GDP and 27.3 per cent of public sector expenditure.

There were some interesting changes. Local capital expenditure was decimated, falling by some 79 per cent during the period. The proportion of local expenditure funded by block grant fell from 61 per cent in 1979 to 42 per cent in 1990 whilst the contribution from specific grants increased to 35 per cent in 1988. Local authorities compensated for the loss of grant income by increasing their rates. The contribution of rates to local expenditure rose from 39 per cent in 1979 to 52 per cent in 1989. Resources were redistributed between local services. Some services (e.g. the police) experienced a real and substantial increase in resources whereas others (e.g. housing) experienced dramatic cuts. There was also a redistribution of resources away from the metropolitan councils towards the county councils. Finally, none of the foregoing figures should be interpreted to mean that the increase in local expenditure kept pace with the demand for local services. This chapter is concerned with local government finance at the aggregate level (on individual services see the other chapters in this book and Hills 1990).

Assessing the accountability objective is difficult because the community charge was in operation for so short a period. Rallings and Thrasher (1991: 182) conclude that 'the poll tax was not itself the prime cause of the variation in results' in the 1990 local elections. However, the key point is that the Government abandoned the objective. Charge capping served to obscure the link between receipt of and payment for a service. Transitional grants (or safety nets) were used to avoid dramatic increases in community charge in selected areas. In

Table 4.1 Local authority expenditure, 1979–89

Local authority expenditure	1979/80	1980/81	1981/82	1982/83	1983/84	1984/85	1985/86	1986/87	1987/88
current prices (£m)	22,425	24,986	26,580	29,132	33,950	34,950	35,363	37,872	40,926
1975 prices (£m)	13,536	12,137							
1980 prices (£m)	24,561	23,492	23,341	23,978	25,950	26,021	25,111	26,101	28,206
% of GDP – market	10.5	10.3	10.0	10.1	10.6	10.4	9.7	9.7	10.4
% of GDP – factor	12.1	11.9	11.8	11.8	12.4	12.0	11.3	11.4	12.2
% of public sector	28.3	28.2	26.7	26.3	28.1	27.5	26.4	26.6	27.2

Source: CIPFA (1989).

an effort to avoid a repeat of 1990's political outcry aganist large community charge bills, the revenue support grant was increased by some £4 billion in 1991/92, an increase paid for by raising VAT from 15 to 17.5 per cent. The grant took the form of a per capita subsidy of up to £140 per person. The Government also capped 'over-spending' local authorities in 1990/91 and threatened to do so again for 1991/92 if local authorities did not pass on the benefit of the increase in grant to community charge payers (Gibson 1990: 247). Thus, when electors failed to spot the link between services and tax bills or, in an aberrant moment, voted for high levels of expenditure, the Government stepped in and remedied the oversight by setting the poll tax at the correct level. It would seem that accountability was the objective of poll tax only when electors did not vote for increased expenditure. It is difficult to avoid the conclusion that the sole objective of community charge was cuts in local expenditure.

It is also doubtful that the Government succeeded in burying socialism. Since the 1987 general election, Labour has increased its share of the vote in the European, local and several by-elections and increased both the total number of seats and the number of local authorities under its control. The most plausible conclusion is that the partisan actions of the Government politicized central–local fiscal relations to the benefit of the Labour Party and to the cost of the Conservative Government which had to manage an ever more recalcitrant system.

Such a brief evaluation of Government policy is possible because the major objectives were both simple and clear. Obviously a number of sub-objectives were achieved; for example the GLC, the MCCs and domestic rates were all abolished. But these actions formed part of a larger picture. The GLC was abolished as part of the effort to control local expenditure but expenditure continued to increase even in the metropolitan areas. The domestic rates were abolished to enhance local accountability but the system remains ambiguous and complex. The grant system was simplified but then modified to shore up the ailing community charge and the transition to the council tax. No matter what sub-objectives the Government espoused, they too were compromised, if they did not founder, on the failure to achieve its macro-objectives. For example, the community charge was supposed 'to remove the inequities of the present rating system'. Unfortunately, the community charge is more regressive than the rates (Bramley 1987; Gibson 1990: 93; Smith 1991), introduced marked regional disparities (Barnett et al. 1990), and increased the tax bill of 55 per cent of electors (Gibson 1990: 212). For a critical appraisal of other sub-objectives of the poll tax see Gibson (1990: 170–1) and Bramley et al. (1989). However, this discussion has focused on the intended consequences of Government policy. There were also several unintended consequences which were products of the implementation gap.

Explaining the implementation gap

In order to understand the outcome of the local government finance measures of the 1980s, it is necessary to explore the interaction between national economic problems, party ideology, party politics and the process of implementation.

Interventions in local government finance do not reflect the Government's concern with the state of local government but with the perceived imperatives of national economic management. In the case of the Conservative Government, concern with inflation, the public sector borrowing requirement and the level of public expenditure shaped policy on local government. Although the Labour Party had a similar definition of Britain's economic problems between 1975–79, the Conservative Party's response to relative economic decline was clearly shaped by ideology.

The control of local expenditure was a long-standing concern of the Treasury, but the initial emphasis on monetarism followed by the policies on privatization, poll tax and the scale of contracting-out were distinctively Conservative. These policies reflected the thinking of the New Right and its various think tanks. Economic problems provided the stimulus to intervene. Party ideology shaped the form and extent of that intervention. However, the logic of the ideology did not always dominate policy decisions. On local government finance, the dictates of monetarism required control over local capital, not current, expenditure. As Enoch Powell wrote (*Sunday Express*, 11 October 1981):

> By all means limit Exchequer grants and Government loans; but every monetarist knows that the rates cannot cause inflation and councils cannot print money. So why set every elected council by the ears from one end of Britain to the other? It doesn't add up. (see also: Jackman 1982)

The control of local expenditure was a substitute for the failure to control central expenditure. The monetarist rationale was so much window dressing.

Controlling local expenditure sounds like a straightforward objective. In fact the Government was pursuing conflicting objectives because it also sought to 'bury socialism' or, to adopt a less partisan tone, to apply the cuts in local expenditure *selectively*. A policy instrument existed for across-the-board cuts (see below) but it would have affected Conservative and Labour controlled councils alike. Brutal simplicity did not appeal to the Government! Consequently, it had to devise a *new* policy instrument which would simultaneously discriminate against 'overspenders' (i.e. Labour controlled councils) and deliver 'cuts' in the aggregate level of expenditure. This task proved difficult. It may even be impossible.

Political parties give expression to ideology and are a major source of policy initiation, a counter-weight to the inertia of Whitehall and established interests. They are also the focal point of conflict. Conservative policies politicized and polarized central–local financial relations.

The focus on grant cuts for 'overspenders', the abolition of the GLC and MCCs, and the choice of local authorities for rate capping were all seen as partisan policies and provoked a suitably intemperate response. The Labour Party controls a substantial proportion of local councils. Local government was the arena in which the electoral fortunes of the party were revived, the test bed for socialist policies, and the main source of opposition to the Government. In sum, local government was a pawn in an increasingly polarized national party political game.

The poll tax simply increased the already high level of conflict. The new tax created more individual losers than winners and poll tax levels were seen as high, a judgement shaped by the Government's serious underestimate of the likely average tax level. Poll tax became a political liability of the first order and made its own significant contribution not only to the instability in central–local fiscal relations but also to division and dissent within the Conservative Party.

The reform of local government finance was an epiphenomenon of national economic management. Ideology did not consistently inform policy. The Government pursued conflicting objectives. Central–local fiscal relations were politicized. If all this were not enough, the process of implementation added some daunting problems of its own.

First, the Government either did not anticipate, or ignored, the constraints imposed by the 'dual polity' (Bulpitt 1983: 3; Rhodes 1991a: 93–4). A dual polity exists when national and local political elites are insulated from each other and the centre seeks autonomy from local affairs in order to concentrate on 'High Politics'. In other words, Britain has a non-executant centre (i.e. it does not directly deliver the bulk of government services) and it relies on hands-off controls to manage the agencies (including but not restricted to local authorities) which are responsible for service delivery. In sharp contrast to the French system, Britain has neither a Napoleonic tradition of using field agents (or prefects) to supervise local authorities nor a system of *cumul des mandats* whereby politicians accumulate electoral offices leading to the close interpenetration of national and local elites. None the less, the Government was determined to control *individual* local authorities. It adopted a command, or bureaucratic, operating code. It ignored the maze of interdependencies which characterize British service delivery systems. It lacked the hands-on means to impose its policies. It never contemplated introducing an organizational infrastructure of field agents to supervise implementation. In short, it did not have the necessary policy instruments to implement its policy. And in the course of this exercise it politicized relationships, further eroding the 'responsibility ethic' of local authorities.

Second, the Government not only created inappropriate policy instruments, it also used existing policy instruments inappropriately. The 'classic' mechanism for reducing local expenditure is the reduction in government grant. In other words, the grant system must place local authorities under fiscal pressure so that, when deciding on their preferred level of local expenditure, the required rate increases hurt local rate payers. The Government's grant settlements signally failed to exert such pressure. As Gibson (1985: 63) demonstrates the grant settlements gave local authorities a 'rate holiday'; for example, the 1983/84 grant settlement meant that 'on average local authorities could have *reduced* their rates by nearly 2 per cent at a time when the expected rate of price inflation was in excess of 5 per cent' and still have met the Government's expenditure plans. There were reductions in grant but on such a scale and at such a pace that they exerted no real fiscal pressure on local authorities. Of course, reductions which hurt would have brought howls of anguish from Conservative, as well as Labour, controlled councils. By the mid-1980s it had given up trying to exert even minimal fiscal pressure and by the 1990s it was *increasing* grant to reduce poll tax bills.

Third, the policy networks, or professional-bureaucratic complexes, were an important brake on the Government's ambitions (Rhodes 1988: 77–87 and ch. 4; Rhodes 1990; Rhodes and Marsh 1992). Policy-making in British Government is characterized by function-specific networks comprising central departments, professions and other key interests. Outside interests are institutionalized in government, relationships are routinized and the policy agenda is stabilized. Policy change is incremental. These networks, especially the professions, were 'handbagged' by the Thatcher Governments. Unfortunately, their co-operation was integral to the effective implementation of policy. A pattern of authoritative pronouncement by the centre followed by policy slippage in implementation became all too common (see the bulk of the chapters in this book as well as Rhodes 1991 and Marsh and Rhodes 1992).

Local government finance was no exception to this pattern. Indeed, the problem was exacerbated in this policy area by the decision to downgrade the role of the Consultative Council on Local Government Finance. At the very time when the Government was introducing hands-on controls of local expenditure, the Treasury effectively abandoned its only point of contact with local authorities. Given the ease with which local authorities ignored or evaded Government policy, the phenomenon of repetitive legislation, the frequency of legal challenges to government policy and the search for judge-proof legislation (see, for example, Loughlin 1986), the price for not consulting was high.

Fourth, the theory of accountability which underpinned the community charge was defective in several respects. Thus, Gibson (1990: ch. 10) shows that rate increases did affect local election results. In particular, he demonstrates that electors were sensitive to rate increases and did penalize high spending councils. The Government itself has admitted that it had no evidence on the relationship between paying rates and the propensity to vote (Gibson 1990: 191). Barnett *et al.* (1991: 45) also conclude that 'there is no evidence to indicate widespread lack of accountability in the domestic sector'. In sum, the community charge could not repair a lack of accountability because it did not exist.

Finally, the poll tax had a number of implementation problems of its own. At the outset, the Government scored several own goals. It chose to introduce the tax in one fell swoop rather than gradually. For the first year of the poll tax, it reduced grant to local authorities. It predicted an average tax level of some £220 per head, a figure substantially below the actual level of £357. All of these factors dramatized the arrival of the tax and magnified the adverse political consequences. At a more prosaic level, the tax was administratively cumbersome, requiring the employment of some 15,000 more staff than the rates. It was a costly tax to collect. Ridge and Smith's (1990: 24) survey found that costs of collecting the community charge were double those of collecting the rates. Allied to the problems of compiling and updating the register, and enforcement and non-collection, the administration of the poll tax can only be described as cumbersome and costly. Gibson (1990: 249) estimates that the *extra* cost amounted to £20 per household whilst official estimates ranged as high as £70 (*The Times*, 1 July 1991).

Chapter 1 lists Sabatier's (1986a) major obstacles to effective implementation. This case study of local government finance has shown how several of these obstacles undermined Conservative policy. Two cautions should be noted immediately. First, normally, it takes from five to ten years for the consequences of policy to become clear. The poll tax was an exception to this generalization. Many other changes have been introduced (e.g. uniform business rate) or are envisaged in the near future (e.g. the council tax). It is too early for this chapter to offer a detailed assessment (although its general conclusions will apply). Second, this chapter has adopted a top-down perspective. It is also necessary to build up a picture of a policy from the bottom-up. The implementation structures for local government finance will reveal, in all probability, an even greater degree of divergence from Government policy objectives. But even after noting these reservations, it is clear that the major obstacles were: ambiguous and inconsistent objectives, inadequate causal theory, inappropriate policy instruments, professional recalcitrance, and the lack of support from local authorities. It is a formidable list.

Sabatier (1986b) emphasizes the importance of street-level bureaucrats and an adequate causal theory for effective implementation. Again the case study of local government finance has pinpointed the Government's inappropriate territorial operating code and the recalcitrance of professions as key stumbling blocks. Few policy objectives were implemented as intended by the Government. Local expenditure was not reduced. Socialism was not buried. Local accountability remains as otiose as ever. Policy success requires any government to build implementation into the design of its policies. I have argued that, in several respects, the theoretical underpinnings of the Government's policy were inadequate: for example, in relation to the command operating code, the rates and accountability. Perhaps the greatest of all these theoretical defects was the use of a top-down model of implementation totally at variance with the differentiated, disaggregated and interdependent structure of British government. Failure was built into the original policy design. When policy design and policy implementation do not proceed hand in hand, then a policy mess is an inevitable outcome.

Acknowledgements

I would like to thank Andrew Dunsire (University of York) for incisive criticisms of the first draft of the paper which led to its being rewritten 'top-down'; Peter Smith (University of York) for providing references to the Economics literature on the poll tax; the Nuffield Foundation for financial support; and David Marsh for the usual.

5

Housing

Peter Kemp

Introduction

During the Thatcher years important changes in housing took place which were significantly affected by Government policy. The most obvious example of this was, of course, the sale of council houses to sitting tenants under the right to buy. Indeed, the Conservatives' 1987 general election manifesto described home ownership as 'the great success story of housing policy' since 1979 (Conservative Party 1987: 11).

The aim of this chapter is not to address the question of whether Britain was a better housed nation in 1990 than it was in 1979, important though that is (see Hills and Mullings 1990). Instead the intention is to examine the main housing policy objectives of Margaret Thatcher's three administrations and to assess the extent to which they were successful in achieving those objectives and with what consequences.

The chapter has five sections. The first section outlines the housing policy objectives of the Thatcher Government, while the second examines the extent to which these objectives can be described as 'Thatcherite'. The third section then looks at how successfully these objectives were achieved. The fourth reviews some distributional outcomes of the changes in housing provision, while the final section draws some conclusions about housing policy under Mrs Thatcher.

Aims and instruments

During the first two terms of office the Conservatives concentrated their efforts on extending home ownership; in the third, they switched the focus of attention towards the privatization of rented housing, though extending home ownership remained as the most important goal (Kemp 1989). These phases were preceded by two waves of policy making: the first took place following their return to power in 1979 and the second occurred after their re-election in 1987 (Hills and Mullings 1990).

Home ownership at all costs

The Conservatives came to power in 1979 with a clear manifesto commitment to increase home ownership and, in particular, to give council tenants a statutory right to buy at a discount from the market value. This new right – the sale of council houses had previously been at the discretion of local authorities and subject to a ministerial consent (Merrett 1979) – was provided by the Housing Act 1980.

A programme of low-cost home ownership initiatives was also introduced or extended by the Housing Act 1980, with the aim of providing opportunities for tenants and newly forming households to get onto the so-called home ownership ladder (see Booth and Crook 1986). The promotion of home ownership was also to be facilitated by the continuation of mortgage interest relief.

A second objective was to reduce public expenditure in housing. This was of course integral to the Conservatives' monetarist economic policy discussed in Chapter 2. There were three elements to this theme in housing. The first was that the Government could only spend 'what the country could afford' (which, so far as the Conservatives were concerned, was less than was being spent when they came to power). Second, there was a need for better targeting of the spending, so that assistance only went to those households 'most in need'. This implied a much greater emphasis on means testing. And third, a more efficient use should be made of public spending, in particular by drawing in private finance wherever possible, but also by greater incentives for obtaining value for money in the public sector (Whitehead 1983).

The 1980 Housing Act introduced a new subsidy system for local authority housing. This involved an annual subsidy settlement which enabled the Department of the Environment (DoE) to withdraw subsidy from local authorities by assuming that they would increase their rents in line with a guideline amount (Hills and Mullings 1990; Malpass 1990). Under the Local Government Planning and Land Act 1980, local authorities were able to augment their permitted capital expenditure by employing their receipts from land and house sales, but these receipts were taken into account when the permitted expenditure allocations were drawn up and restrictions were applied to the proportion of the receipts which they were permitted to use (Forrest and Murie, 1988).

In these ways, central control was increased over local authority housing finance, which along with the 'right to buy' (RTB) and the increasing emphasis on housing associations, contributed to what Murie (1985) called the 'nationalization of housing policy'.

A third objective of the Conservatives was to minimize the role of local authority housing. In large measure, this objective was to be the intended outcome of the first two objectives in that the sale of council houses would reduce the size of the existing stock, while reductions in local authority housing capital spending would minimize additions to it from new building. Indeed, council house sales killed three birds with one stone: not only did it increase home ownership and reduce the size of the council stock; it also facilitated – because the receipts from sales, given public expenditure accounting rules, could be offset against gross capital spending – a reduction in the net expenditure figure (Forrest and Murie 1988).

This objective was about more than just the size of the sector, it was also about its role. The Conservatives argued that council housing should focus on those with 'special needs', such as the elderly and the disabled, and perhaps also the unemployed – that is, those who could not fend for themselves in the market – rather than provide for general housing needs, which should instead be catered for by private enterprise.

A fourth objective was to halt the decline of the privately rented sector. To this end, the Housing Act 1980 eased rent and eviction restrictions on private landlords (see Crook 1986; Kemp 1988).

These key objectives did not exist in a vacuum but reflected the Conservatives' wider policy stance, including the objectives of reducing public expenditure and rolling back the state, and their approach to central–local relations, subjects which are examined elsewhere in this book. They were also a response to – and were designed to influence – the restructuring of housing provision that had been taking place in Britain for over 70 years. With the decline of private renting, housing provision had been increasingly polarized between owner occupation and council housing. By 1979, these two tenures accounted for 86 per cent of all dwellings in Britain. The Conservatives have promoted home ownership so vigorously partly because, with the inexorable decline of private renting, it seemed the only large-scale private alternative to public housing (Kemp 1989).

Demunicipalization

The Conservatives' manifesto for the 1987 general election announced a new programme aimed at transforming the provision of rented housing. The subsequent white paper on housing outlined its new approach and listed four objectives: to continue to encourage home ownership; to 'breathe new life' into the 'independent rented sector', by which it meant private renting and housing associations; to give council tenants the right to opt for alternative landlords; and to target public money more effectively (DoE 1987).

The main thrust of the proposals and subsequent legislation was the demunicipalization of rented housing provision (Kemp 1989). The Secretary of State for the Environment said that a central objective of the white paper was 'an increase in the choice available to those who do not want or could not afford to own their own homes and in particular the breaking up of the local authority monopoly in social rented housing, (Ridley 1988: 1). The Government hoped to achieve a significant reduction in the role and importance of local authorities as landlords and as suppliers of new housing, and an increased role for other providers such as housing associations and private landlords. Local authorities were to be confined to, at best, an enabling role, facilitating provision by others. Housing associations were a convenient vehicle to take over from councils as the main provider of subsidized housing to rent (Coleman 1989).

This shift in the orientation of housing policy was in part a response to the progress of the RTB. From 1982 sales of council houses under the right to buy had begun to decline. Although the level of discounts was raised in 1984 and in 1986, it seemed that the initial high level of sales after the 1980 Act would not be regained. Home ownership appeared to be approaching its maximum feasible level. Housing Minister William Waldegrave (1987: 8) argued that 'the next great push after the right to buy should be to get rid of the state as a big landlord'. If council tenants could or did not want to buy their homes, then other buyers would have to be found. The shift to selling tenanted estates was therefore a logical next step to maintain the privatization momentum in housing (Kemp 1990).

The Housing Act 1988 introduced two main mechanisms for demunicipalizing the existing stock of council housing. First, it gave approved landlords the right to bid for council properties, and council tenants the right to opt out of such transfers. Second, it introduced Housing Action Trusts (HATs) based on the Urban Development Corporation model which the government had used as part of its inner city regeneration programme. HATs were to take over council housing in selected estates, carry out improvement works and then pass them on to other landlords. They were to be imposed on the local authorities concerned without consultation, though during the passage of the Housing Bill the Government was forced to concede to tenants the right to a ballot on whether the HAT should go ahead.

The Local Government and Housing Act 1989 introduced changes to the revenue and capital funding of local authority housing. On the revenue side, it prohibited authorities from subsidizing their rents out of the general (rate) fund. By adjusting the way subsidy on housing benefit payments is calculated, the Act gave the Government a new lever over rent increases (Malpass 1990). On the capital side, the new regime involved tighter restrictions on authorities' use of capital receipts from the sale of dwellings and land and new controls on their borrowing (Hills 1991).

Other changes were made to stimulate supply by alternative providers of rented housing such as private landlords and housing associations. The Housing Act 1988 deregulated all new lettings by private landlords. And in order to give a 'kickstart' to investment in privately rented housing, the Finance Act 1988 extended the Business Expansion Scheme (BES) to include companies letting on assured tenancies at market rents. The BES gives generous tax relief to investors buying shares in these companies (Crook et al. 1991).

The Housing Act 1988 also deregulated new housing association lettings, putting them on the same basis as those by private landlords. Associations were to be made increasingly reliant on private rather than public loans, average grant levels were to be reduced and other changes made which exposed them much more than previously to risk (Hills 1991). In this way, housing associations were to be more subject to what the white paper called 'the disciplines of the market' (DoE 1987); more quasi-private than quasi-public agencies.

Finally, the Local Government and Housing Act 1989 introduced means testing of home improvement grants, a simplified array of grants, and a new fitness standard partly based on the Scottish tolerable standard.

How Thatcherite?

The extent to which all of this represented a change of direction or only modified continuity with the past has been the subject of debate. Malpass (1990), for example, has argued that 1979 did not represent a sharp watershed but rather that there were many important continuities as well as discontinuities with the past. In reviewing the impact of Thatcherite housing policy between 1979 and 1990, therefore, it is necessary to examine the extent to which policy can in fact be described as Thatcherite at all. But as Marsh and Rhodes (1989) stress the term 'Thatcherite' is not well defined or agreed upon. We therefore confine ourselves here to examining whether there was anything different or distinctive about housing policy under Mrs Thatcher compared with previous administrations.

The promotion of home ownership

Promoting home ownership has been a Conservative objective since the early 1920s (see Merrett 1982), for political as well as for housing reasons (Holmans 1987). The historic continuity with previous Conservative housing policy goals was acknowledged by the Prime Minister in the 1979 Queen's Speech, when she announced that:

> Thousands of people in council houses and new towns came out in support of us for the first time because they wanted a chance to buy their own homes. We will give every council tenant the right to purchase his own home at a substantial discount on the market price and with 100% mortgages for those who need them. This will be a giant stride towards making a reality of Anthony Eden's dream of a property owning democracy. (quoted in Forrest and Murie 1988: 55)

If the promotion of home ownerhsip was not a distinctively Thatcherite policy, neither was it an exclusively Conservative one: Labour Governments have always been favourably disposed towards owner occupation (Kemp 1991). Where Labour and the Conservatives differed was over the sale of council houses. Labour Governments generally preferred a discretionary approach to sales which allowed local authorities to make decisions based on their knowledge of local conditions and, until 1983 was committed to repealing the statutory RTB (Forrest and Murie 1988). But even with the RTB it is worth noting that in the 1974 general elections the Conservatives under Heath were committed to introducing a statutory right to buy scheme if they were returned to office.

What was distinct about Thatcherite housing policy was not the desire to increase home ownership as such, but rather the single mindedness with which this objective was pursued and its elevation to the primary goal of housing policy above all else, especially during the first two terms of office. Indeed, under Mrs Thatcher's Governments, policy became obsessed with tenure rather than with the traditional housing policy concerns about the quality and quantity of supply (Malpass 1990).

Cutting back public expenditure on housing

Harloe and Paris (1984) pointed out that real reductions in public expenditure on housing began under Labour as part of the 1976 IMF loan agreement. But what Labour did with reluctance, the Conservatives under Mrs Thatcher did with conviction. As Holmans (1991: 21) has pointed out, the 1976 cuts and previous reductions in expenditure plans were a response to short-term economic pressures, but a 'settled long-term policy of holding down public expenditure in its own right with a high degree of priority was a post-1979 policy change'.

Minimizing the role of local authority housing

The Conservatives have never been enthusiastic about council housing (Hamnett 1987), seeing it as an unfortunate necessity given the decline of private landlordism. Labour has generally been much more committed to council housing, but since the mid-1960s both parties have seen it as something of a second best to home ownership.

Refocusing council housing on special rather than general needs has been a familiar Conservative objective (Malpass and Murie 1990) but the much more interventionist policy of demunicipalization pursued after 1987 was new. Their aim was not only to shift *new* rental provision away from local authorities, but also to transfer as much as possible of the *existing* stock to alternative landlords. This was certainly an approach that was different from previous Conservative and Labour administrations. As Malpass (1990) has pointed out, Mrs Thatcher's Governments exhibited a degree of hostility towards local authority housing that had not previously been seen.

Reviving the private landlord

Reviving the privately rented sector has long been an aim of Conservative (though not Labour) administrations. The Conservatives deregulated parts of the sector in 1923, 1933 and 1957, though the Heath Government failed to do so. Thus it was not peculiar to Mrs Thatcher's Governments. More novel was the introduction of tax incentives in the Finance Acts of 1982 and 1988, aimed at stimulating investment in private housing to let (Kemp 1988; Crook *et al.* 1991). Previous attempts to revive the private landlord were based very largely on deregulating rents. Thus while the objective was not new, subsidizing the private landlord was a distinctively different policy instrument of Mrs Thatcher's Governments.

Implementation

Expanding home ownership

The Conservatives were successful in extending home ownership. It expanded from 55 per cent of all dwellings in Britain in 1979 to 67 per cent in 1989 (Table 5.1). The RTB accounted for about two-fifths of the increase. Also important was the deregulation of financial markets – a non-housing objective of the Government – which made mortgage funds more easily available and helped to increase the amount per dwelling which lenders were willing to advance (Maclennan and Gibb 1990). At the same time, real growth in average earnings throughout the 1980s will have made home ownership possible for a significantly greater number of households than previously. On the supply side, the lack of rented housing may have pushed some households into home ownership who might otherwise have rented.

On the other hand, the 1980s were a decade of high real interest rates (in contrast to the 1970s when real interest rates were negative) and low inflation, both factors which disfavour home ownership compared with renting and which were an explicit product of government macroeconomic policy. Thus while housing policy in the 1980s consistently favoured home ownership, macroeconomic policy did not.

Since surveys consistently show that owner occupation is the preferred tenure of most households, the Conservatives were pursuing an objective that was in tune with the wishes of the people. But in the case of council tenants

Table 5.1   Distribution of housing between tenures in Britain

December	Owner occupied %	Rented privately %	Rented from housing associations %	Rented from local authorities %
1979	55	12e	2e	31
1983	60	10	2	28
1987	64	8	3	25
1989P	67	7	3	23

Notes: e = author's estimates; P = provisional.
Source: DoE (1990: table 9.3).

they were prepared to pursue the objective by allowing them to buy at a subsidy of up to 60 per cent on houses and 70 per cent on flats. This, combined with the fact that, for most of the postwar period, houses and flats have been appreciating assets, makes it hardly surprising that the right to buy was a significant success.

Moreover, the RTB was an instrument that was triggered by the tenant, not by the local authority. In that sense, implementation was shared between the beneficiary and the formal implementing agency at local level. In addition, the Housing Act 1980 gave considerable powers to the Secretary of State to intervene (including the appointment of commissioners if necessary) where it appeared that local authorities were taking excessively long to process RTB applications, powers that they used in the case of Norwich City Council (Forrest and Murie 1988).

Reducing public expenditure on housing

The Conservatives were also very successful in achieving real cuts in public expenditure (as defined by the Treasury) on housing. This success was helped by the RTB. Capital receipts from the housing programme totalled £17.6 billion or 43 per cent of the entire proceeds from privatization between 1978/79 and 1988/89 (Forrest and Murie 1988). When this is set off against the gross capital expenditure figures, the result is a net capital spending reduction of 75 per cent over the same period (Hills and Mullings 1990).

The effects of such a very large cut in capital expenditure take some time to show because the total stock of houses changes only very slowly (Ball 1983). And unlike cuts in social security or MIRAS there are no immediate cash losers from reductions in gross capital expenditure, whose financial hardship can be directly traced to such cuts. Instead, it is less easy to identify the losers and they are affected only indirectly. Political opposition to the capital spending reductions has consequently been relatively muted.

Since most new local authority housing has been built on contract by the private sector, the construction industry has clearly lost out from this massive cut in capital spending during the Thatcher years. They have been torn between support for the general policy of deregulation and privatization pursued by Mrs Thatcher's Government and the negative effect it has had on their markets. This presumably made it easier than it otherwise would have been to brush aside any objections from the construction lobby to reducing public expenditure in housing.

Net current expenditure (essentially, subsidies to local authority rents) was also reduced, by 60 per cent in real terms during the Thatcher years (Table 5.2). But this fall was offset almost entirely by an increase in housing benefit expenditure. The latter was in part a function of the former: reduced subsidy meant higher local authority rents, which in turn meant increased expenditure on housing benefit. In this way, the DoE was able to reduce its spending total at the expense of the Department of Health and Social Security (DHSS)/

Table 5.2 Real net public expenditure on housing (in 1987/88 prices)

Financial year	Net current (GB)	Housing benefit (GB)	Net capital (GB)	Total public expenditure (UK)	Mortgage tax relief (UK)
			£ billion		
1978/79	3.5	1.8	5.3	11.2	2.6
1988/89	1.4	3.6	1.3	7.0	5.2
% change	−60	+200	−75	−37	+200

Source: Hills and Mullings (1990: 147).

Department of Social Security (DSS) which took over full responsibility for housing benefit in 1982/83. However, this switch fully reflected the Conservatives' aim of shifting subsidy from bricks and mortar to people.

Overall, public expenditure on housing fell by more than a third in real terms, from £11.2 billion in 1978/79 to £7.0 billion in 1988/89 (in 1987/88 prices). Yet if the definition of expenditure is widened to include tax reliefs, then a rather different picture emerges. The cost of mortgage interest relief increased by 200 per cent in real terms over the same period. With this wider definition, expenditure fell by only 12 per cent.

Reducing the role of local authority housing

Under Mrs Thatcher, local authority completions fell to their lowest peace time level since 1920. Between 1979 and 1989 output fell by 80 per cent. Yet this was not wholly the result of government policy. Holmans (1991) has argued that there was in any case a fall off in the demand for council house building by local authorities, but that capital controls took local authority building below a level to which it would have fallen of its own accord.

The net result of reduced new construction by local authorities and the sale of over a million existing dwellings was that the local authority sector fell in absolute size and as a proportion of the total housing stock for the first time in its history (Forrest and Murie 1986). Table 5.1 shows that local authority housing declined from 31 to 23 per cent of the total housing stock between 1979 and 1989.

The post-1987 demunicipalization drive has had less success, though it is too early to provide anything more than an interim assessment at this stage.

All six of the local authority housing estates earmarked by the DoE (without consulting either the councils or the tenants concerned) for HAT status failed to get off the ground after the tenants rejected the proposals despite the promise of extra cash for estate improvement works if they voted in favour of them.

Subsequently, attracted by the cash earmarked for HATs, two councils have persuaded their tenants and the DoE to agree to the setting up of a HAT to help improve conditions on problem estates in their area, but on different terms from those envisaged for the original six estates selected for HAT treatment by the Government. These 'voluntary' HATs involve a role for the local council whereas the original HAT concept did not.

Tenants' Choice has attracted very little interest from either alternative landlords or council tenants. The Government assumed that disgruntled council tenants would rush at the opportunity to change their landlord. But while council tenants are keen enough to enter the market at a reduced price when the commodity on offer is the ownership of their own home, they do not when it comes to renting it. The advantages to them in renting from a private sector landlord appeared limited but the disadvantages – much reduced security of tenure, a more punitive attitude to arrears and the prospect of higher rents – seemed significant.

One unplanned outcome of the new demunicipalization drive, however, was the emergence during 1988 of wholesale, 'voluntary' stock transfers (VSTs). These involve a local authority in selling its entire stock to a new landlord, generally a housing association established by the council for the purpose. By April 1991, 16 VSTs had taken place (Table 5.3) and more were underway, suggesting that a bandwagon effect was beginning to occur.

VSTs are an example of local government implementing the government's demunicipalization objective but using an instrument fashioned by the locality not the centre. Many of the pioneer VSTs involved small, Conservative controlled authorities in the south of England with a small stock of council housing. The stock transfer proposals to date have all come from the

Table 5.3   Wholesale voluntary stock transfer

Local authority	Date of transfer	No. of dwellings
Chiltern	December 1988	4650
Sevenoaks	March 1989	6526
Newbury	November 1989	7053
Swale	March 1990	7352
Broadland	May 1990	3721
North Bedfordshire	June 1990	7472
Medina	July 1990	2825
Rochester	July 1990	7981
South Wight	July 1990	2119
Mid Sussex	November 1990	4554
East Dorset	December 1990	2245
Tonbridge and Malling	January 1991	6382
Ryedale	February 1991	3353
South Bucks	March 1991	4942
Christchurch	March 1991	1542
Suffolk Coastal	April 1991	5365

Source: DoE, personal communication.

councillors and officers, not the tenants (Kemp 1990). It is not yet clear why in some local authorities the tenants voted in favour of a stock transfer while in others they did not.

The revival of private renting

One respect in which the council sector did not decline was in its share of the rented housing stock. As Table 5.4 shows, they maintained their share of rented housing between 1979 and 1989, while private landlords lost market share. Thus the Thatcher era saw a *deprivatization* of rented housing (Kemp 1990). Indeed, the privately rented stock decreased by one third.

It is too early to assess the impact of the deregulation of new lettings on private renting housing, but the Business Expansion Scheme (BES) has been a limited success. The first two years saw £543 million invested in BES companies, producing about 10,000 dwellings. But the cost of this has been high at well over £200 million in tax revenue foregone (Crook *et al.* 1991). Without the tax relief, this new investment would not have occurred. It seems likely that the BES will produce only a minor and short-lived wave of new investment (Kemp 1989).

The policy objective of reviving private renting thus largely failed. In part this was hardly surprising as it had been declining for more than half a century when Mrs Thatcher came to power. Even so, the policy was based on inadequate causal assumptions. Committed to the market, the Conservatives believed that, once set free from rent regulation, the market for private renting would revive. Yet deregulation was only a necessary and not a sufficient condition for revival (Kemp 1988). An important reason for the continuing decline of the sector has been that the housing tax and subsidy system favours home ownership at the expense of private renting. A significant revival of private renting would have required the abolition or substantial reduction of the tax privileges of home ownership. Thus the objective of reviving private renting to some extent clashed with that of extending home ownership.

Table 5.4   The provision of rental housing in England

	1979		1989P	
	000	%	000	%
Local authorities	5,140	67	4,161	68
Housing associations	368	5	548	9
Private landlords	2,168	28	1,449	24
All rented dwellings	7,676	100	6,158	100

Notes: P = provisional.
Figures may not sum to 100 due to rounding.
Source: DoE (1990: table 9.3).

Gainers and losers

The gains and losses from the housing policy and provision changes during the Thatcher years were not evenly distributed and varied by tenure.

Those who bought their council house at a discount from the market value generally benefited from Conservative housing policy. In 1990 the average discount was 53 per cent and the total value of the discounts in that year alone was £2.5 billion. It was inevitably the better off tenants living in the better houses in the better areas who tended to buy (Forrest and Murie 1988). In this way the RTB contributed to the growing 'residualization' of local authority housing (Malpass 1990).

Owner occupiers more generally were able to benefit from untaxed capital gains resulting from the real increase in house prices that took place during the period. Many also benefited from the process of 'equity withdrawal': Lowe and Watson (1989) estimated that equity withdrawal on inheritance and moving house amounted to £16 billion in 1988, equivalent to 2 per cent of personal disposable income. This and the house price boom of the late 1980s is believed to have fuelled inflation and indirectly helped produce the interest rate hike and subsequent recession at the close of the Thatcher era (Muellbauer 1990; Maclennan *et al.* 1991).

The Government's use of high interest rates as its single most important economic tool in its anti-inflation strategy helped to push some home owners into arrears and repossession through the resulting increased mortgage rates and higher unemployment. Here again, macroeconomic policy and housing policy have had important interactions with negative consequences for some home owners.

If for most home owners, however, the outcome of Conservative policies was beneficial, for many council tenants who remained in the rented sector, the outcome was less rosy. The sector as a whole underwent further residualization, a process that had been gaining pace for many years before 1979 but which accelerated after then (Malpass 1990). Table 5.5 shows that council tenants were increasingly among the poorest households. Rent to income ratios also increased (Hills and Mullings 1990), partly because of real increases in local authority rents and reductions in the generosity and scope of housing benefit.

Table 5.5   Council tenants in the distribution of income in Britain

Percentage of council tenants who were among the:	1968 %	1978 %	1988 %
Poorest 30% of all households	31	42	61
Middle 20% of all households	23	23	21
Richest 50% of all households	46	35	18
All council tenants	100	100	100

Source: Wilmott and Murie (1988: 31).

While mortgage to income ratios also increased in this period (Hills and Mullings 1990), home owners' outgoings tend to decline in real terms over time, but tenants face increasing rent levels. Moreover, home owners have generally benefited from considerable capital gains. Some authors have argued that an important social, economic and political division – or 'consumption sector cleavage' – has opened between those households who have bought their home and those who can not, with the former able to benefit from the material and psychological benefits of home ownership and the latter forced to remain in a second-class form of housing and unable to enhance their wealth through the capital appreciation of their home (Saunders 1990).

Whether this new 'two nations' (Hamnett 1984) in housing provision – which has in part at least been accelerated by Government policies – reflects inevitable features of the two main tenures or contingent and historically specific factors, is a matter of debate (cf. Saunders 1990, and Forrest et al. 1990). What is clear, however, is that it refers only to those who are housed. Yet during the 1980s the number of homeless people increased considerably, creating a 'third nation' in housing.

As Table 5.6 shows, the number of households accepted for rehousing because of homelessness increased from 53,110 in 1978 to 126,680 in 1989 or by 139 per cent. The number placed in bed and breakfast or other forms of temporary accommodation pending enquiries or prior to permanent housing, increased from less than 3,000 to nearly 38,000 over the same period.

The 1980s also saw a significant but not well quantified increase in homelessness among single people and childless couples who were not eligible for rehousing under the Housing Act (Conway and Kemp 1985; Clapham et al. 1990). Towards the end of the period there was also a sharp increase in rough sleeping and vagrancy, particularly in central London.

Table 5.6 Homeless households accepted for rehousing by local authorities in England, 1978–89

Year	No. of households
1978	53,110
1979	57,200
1980	69,920
1981	70,010
1982	74,800
1983	78,240
1984	83,190
1985	93,980
1986	102,980
1987	112,730
1988	117,550
1989	126,680

Source: DoE Quarterly Returns, 1979–90.

Table 5.7   Local authority housing in England and Wales, 1976–89

	New building	Sales	Total Stock 000s	%
1976	112,028	5,313	5,285	29
1977	108,483	13,020	5,398	29
1978	87,799	30,045	5,463	29
1979	69,734	41,720	5,448	29
1980	70,830	81,483	5,425	29
1981	49,339	102,720	5,361	28
1982	30,213	202,045	5,180	27
1983	29,986	141,457	5,056	26
1984	29,193	103,177	4,969	25
1985	23,515	92,294	4,886	25
1986	19,472	88,718	4,811	24
1987	16,375	105,107	4,708	23
1988	16,505	155,556	4,563	22
1989P	13,497	170,691	4,393	21

Note: P = provisional.
Source: DoE (1990: tables 9.3 and 9.6).

The causes of this increase in homelessness are complex (see Greve 1990) and include social and demographic changes as well as the increase in unemployment in the 1980s. But to some extent it was an unintended consequence of Government policies. The supply of housing to rent fell considerably, in part because of Government capital spending controls (see Table 5.7). Changes in social security, particularly affecting young adults and those living in temporary accommodation, were also important factors in the rise in single homelessness (Thornton 1990).

For much of the 1980s the relentless rise in homelessness was neglected by Government. There is no reference to it, for example, in the 1987 housing white paper (DoE 1987). But in response to growing public concern about the increasingly visible growth in street homelessness, the Government introduced several temporary initiatives to tackle the problem in 1990 and 1991.

Taking stock of an era

Housing is usually seen as one of the areas in which Mrs Thatcher's Governments were able to successfully implement policy and achieve their objectives. The key indicators of this success are the extensive take up of the RTB and the growth in home ownership more generally since 1979; as well as the substantial reduction in public spending, unlike many other areas of the welfare state (see Hills 1990).

Yet beyond these headline policies, there were significant areas of policy failure or of only qualified success. Most clearly of all, the Conservatives failed to revive the privately rented sector, which instead shrank by a third between 1979 and 1989. While the deregulation measures in the Housing Acts of 1980 and 1988 were successfully introduced, by themselves they were not sufficient to achieve the stated objective, which was in any case partly in conflict with their prime goal of expanding home ownership at all costs.

The policy of demunicipalizing the existing stock of rented housing, embodied in the Housing Act 1988, got off to a poor start. By mid-1991 there had been almost no interest in Tenants Choice either by tenants or by alternative landlords. Like the RTB, Tenants Choice did not require the acquiescence of local authorities but, unlike the RTB, few tenants proved willing to be, as one Housing Minister put it, 'helped out into the market' (Waldegrave 1987: 9).

The policy of imposing HATs on councils and tenants failed. Although two 'voluntary HATs' were subsequently negotiated they were a significant departure from the original conception, and involved negotiation and compromise between central government and the local authorities concerned.

A small but growing number of councils transferred their entire stock to new housing associations. VSTs represented a very significant development and probably exceeded the Conservatives' expectations, not in aggregate but at the individual local authority level, for HATs and Tenants Choice were aimed at estates rather than the entire stock. This is a case of a policy evolving during its implementation (cf. Ham and Hill 1984). For although the transfers have been presented as a way of getting around capital spending controls, of avoiding large rent increases and of preserving the rented housing stock from the ravages of the RTB, it was Government restructuring of the financial environment and their ideological assault on council housing, which helped persuade the mainly Conservative local authorities involved to jump the municipal housing ship.

The failure to date of Tenants Choice, the re-design of HATs and the emergence of VSTs show that even a centralizing government with a clear objective – getting rid of council housing – cannot necessarily implement its policies without negotiation and compromise. The RTB was an exception to this, but that was partly because one of the implementing actors – the tenants – were also significant beneficiaries from it. With Tenants Choice and with HATs as originally conceived, that appeared not to be true. Indeed, they were partly based on the assumption that tenants would want to take up the schemes when in fact many of them were deeply opposed to them.

While the objectives were clear if not always consistent, housing policy under Mrs Thatcher was never a true, market liberal approach. Instead, it inevitably reflected significant elements of pragmatism and electoral calculation, most obviously over the preservation of mortgage interest relief.

From the 1979 general election onwards the Conservatives dominated the housing policy agenda and (except in 1985 when there was some policy drift) consistenly maintained the initiative during the Thatcher years. Labour were generally on the defensive and did not have a well-developed alternative.

Following the 1983 election they committed themselves to maintaining the RTB, largely it seems for electoral reasons and, more recently, said their support for more building by local authorities was for pragmatic reasons only and 'not because there is any intrinsic superiority' in the public sector (*The Guardian,* 30 June 1990).

Towards the end of the 1980s, however, the Government was put on the defensive over the rise in homelessness particularly in rough sleeping in central London. This was in part an unintended consequence of their housing and other policies, especially in social security. Such was the public concern that the Government introduced a number of temporary initiatives aimed at getting homeless people off the streets and into temporary accommodation but which are unlikely to provide a permanent solution to the problem. Sadly, the most visible legacy in housing from the 1980s, at least in the capital, was the growth in vagrancy and rough sleeping among single people.

6

Social security

Jonathan Bradshaw

Introduction

A curious aspect of New Right ideology is that despite its fervour and seeming moral certainty it is difficult to discover an explicit set of objectives against which to evaluate the social security policies implemented by the Government of Margaret Thatcher during the period 1979 to 1990. What criteria should be used to evaluate the achievements of the Thatcher era in social security? As other writers have pointed out (King 1987) the collection of ideas commonly associated with the New Right contain an eclectic range of economic, political, moral and social beliefs and principles. Without doubt, a dominant principle is economic and political liberalism, which is expressed in a belief in the free market, individual liberty and a reduced public sector. However conservatism is also a strong influence. Conservatives also believe in the retrenchment of the welfare state and are anti-government but in addition emphasize traditional structures – the family, responsibility, work, self-reliance, religion, philanthropy, female dependency, the authority of men, and so-called Victorian values.

It is difficult if not impossible to explicate the implications of these ideas for a specific area of policy such as social security. However, a set of beliefs did have implications for social security policy, directly and indirectly through their implications for economic policy and public expenditure. These beliefs were: that public expenditure was too high and crowding out private consumption and investment; that high levels of taxation required to fund public services and benefits were restricting choice and freedom, reducing incentives to work and save, undermining enterprise and increasing dependency; that if individuals were given greater incentives they would work harder and the benefits would trickle down to the less fortunate. There was also the view that the welfare state had become a vast self-serving bureaucracy and that it was time to turn back to the traditional family, voluntary effort, and private and occupational provision to meet need.

In the absence of a coherent theory that could be applied consistently to social security policy, it is probably best to examine the explicit, stated objectives of the Conservative Government in relation to social security policy. There are the manifestos. These, however, have tended to be exceptionally vague in their commitments in social security. For example the 1979 manifesto stated that social security was too complicated, that the Party intended to move towards their original tax credit proposals, that they would tax short-term benefits, 'act more vigorously against fraud and abuse' and support child benefit (Conservative Party Manifesto 1979: 27).

A better source is the social security chapter of the annual White Paper on public expenditure which contains a list of the criteria against which potential changes to benefit policy are assessed. The list contains some of the criteria that you might expect to find – the need to encourage independence and incentives to work, the extent to which benefits are directed to those most in need, the effect on family stability. But in general the list of criteria has an executive, operational, non-ideological feel to it. It changes little from year to year and admits

> The list is not exhaustive and not every item is necessarily applicable in every case of policy development. In many cases it is necessary to strike a balance between various objectives. (DSS 1991: para. 8)

The best source of social security objectives, with perhaps a firmer ideological dimension, are three major White Papers on social security. They each give a rather different picture of Conservative aspirations.

First, the White Paper resulting from the Fowler Reviews of social security, *The Reform of Social Security: Programme for Action* (DHSS 1985) argues that social security needs to be reformed for five reasons: it is too complex; it fails to give effective support to those in greatest need, including low-income families with children; the interaction of taxes and benefits trap people in poverty; social security prevents people making their own provision and exercising freedom of choice in respect of pensions; and pensions are going to cost too much for future generations. The paragraphs (1.5–1.7) in the White Paper on the objectives of the proposals allude to some of the more important determinants of Conservative social security policy:

> financial issues of pensions policy should be faced now, leaving future generations with the freedom to decide how best they want to allocate the resources which are then available . . .

> We believe resources must be directed more effectively to areas of greatest need . . .

We want a system that is simpler to understand and better managed.

We want sensible co-operation between the social security and the tax system.

We want a system which is consistent with the Government's overall objectives for the economy.

In these statements we find evidence of a belief in privatization, selectivity, managerialism, incentives and last, but certainly not least, the needs of the economy.

Social security accounts for one third of all public spending. It cannot be ring fenced from the requirements of sensible management of the economy as a whole. (para. 1.6)

Second, the White Paper on maintenance *Children Come First* (DSS 1990a) is interesting because it is the product of Mrs Thatcher's strongly held personal view that 'No father should be able to escape from his responsibility' (George Thomas Society Lecture, 17 January 1990). The White Paper has a number of objectives:

1 that absent parents honour their legal and moral responsibilities to their children;
2 the maintenance system is made effective;
3 lone parents' work incentives are increased;
4 dependence on income support (and public expenditure) is reduced.

The scheme proposed in the White Paper gives the state a stronger role in one of the most intimate aspects of a personal relationship. It establishes the obligation of an absent parent to support the caring parent as well as the children, giving first priority for whatever financial resources are available to the first partnership and thereby effectively, though not explicitly, discouraging illegitimacy, separation, divorce, repartnering and second children.

Third, the White Paper on benefits for disabled people *The Way Ahead* (DSS 1990b) covers a client group where the imperatives of ideology are rather less explicit. In this case

The main needs are clear: better coverage of assistance with the extra costs of being disabled; better help for those disabled people who wish to increase their independence by working; and a better balanced structure of benefits to support those who cannot work, giving greater emphasis than now to those who are disabled from birth or in their early years. (Foreword)

Between them these three white papers indicate the range and variety of the objectives to be found in Thatcherite social security policy. However before turning to consider to what extent they were achieved it is worth reminding ourselves of the nature of social security policy.

The nature of social security

Social security is by far the single largest proportion of public expenditure, taking 33 per cent of the total, or 10.1 per cent of GNP in 1989–90. Total expenditure was £52.6 billion in 1989/90, compared with, for example, £20.1 billion for health, £20.3 billion for defence and £5.7 billion for education. The vast bulk of this expenditure goes in transfer payments to beneficiaries. Administration only represents 5.6 per cent of total expenditure. There are 16 different contributory benefits and 12 non–contributory benefits administered by 83,000 civil servants and an unknown number of local authority officials (administering housing and community charge benefits). Unlike other policy areas covered in this volume, policy-making in the social security area is inevitably top-down, central government led, with very little room for constraint or contribution from other agencies such as local government. There is only a tiny element of administrative discretion that could intervene between policy intention and effect. So subject to political, financial and operational constraints the policy-maker has a relatively open arena in which to work.

There is a great variety of tasks performed by social security

> Social security benefits meet many needs: some provide an income for people who have little or no earnings because they are elderly, unemployed or sick, or because they must look after children or elderly or disabled people. Others provide help with housing costs or the cost of bringing up children; pensions for retirement pensioners and income for widows; assistance with the extra expense of disablement; and compensation for injury, disease or death caused at work or by service in the armed forces. (para. 3, HM Treasury 1990b)

Thus social security expenditure is the most important vehicle for the distribution and redistribution of resources to individuals and families in need. In 1987 cash benefits represented 75 per cent of the gross income of the bottom decile of households and 15 per cent of the gross income of all households. For certain types of household it is particularly important. For single pensioners cash benefits represent 61 per cent of gross income, for lone parents with children 59 per cent of gross income (*Economic Trends*, May 1990). One benefit, income support, determines the living standards of one person in seven in the UK, including 16 per cent of elderly people, 79 per cent of unemployed people, 21 per cent of the long-term sick and disabled and 72 per cent of lone-parent families.

So social security is huge and vitally important to the living standards of many of the most vulnerable people in our society. As if this was not a sufficient constraint on a Government with aspirations to 'roll back the frontiers of the state' what happens in social security is not only determined by policy-makers. Trends in social security expenditure are very much determined by external forces, principally demographic and economic factors. For a Government seeking to cut public expenditure, the 1980s have not been particularly kind demographically or economically.

Demographic trends

There have been four major *demographic trends* affecting social security expenditure.

First, a steady increase in the number of *retirement pensioners* from 8.9 million in 1980 to 9.9 million in 1990. This, and the increase in numbers retiring with eligibility to the state earnings related pension scheme (SERPS), has led to a real increase in expenditure on elderly people of 24 per cent between 1978–79 and 1989–90 (HM Treasury 1990b).

Second, changes occurring in *family form* have put increased pressure on social security. Both the increase in the rate of divorce and separation and in the proportion of children born out of wedlock have led to a sharp increase in the number of lone-parent families. The change in the structure of lone parents (fewer widows, more single lone parents), and the state of the labour market have led to a massive increase in dependence on social security. In 1979 only about a third of lone parents were dependent on supplementary benefit, in 1989 nearly three quarters were receiving income support.

Third, there has been a large increase in the numbers of people receiving *disability benefits* during the decade, for example the number of beneficiaries of invalidity benefit increased from 620,000 in 1980 to 1.2 million in 1989/90. No doubt the real increase of 63 per cent in expenditure on benefits for sick and disabled people between 1978/79 and 1989/90 has been due to improvements in take up, changes in policy and the level of unemployment (see below), but demography has played its part.

All these demographic changes have led to upward pressure on expenditure. In contrast, with declining *fertility* rates, the number of children has declined from 13.6 million in 1976 to 12.2 million in 1989/90 and together with the real decline in the value of the benefit, expenditure on child benefit has fallen.

Economic factors

There are two main *economic factors* which have influenced social security policy during the Thatcher years.

First, and by far the most important, has been the level of *unemployment* caused by a decline in labour demand and the abandonment of 'full employment' as a postwar Keynesian commitment. Although labour demand began to pick up after 1983, labour supply increased due to larger cohorts of young people entering the labour market up to 1986 and the increased economic activity of mothers. Between 1978/79 and 1989/90 real expenditure on benefits for the unemployed increased by 46 per cent. Although expenditure in total on the unemployed has declined in real terms since 1986/87 with the fall in unemployment, unemployment is still very high compared with 1960s and 1970s and has been increasing again since spring 1990. During the 1980s, we have learnt that unemployment not only affects expenditure on unemployment benefit. The massive increase in expenditure on invalidity benefit has almost certainly been due in large part to people leaving employment before retirement age and instead of signing on as unemployed, registering with their GPs as long-term sick. Unemployment also affects the level of claims for family credit, housing benefit and income support by lone parents.

Second, associated with the level of unemployment is the level of *real earnings*. Although over the period earnings have moved substantially ahead of prices, differentials in earnings have widened, and opportunities for overtime and second earners have been reduced. The result has been an increased number of low-paid earners and an increased dependence on benefits (family credit and housing benefit) which supplement the earnings of those with employment income.

Evaluation

Having set the scene by showing the context in which Mrs Thatcher's Government's social security policies have operated we turn now to consider the extent to which Thatcherite policies have been implemented in the field of social security and what impact they have had.

First, it is worth pointing out that there has been no shortage of legislative effort. The practice of *laissez faire* has not permeated social security. Since 1979 there have been almost annual Acts concerned with social security policy as well as countless changes in regulations and policy. There have also been major changes in administration, most notably a huge investment in information technology in the Operational Strategy and more recently the DSS has pioneered the Next Steps Strategy and devolved administrative responsibility to agencies. Quality of service has become the guiding precept – postal claims have been introduced, visiting has been more or less abandoned, the DSS welfare function reduced and there is a new Department logo.

What has been the overall consequence of this effort, and what general themes can be discerned?

Public expenditure on social security

A central element of Thatcherite policy has been the attempt to reduce public expenditure in order to cut taxation. The policy was perhaps best expressed in the Treasury White Paper in 1984:

> The growth of public spending has over the last twenty years been the motive force which has driven ever upwards the burden of taxation on individuals and companies alike. The government believes that it is necessary to reverse this process, to decide first what can and should be afforded, then to set expenditure plans for individual programmes consistently with that decision. (HM Treasury 1984)

Social security has been one of the main reasons that this policy has never been achieved. Between 1979 and 1990, social security expenditure has risen in cash terms by £38.2 billion and in real (1987/88) terms by £14.2 billion. It has increased as a proportion of all public expenditure until 1988/89 and as a proportion of GNP until 1987/88. We have already seen that the main reasons for this failure to achieve cuts in social security are due to extraneous factors, mainly unemployment and demographic processes. However, there are also policy reasons.

With rising numbers of social security claimants the only way to reduce benefits would have been to make substantial cuts in the real level of benefits and the Government balked at this option. During the period 1979–88, 38 changes in the rules governing unemployment benefit were made, most of them for the purpose of reducing the social security costs, but also to increase work incentives. Atkinson and Micklewright (1989) have estimated that the cumulative effect of these efforts were to save £465 million. The 1986 social security reforms were officially intended to be financially neutral: cuts in housing benefit were to offset increases in expenditure on income support and family credit. But an outcry about the effects of the new housing benefit tapers led to a relaxation of the capital rules which effectively cancelled out the savings. During the reviews child benefit was considered as a source of saving by abolishing or changing it. Child benefit has been frozen, unfrozen, frozen again, been under constant threat, but still survives (and after the period covered in this analysis was increased and linked to a price index). In this, as in other areas of policy, anxiety about the social and political costs of policy changes weighed against the radical cuts that Thatcherite fiscal policy called for. It came down to the familiar battle between a Treasury demanding cuts from the Department of Social Security and Secretaries of State for Social Security (with perhaps the exception of John Moore), stoutly defending their budget and the matter being resolved by some incremental change.

Arguably social security expenditure would have been very much higher than it was without Thatcherite policies. The principal saving came from the decision, made early in office, to break the link between the uprating of benefits and earnings. There is no recent official estimate of how much this has saved, though by 1985 it was over £6 billion. Other smaller savings have come from the failure to uprate benefits fully in line with prices (see below), the abolition of earnings related to unemployment and sickness benefit, continuous increases in the tapers and other cuts in housing benefit, the freezing of child benefit and the abolition of the maternity and death grants. Other notable changes that led to savings in public expenditure were the replacement of single payments in supplementary benefit with the Social Fund which succeeded in putting a cap on discretionary payments at the margin of income support. This is the first time that cash limits have been introduced into social security.

Offsetting these savings have been increases in expenditure led by policy changes. Some of these changes have not been of the Government's volition.

Thus decisions of the European Court led to the extension of Invalid Care Allowance to married women and the abolition of the housework test in the non-contributory invalidity benefit (now severe disablement allowance). The changes currently being implemented to benefits for disabled people will in the medium term add at least £300 million to public expenditure. There have been a host of other small changes in social security that have led to increases in expenditure. There has been a recent notable increase in tax expenditure through the massive take-up of personal pensions. This has unexpectedly lost the exchequer over £2 billion and the National Audit Office (1990) estimate that this will rise to £6 billion over a five-year period. Although this will not show as public expenditure in the public accounts, it will effect the public sector borrowing requirement in exactly the same way. The abolition of the earnings related supplement to invalidity benefit will also eventually lead to substantial savings.

What have been the effects of these changes for individuals and families? There is no doubt that the effects have varied over the period and varied for different groups. In general pensioners and some people with disabilities have fared better than the unemployed and families with children. Young people have suffered most, experiencing on top of high rates of unemployment, the abolition of rights to benefits for 16 and 17 year olds, the abolition of rights to income support and housing benefit for students and a reduction in the level of benefits for most claimants under 25. Children also appear to have suffered: there is evidence that their diets have deteriorated, their heights have stopped increasing, more of them are homeless, there is a greater incidence of child-hood sickness and the reduction of the infant mortality rate has slowed down (Bradshaw 1990).

To provide evidence of the overall impact of these changes we have three sorts of data: on trends in the level of benefits, on the incidence of poverty and on inequality.

The level of benefits

First, in Table 6.1, we show what has happened to the levels of selected benefits between November 1978 (the last uprating of the Labour Govern-ment) and April 1990 (the last uprating of the Government led by Mrs Thatcher).

The picture that emerges from Table 6.1 is fairly consistent regardless of the benefit. The real value of benefits has fallen between November 1978 and April 1990, though not by very much. The exception to this is child benefit which in April 1990 was worth £2.13 per child less than its real value in November 1983. The level of benefits as a proportion of average male earnings have fallen more sharply because, since 1980, they have only increased in line with prices while earnings have moved ahead of prices. In fact the comparison with average male earnings underestimates the gap that has emerged between the incomes of households dependent on benefits and households with earnings

Table 6.1   Rates of benefit

		Value of benefit	
		At April 1990 prices £p.w. at date of uprating	As a % of average earnings
Standard rate retirement pension (single person under 80)	November 1978	47.52	20.4
	April 1990	46.90	15.9
Standard rate of unemployment benefit	November 1978	38.38	16.4
	April 1990	37.35	12.6
Standard rate of invalidity pension	November 1978	47.52	20.4
	April 1990	46.90	15.9
Child benefit (one child)	April 1979	9.22	3.9
	April 1990	7.25	2.5
		(at April 1987 prices)	
SB long-term rates (couple)	April 1978	58.73	32.9
	April 1987	61.85	27.6
		(at April 1990 prices)	
Income support (couple)	April 1988	57.62	20.9
	April 1990	57.60	19.5

Source: DSS *Abstract of Statistics for Index of Retail Prices, Average Earnings, Social Security Benefits and Contributions.* Analytical Services Division, DSS (1990).

because there has been an increase in the number of households with two earners. Arguably the most crucial benefit is income support, because so many people are dependent on it, and it provides the minimum floor to the social security system. It is difficult to show what has happened to the rates of this benefit over time because of the change from supplementary benefit to income support in April 1988. The Social Services Committee (1989) compared the income support rates introduced in April 1988 with what the supplementary benefit rates would have been if they had been uprated in line with inflation between April 1987 and 1988 and taking account of the fact that 20 per cent of rates and water rates have to be covered by the income support scales. They found that most family types were structural losers (there was transitional protection for actual losers). Even the small gains for couples with children would not have been enough to compensate them for the loss of single payments due to the introduction of the Social Fund.

Low incomes, poverty and inequality

The second sort of evidence on the outcome of Government policy are statistics on low income. These are unfortunately not up to date – the latest figures available at the time of writing are for 1987. There is also a tremendously

Table 6.2   Households below average income,* 1979

	1979 %	1987 %
Married pensioners	18	27
Single pensioners	9	23
Married with children	9	20
Married without children	4	10
Single with children	29	47
Single without children	6	15
Pensioners	14	25
Full-time workers	3	8
Sick or disabled	32	32
Lone parents	44	58
Unemployed	47	59
Other	27	32
All	9.4	19.4

Note: ★ Proportion of individuals with income below 50 per cent of the average. Income after housing costs.
Source: DSS *Households below average income: a statistical analysis 1981–87.* Government Statistical Service (1990).

arcane dispute between aficionados of 'poverty statistics' about the pros and cons of different series. The Government have been very critical of the official low-income statistics (which relate income to benefit level), for the good reason that when benefit levels are increased the number defined as living in poverty increases. But it was not necessary to abandon them entirely, as they did, after the 1985 analysis. The Institute for Fiscal Studies (1990) carried on the analysis to 1987 but were unfortunately not able to reconcile their results with the Government's.

The new DSS series Households Below Average Income (HBAI) relates income to the average. Table 6.2 shows that the number of persons living in families with incomes below 50 per cent of the average increased from 9.4 per cent in 1979 to 19.4 per cent in 1987.

However, the Government would argue that if the comparison is made in real terms the picture is not so bleak. This can be seen in Table 6.3 which shows that it is really only married couples with children whose proportion with incomes below 50 per cent increased in real terms. Overall the proportion of people with real incomes of less than half the 1979 average remained constant.

The third source of information on the distribution of income is provided by the Central Statistics Office (CSO) annual analysis of the effects of taxes and benefits on household incomes (*Economic Trends*, May 1990). The latest data is for 1987 and so excludes the impact of the social security reforms of 1988 and the tax-cutting budget of the same year. It is debatable which measure of income should be taken. The difference between gross income and

Table 6.3   Households below average income,* 1979 real terms

	1979 %	1987 %
Married pensioners	18	6
Single pensioners	9	7
Married with children	9	12
Married without children	4	6
Single with children	29	15
Single without children	6	9
Pensioners	14	6
Full-time workers	3	4
Sick or disabled	32	14
Lone parents	44	18
Unemployed	47	43
Other	27	19
All	9.4	9.4

Note: * Proportion of individuals with income below 50 per cent of the average. Income after housing costs.

original income (that is after the addition of social security benefits) is probably most appropriate for this analysis. Whichever measure is taken the share of income of the bottom two quintiles has fallen and that of the top two quintiles has risen. Inequality, as measured by the Gini coefficient, has increased. It can be seen that the effect of social security is to reduce inequalities. But given the increase in inequalities in original income between 1979 and 1987, even after the effects of social security benefits have been taken into account, inequalities

Table 6.4   Share of income by quintile group, 1979–87

		Quintiles					
		1st	2nd	3rd	4th	5th	Gini coefficient
Original income	1979	0.5	9	19	27	45	45
	1987	0.3	6	16	27	51	52
Gross income	1979	5.5	11	17	25	41	35
	1987	5.1	10	16	24	45	40
Disposable income	1979	6.5	12	18	25	39	33
	1987	6.1	11	17	25	42	37
Post-tax income	1979	6.1	11	18	24	40	35
	1987	5.1	10	16	24	45	40
Final income	1979	7.1	12	18	24	38	38
	1987	6.2	11	17	24	42	36

Source: CSO (1990).

have increased. Social security interacts with fiscal policy in determining the final distribution of income. A variety of factors have led to the tax/benefit system becoming vertically less progressive. These include tax thresholds only rising in line with prices in recent years; very substantial cuts in the rates of income tax on higher incomes; increases in national insurance contributions; huge increases in tax expenditures, principally tax relief on mortgage interest payments; real increases in rents, poll tax and water rates; and a shift to indirect taxes. The overall effects of these changes is that the distributional affect of direct and indirect taxes is now neutral.

Having reviewed the macro or overall impact of the Conservative Government's social security policies in the 1980s we now turn to consider some of the more specific themes.

Selectivity

As we saw earlier in this chapter, the aspiration to concentrate help where it is most needed (also known as targeting or selectivity) has been an objective of Conservative social security policy. The role of means tested benefits expanded. Barr and Coulter (1990) estimate that real (1987/88) expenditure on means tested benefits (including housing benefit) increased by 171 per cent between 1979 and 1989 while expenditure on insurance benefits increased only 17 per cent over the same period. This occurred for a variety of reasons: the uprating of benefits in line with prices rather than earnings, the freezing of child benefit during some of the period, the real increases in rents, the abolition of earnings related supplement to unemployment and short-term sickness benefits, the introduction of means tested maternity and death grants, the introduction of income support and the replacement of family income supplement by family credit.

However, the really big increase in means testing was not the result of purpose and policy but the consequence of unemployment and demographic change. The level of unemployment led to the marginalization of the national insurance unemployment benefit system. Unemployment benefit only lasts a year and with increasing unemployment among young people who had never contributed, and long-term unemployment exhausting entitlement, the proportion of the unemployed receiving income support increased to 79 per cent in 1989/90. Both the number and proportion of lone parents dependent on income support also rose very rapidly. However, and equally significant, there was no increase in the proportion of retirement pensioners and the sick and disabled receiving targeted benefits. In fact with increases in the proportion of pensioners retiring with entitlements to occupational pensions and the state earnings retirement pension (SERPS), the proportion receiving income support fell. The proportion of the sick and disabled on income support remained constant although their numbers increased. The number of families receiving family income supplement doubled as a result of labour market effects and the number receiving family credit doubled again as a result of a widening in the eligibility criteria.

The Government sought in the context of the Social Security Review to expand the role of some selective benefits further but political support for SERPS, child benefit and the contributory and non-contributory benefits for disabled people was too great. They were also, no doubt, constrained by the two great defects of means tested benefit (apart from their greater administrative costs).

Take-up

The Government has struggled hard to improve the take-up of means tested benefits by simplifying them, by improving their operation and by publicity campaigns. They do appear to have been successful in increasing the proportion of the eligible case load receiving supplementary benefit from 75 per cent in 1981 to 84 per cent in 1985. However the proportion of those eligible receiving housing benefit was only 79 per cent in 1985 (but 90 per cent of expenditure was taken up). The take-up of family credit was, despite a massive television advertising campaign, still thought to be claimed by only half of those eligible.

'Poverty trap'

With the increase in the numbers on housing benefit and family income supplement and the increase in national insurance contributions offsetting much of the benefit of reductions in the standard rate of income tax, the number of families experiencing marginal tax rates in excess of 100 per cent increased to 70,000. Following the reforms implemented in 1988 and the change to assessment of means tested benefit on a net basis, no one should now experience marginal tax rates in excess of 100 per cent, but this has been achieved at the cost of increasing the number with marginal tax rates in excess of 70 per cent from 290,000 to 445,000 (before the 1989/90 budget and 415,000, after the 1989/90 budget). So the intensity of the poverty trap has been reduced at the expense of increasing its extensiveness.

The emphasis on selectivity in social security policy can be contrasted with the Government's approach in fiscal policy where the benefits of tax allowances increased in volume for all tax payers but continued to benefit higher rate tax payers most.

Incentives

Ancient anxieties about the behavioural effects of benefits have taken on slightly new colours during the Conservative years. Aspirations to uphold the value of work and traditional family forms have begun to be articulated in the wider context of the 'dependency culture'. American writers on the underclass especially Charles Murray caught the imagination of Ministers perhaps most notably John Moore, who in a speech to the Institute of Directors said,

We believe that dependence in the long run decreases human happiness and reduces human freedom . . . Therefore the next step forward in the long evolutionary march of the welfare state in Britain is away from dependence towards independence . . . Everyone knows the sullen apathy of dependence and can compare it with the sheer delight of personal achievement . . . Two things need to be done. The first is the most important. It is to change the climate of opinion. (Institute of Directors Annual Lecture, 8 June 1988)

The Conservative Government can claim to have achieved a sharp reduction in the unemployment trap – the overlap between unemployment benefits and net income from work. Thus the number of working heads of tax units with replacement rates above 100 per cent fell from 60,000 in 1985 to 20,000 in 1988/89 and the number with replacement rates in excess of 70 per cent fell from 1.9 million to 745,000 over the same period. This improvement in the unemployment trap was achieved by cuts in benefits to the unemployed (unemployment benefit for a couple plus two children as a proportion of average income fell from 48.6 per cent in 1979 to 37.8 per cent in 1990), the abolition of earnings related supplement to unemployment benefit, and the taxation of unemployment benefit. It was also assisted by improvements to in-work benefits (family credit and housing benefit) and the growing gap between earnings and prices.

These were not the only efforts to affect the dependency of the unemployed on benefit. There was a massive transfer of unemployed people to make-work and training schemes. Eventually all 16 and 17 year olds lost any entitlement to income support when the Youth Training Scheme was extended to two years in 1987. As part of the introduction of income support, benefit levels for most 18–24 year olds were reduced, partly on the assumption that they were likely to be non-householders, i.e. living at home. The Employment Training Scheme eventually paid benefits plus an allowance to 190,000 long-term unemployed people. Successive changes reduced and then finally abolished students' entitlement to income support and housing benefit. Long-term unemployed claimants are now subject to a compulsory Restart programme if they have been unemployed for two years.

These changes in benefit entitlement for young people (in addition to the earlier changes made to housing benefit for young adults living with their family) have transferred a considerable proportion of responsibility for dependent young people from the state to their families. Where there are no families or family relations have broken down, considerable hardship has resulted from this policy.

It is not clear whether any of these measures have actually changed behaviour. Despite economic theory and sophisticated economic analysis there is still little evidence, even in a buoyant labour market, that high replacement rates affect incentives to work. Nevertheless, Ann Widdecombe, parliamentary secretary, claimed:

I believe our success in cutting away the penalties on hard work and self
reliance that littered the old benefit system will stand as one of the
enduring social and economic achievements of the 1980s. (DSS press
release 91/34)

Apart from the status of young people, the Government has become
increasingly concerned about the family and, recently, especially about lone
parents' dependence on social security. Already the measures that have been
described earlier are in hand to increase the proportion of absent parents
supporting lone-parent families with maintenance payments. While these
could affect behaviour in respect of child rearing, marriage and divorce, they
appear to be primarily concerned with reducing benefit costs by increasing the
labour supply of lone parents. In this objective Conservative values face a real
conflict between traditional views about the role and responsibilities of mothers
to (stay at home and) care for children and their aspirations to reduce dependency on the state by getting them to work. So far they have maintained the
lone parents' entitlement to benefit without a requirement to work and regardless of the age of the youngest child. Lone parents, it is claimed, should have a
choice whether to work or stay at home. In practice there is very little choice.
The tax/benefit system, and the absence of free or subsidized child care,
present substantial barriers to labour-force participation – quite apart from the
state of labour demand. As a result, the dependence of lone parents is increasing. A Conservative Government (indeed any government) in the 1990s still
has to resolve these competing values one way or the other.

Privatization

The encouragement of increased independence and self-reliance in Conservative ideology goes hand in hand with an emphasis on private provision.

Social security has been responsible for funding a massive expansion in
private residential and nursing homes for the elderly, but this expansion was
certainly not an objective of policy and repeated efforts have been made to
curtail it, culminating in the decision to transfer the budget and responsibility
for funding the care of people in residential homes to local authorities. Also this
is a private *outcome* of social security. What we are really concerned with is
private *inputs*. In the case of social security, this means personal, voluntary or
occupational provision.

To the extent that the state withdraws from supporting claimants by
cutting benefits or abolishing entitlements, the burden has to be picked up
personally – by the claimant in increased debt or reduced living standards or by
their relatives or by the voluntary sector or employers. We have already discussed some ways in which there has been a transfer of financial dependence
from the state to parents. We have seen what has happened to benefit levels:
many claimants are absolutely worse off than they would have been and many,
many more are worse off comparatively. Certainly there is evidence that debt

among claimants is very high (Bradshaw and Holmes 1989; Berthoud and Kempson 1990) and evidence that the number of claimants with direct deductions from their benefits has increased. A major contribution to this, and any transfer to the voluntary sector that has taken place, has been the Social Fund. This replaced single payments in 1988 with a cash limited, largely loan based scheme. The Social Fund represents 0.36 per cent of the total social security budget in 1990/91 and has probably caused more controversy than any other single element in social security since 1979. This is because it has left people in urgent need without support, increased their indebtedness and thrown extra burdens on the voluntary sector (and local authorities).

There are two ways in which social security provision has been *occupationalized* or *privatized* during the last ten years. First, employers have been given responsibility for paying sickness benefit and maternity allowance. The intention was to make employers entirely responsible, but this was vigorously opposed by employers and until 1991 it was purely a transfer of administrative responsibility in that employers were fully compensated financially by a reduction in their national insurance contributions. However, from 1991/92 the Government plans to move to only 80 per cent reimbursement for sickness benefit on the basis that 90 per cent of employees are already covered by occupational sickness benefit.

By far the most important element of privatization in social security has been the introduction and roaring success of personal pensions. Occupational pensions had been an increasingly important element in social security provision for old age, but by the early 1980s occupational cover was stagnant. In his 1985 Green Paper proposals for the reform of social security, Mr Fowler intended to boost the role of private and occupational provision by *inter alia* abolishing the state earnings related pension scheme (SERPS). SERPS had emerged from decades of inter-party haggling over pensions policy and there was widespread opposition (not least from the private pensions industry) to Mr Fowler's attempts to abandon a scheme that had been introduced with all party support. Fowler was forced to back down on his plans to phase out SERPS and instead set about reducing the costs of SERPS by modifying it. In addition he introduced new incentives for occupational and personal pensions, including an extra 2 per cent rebate on contributions for those who contracted out of SERPS for the first time before the end of 1992/93. The Government Actuary had assumed that there would be 750,000 personal pensions in force, but by April 1990 there were over 4 million and it is now expected the number will rise to 6 million. Nearly all of these qualified for the extra rebate for opting out of SERPS and this, together with the lost contributions, cost the national insurance fund £2 billion. It went rapidly into deficit and was only rescued by the Social Security Act 1990 removing the cost of industrial injuries benefit from the fund, compensating the fund for the loss of contributions in statutory sick pay and statutory maternity pay from the general exchequer, and merging the redundancy payments fund, which contains £1 billion. Without these changes the House of Commons (1990) estimated that contribution rates would have had to be 2.8 per cent, 4.0 per cent and 3.3 per cent higher in 2010, 2030 and 2050 respectively because of the unexpected success of personal pensions. The cost is still growing and may reach £6 billion by 1993. As with other areas of policy, the general tax payer has paid for the success of privatization.

Conclusion

In evaluating the implementation of policies by the Government of Mrs Thatcher perhaps social security is a special case. A special case in the sense that whatever any particular government aspires to do, social security practice (and expenditure) is largely determined by predetermined entitlements, the state of the economy and demographic patterns. Mrs Thatcher's Government's policies in the field of social security were all determined in the first instance by these 'extraneous' factors, in particular high levels of unemployment and changes in the structure of family life. Indeed it could be claimed that social security enabled a policy of mass unemployment to be pursued as an anti-inflation measure without generating public unrest.

It is also difficult to discern consistently clear social security objectives in New Right ideology. There are certain themes or slogans – privatization, selectivity, managerialism, incentives and certain values relating to independence, the family, work and so forth – but no very clear overriding goal. The simple nostrums of right-wing ideology were at variance with the reality of social security. Furthermore, social security was not the focus of attention of Conservative thinkers. The minds of the members of right-wing think tanks were focused on other areas of policy, they lacked knowledge, understanding and interest in social security. There was only one Secretary of State for Social Security from the Thatcherite wing of the party, John Moore, and he did not last long. Far from boasting about the scale of the cuts in benefit and the extent to which individual initiative had been encouraged, Ministers were more inclined to assure Parliament that the poor were being looked after better than ever before as a result of record levels of expenditure!

Perhaps the most substantive objective in social policy of the Thatcher era was to cut public expenditure. Despite this, social security expenditure increased in absolute terms, real terms, and for the most of the period as a proportion of GNP. Nevertheless, despite this increase in expenditure, there was an increase in poverty and greater inequality. Inequality is not something that Conservative Governments should in ideology be much concerned with, but they have certainly been concerned with poverty, challenging the concept and redefining the evidence. However, there is no doubt that more people have been living on low incomes in comparative terms. Benefits have fallen in value and beneficiaries' income compared with earnings have reduced substantially. This, together with an increasingly regressive tax system, has meant that the rich have got richer and many of the poor have got poorer.

In ten years the social security *structure* has changed. Indeed it has been changed constantly by small acts and acts which it has been claimed are very substantial. At the end of the day, however, it is really not much different from what it was. The essence of the contributory scheme remains. There has, as ever, been an extension of means testing. There have been changes that have diminished the benefits available to the unemployed and to young people. There have been changes that have increased the incomes of people with disabilities and those with low wages. Families with children have not done as well as the Government might have wished. The gap between two nations in old age has grown – younger, two-person, home owners, with occupational pensions and some SERPS entitlement have gained, while the rest have lost. The structure of social security in the UK has become less European in that it has become more income related. However, it has neither become as residual and ineffective as the social security system in the USA, nor has it achieved the vigour and coherence of the wholly means tested system reformed by a Labor Government in Australia.

From an academic perspective the analysis of this period has confirmed three hypotheses.

First, social security is deeply impervious to change (at least from the radical right). It is ingrained in our culture, economy and system of exchange to such an extent that governments can only succeed in tampering at the margins.

Second, the reasons for this are that social security is recognized by a substantial body of opinion as essential to our civilized society. Social security benefits are not just the result of able pressure groups operating on behalf of claimants in Whitehall. It is not merely an outcome of executive action – the civil servants running the system. Nor has social security been sustained only by MPs, Conservative as well as Labour representing their constituents' interests or the House of Lords who, acting as a restraining influence have kicked a number of the Government's proposals into touch. Social security has survived because like other social policies it has been sustained by a substantial proportion of the electorate – certainly those who stand to benefit – but also those who do not. There is evidence (Taylor-Gooby 1990) that the majority would rather see improvements in benefits before cuts in taxation and that support for this view has been increasing in the 1980s. The popularity of different benefits varies – pensions are the most popular. But faced with a proposal to cut benefits for any group, the majority of the general public will resist supporting it. Faced with these views, the pensioners vote, the high level of unemployment and anxiety about civil strife, the Government moderated its ideological aspirations.

Third, for a radical Government seeking to make reforms to the social security system, the Treasury has a devastatingly unhelpful influence. Even if it is accepted that it is inevitable that social security should be a handmaid to economic management and that this is the responsibility of the Treasury, their influence is still maligned. They are short-term thinkers, focused on a public expenditure round, incapable of planning or strategy in the longer term. The Treasury supported by the Prime Minister dominated DSS policy (but not the Inland Revneue which carries on seemingly impervious to Government objectives or at least the need for a joint approach to social policy). Almost all reforms had to be revenue neutral. Short-term gains had to be paid for by short-term losses. More radical policies that might have led to savings in the long-term had to be eschewed because of the costs that would be involved in avoiding politically damaging short-term losses. As a result policy change remained incremental and modest.

The view you take of Thatcherite social security policy depends on your own political persuasion. A generation of young people has *experienced* Thatcherite social security policies: they have been denied benefits, had to claim benefits and had benefits cut. Huge numbers of people have passed through unemployment. The sick and disabled have remained at the boundaries of poverty. Families with children have lost ground. Some pensioners have felt themselves increasingly detached from the living standards of the working population. On the right there is and will be a feeling that the job has been left undone; that there have been achievements on incentives and private pensions, but regret that the essence of the state structure remains and many opportunities were flunked; that they never really got round to social security. The middle of the political spectrum appears to be devoted to big bang reforms of the tax/benefit system – integrated social dividend schemes. While these are the most radical proposals about, they are also the most unlikely to be implementable. The Labour Party on the left has committed itself to improving child benefit and pensions in the short term and other benefits in the long term. It has also proposed to transform the contributory system. There is as yet nothing to convince one that any party has yet recognized that social security, with all its boring details, can be a major vehicle for the transformation of Britain – including its economy.

Acknowledgements

I am grateful for comments on a draft of this chapter from Peter Saunders, Robert Walker, Richard Berthoud, John Ditch, Norman Glass, Peter Kemp and the editors. The defects remain my own responsibility.

7

The National Health Service

Gerald Wistow

Introduction

The National Health Service (NHS) was established in 1948 as an integral part of the postwar social contract between the State and its citizens. Reflecting these origins, its founding principles were those of: comprehensiveness, equity, equality of access, and the provision of services free at the point of use (Royal Commission 1979: para. 2.6; Institute of Health Service Management 1988: 17–18). Forty years on, such universalist principles found few echoes in the rhetoric of successive Thatcher administrations. Rather, they were associated with the kinds of social engineering which those Governments held responsible for the dependency culture and associated economic decline they had set out to challenge and reverse.

At least until 1988, however, the NHS seemed to be immune from, for example, those influences which led to the privatizing of industries whose nationalization coincided with the NHS's birth. The publication, towards the end of the Thatcher years, of a White Paper which included proposals for creating an internal market appeared to suggest the stronger influence of party ideology on policy-making. However, the White Paper emphasized the continuity between its approach and the principles on which the NHS had been founded:

> the Government will keep all that is best in the NHS. The principles which have guided it for the last 40 years will continue to guide it into the twenty-first century. The NHS is, and will continue to be, open to all, regardless of income, and financed mainly out of general taxation. (Royal Commission 1979: para. 1.2)

How far this emphasis on policy continuity is a presentational one – designed to obscure the extent of proposed change in an institution whose poll ratings are exceeded only by the Royal Family – will be a major issue for policy analysis in the post-Thatcher era.

Moreover, policy towards the NHS has not been wholly characterized by continuity and consistency since 1979. Elements of the incoming Government's approach were substantially reversed after 1982 and again modified in 1988–89. As a result, three phrases of policy development may be identified: decentralization and an attack on bureaucracy (1979–82); centralization and the rediscovery of managerialism (1982–89); managed competition and internal markets (1989 onwards). At the same time, however, it should be recognized that the 1979 manifesto contained a number of themes which were to recur repeatedly during the following decade.

Policy objectives 1979–90

The 1979 manifesto argued that the enlargement of the role of the state, together with the dimunition in the role of private enterprise and the individual had 'crippled the enterprise and effort on which a prosperous country with improving social services depended' (Conservative Party 1979). The country's relative economic decline, it argued, could be rewarded only by the Government 'working with the grain of human nature, helping people to help themselves – and others' (ibid.). Economic policy was to have primacy over social policy, which meant giving priority to the reduction of taxation in order to improve incentives, relying more on market forces and enterprise, attacking waste, bureaucracy and over-government, and reducing public expenditure (Jackson 1985a: 33 and 37).

Specific manifesto commitments on the NHS broadly followed this approach. Significantly, however, they included a commitment 'not to reduce spending' on the NHS and to 'make better use of what resources are available'. In support of the latter objective, it proposed to 'simplify and decentralize the service and cut back bureaucracy'. Other commitments included 'ending Labour's vendetta against the private health sector', restoring tax relief on company health insurance schemes and allowing pay beds where demand existed. It also raised the possibility of changing the funding base of the NHS through the insurance principle.

Decentralization and an attack on bureaucracy, 1979–82

In the years immediately following the 1979 election, DHSS ministers were faithful to their manifesto commitments, though the insurance option was less vigorously pursued. Patrick Jenkin, the first Conservative Secretary of State, repeatedly referred to the 'overriding economic imperative' (Webb and Wistow 1981: 35) and emphasized that 'a sound and thriving economy was the foundation of all welfare provision' (DHSS 1979a). An unsympathetic attitude to welfare expenditure was suggested in his comment: 'it is no use having a bleeding heart if you haven't the money to pay for it' (Jenkin 1979a). Yet, in practice, the commitment not to cut NHS spending was more than fulfilled: between 1979/80 and 1982/83, current expenditure on hospital and community health services increased by 3.3 per cent in 'real' terms, after allowing for NHS inflation (House of Commons 1991a). Both the level and adequacy of such spending were, however, to remain major issues of political and public controversy throughout the Thatcher era (see pp. 111–13).

Centre–periphery relations proved to be another area of continuing, though less politicized, debate. In this first phase of Conservative Government, ministers characterized their approach as one of 'disengagement' from over-detailed control and over-bureaucratic management of the service (Webb and Wistow 1981: 31). Within weeks of taking office, Jenkin emphasized:

> The Government wants to see a simpler, more flexible structure in the NHS with Local Health Authorities using their own initiative to respond to local needs, rather than being a conveyor for detailed orders and advice from the Centre. (DHSS 1979b)

Proposals to fulfil the commitments to decentralization and the reduction of bureaucracy were set out in a consultative document 'Patients First' (DHSS 1979a). The Royal Commission on the NHS (1979) which reported earlier the same year, had accepted the widely held view that the Heath Government's 1974 reorganization had produced an over-complex and unwieldy structure. Accordingly, it recommended that either the area or district tier of administration should be removed. The new Government opted to abolish the former in accordance with its wish to focus responsibilty at as local a level as possible. In addition, the new District Health Authorities were required to deliver 10 per cent savings on administrative costs following this simplification of NHS structures.

In his foreword to 'Patients First', Jenkin had set out the underlying objective of freeing local decision-makers from inappropriately detailed interference by either central government or regional health authorities. This objective was followed through in 'Care in Action', a handbook on policies and priorities for the health and personal social services which was published in 1981 (DHSS 1981). Jenkin (1979b) had criticized as dirigisme, inflexible and bureaucratic the practice of the previous decade of specifying service norms or target levels of provision to be achieved within given periods (see DHSS 1971, 1976a, 1976b, 1977). In his view, this resulted in an inevitable loss of initiative 'to the centre from the community at ground level'. Such targets and timescales were abandoned, therefore, though the underlying policy priorities remained broadly the same and represented a continuing commitment to territorial resource equalization, the improvement of standards for 'cinderella' services (such as those for elderly, mentally ill and mentally handicapped people) and a shift in the balance of services from hospital to community based provision. The crucial difference, however, was that there were now to be no detailed standards by which the rate of progress towards these objectives could be assessed.

In practice, mechanisms for reviewing performance and securing accountability for shortfalls against such targets had never been well developed at any level in the service. For this reason, among others, it had proved difficult to counter the dominance of hospital services, especially those in the acute sector (Haywood and Alaszewski 1980; Wistow 1992). However, the Government's approach was not only consistent with its commitment to localism and the removal of detailed central controls. It also made sound political sense to emphasize local rather than national responsibilities for service development and to remove quantitative targets which implied national standards against which the success, or otherwise, of Government policy might be measured. As Klein (1981: 168) remarked, 'the decentralization of blame' is a logical response by central government to hard times. It might be added, that such a logic is perhaps particularly powerful when financial constraint flows directly from the resource policies of the centre itself. Even so, it proved a strategy to which the centre found it impossible to hold. By the time the restructured health service came into being in April 1982, a new Secretary of State (Norman Fowler) was initiating an era of unprecedented central control and intervention.

Centralization and the rediscovery of managerialism, 1982–88

The second phase of Government initiatives in the NHS was dominated by a managerialist agenda and resulted in a potentially more coherent framework of scrutiny and control than had existed in the service's history. In adopting this course, Ministers effectively reversed a major element of their 1979 manifesto commitments. However, this reversal was strongly influenced by their further commitment to protect the NHS from spending cuts. Such protection, together with the increased spending necessary to meet demographic and other changes (see pp. 111–13), could be secured only by demonstrating the effectiveness with which existing resources were being managed. Moreover, and according to Harrison et al. (1990: 80), 'an informal 1979 agreement between ministers to the effect that the NHS should be preserved from reductions in real resources ran out in 1981–82'.

Parliamentary criticisms of accountability arrangements within the NHS were also influential. The newly established Social Services Committee quickly highlighted a central weakness in Ministers' disengagement strategy by questioning the extent to which it was compatible with their accountability to Parliament for NHS expenditure (House of Commons 1980: para. 25). In the same report, the Committee was also moved to 'express forcibly our disquiet that the Department, whilst embracing the rhetoric of greater efficiency, does not appear to be in a position to measure its actual achievement' (ibid.). The following year, the Public Accounts Committee criticized the Department for the absence of 'proper control' over the NHS and argued that, to be meaningful, accountability upwards must be matched by a flow of information about the activities of the districts, which will enable the regions, and in turn DHSS, to monitor performance effectively and to take the necessary action to remedy any serious deficiencies or inefficiencies. (House of Commons 1981: xvii)

Before the Committee returned to NHS matters in 1982, Ministers had already announced a number of initiatives directed directly at such matters. How far these measures were directly due to pressure from the select committees and how far, as Klein (1985: 199) hints, they reinforced emerging thinking within DHSS cannot be clearly established. Griffiths (1991: 2) has indicated that the background to his 1983 inquiry into NHS management 'was the tremendous parliamentary questioning on the waste and inefficiency in the service'. It was clearly also in the interests of the Department in its negotiations with the Treasury to be able to demonstrate that effective monitoring and accountability were in place.

Initiatives to strengthen accountability

In January 1982, Mr Fowler announced an annual review system and a performance indicators package. Other initiatives were soon to follow, including Sir Derek Rayner's efficiency scrutinies, cost improvement programmes, the disposal of surplus land and experiments with private audit (for details, see Harrison 1988: ch. 4). The review system comprised a mechanism through which Ministers could review regional plans and performance against targets agreed the previous year. A similar review of districts was conducted by the region and, after 1984, of units by the district. The performance indicators package was developed to assist this new review process. Though largely dealing with activity levels (outputs) rather than treatment outcomes, the indicators provided a framework for crude comparisons between districts and for identifying areas in which further analysis might be justified (see Harrison 1988: 58). Moreover, they helped provide a framework for negotiating, through the review process, target levels of activity, such as the number of particular cases to be treated or of long-stay patients to be discharged (Klein 1989: 206). Thus the planning norms, discarded as recently as 1981, were effectively replaced by a system of annually agreed and monitored performance targets.

Both of these initiatives were further developed and refined after 1982. They may be criticized for focusing primarily on 'efficiency, economy and conformity to plans' rather than effectiveness (Harrison et al. 1990: 129). Compared with the situation described by the parliamentary committees, however, they represented a significant addition to the machinery for defining and securing departmental objectives. Moreover, and in contrast with the initial, somewhat romanticized thinking about setting the periphery free, they may be seen as part of 'a strategy to centralise knowledge about local performance while decentralising responsibility for the execution of government policies' (Carter 1991: 96). They were rapidly followed by steps to establish a more powerful executive function at all levels in the service.

General management

When the service was re-organized in 1974, management responsibilities at the regional, area and district tiers were vested in multi-disciplinary teams consisting of an administrator, treasurer, nurse and up to three doctors. Decision-making within those teams was by consensus which meant that each member had a power of veto. This arrangement reflected the reluctance of medicine to operate within conventional management hierarchies, as did the creation of medical advisory committees which paralleled the formal management structures at every level. Moreover, the consensus teams at each tier were initially linked by monitoring rather than line relationships. Thus the service, as a whole, operated without a conventional management hierarchy within or between levels. In addition, responsibilities were distributed on the same functional or professional basis at the centre which produced weaknesses in its capacity to manage the service corporately (Regional Chairmen 1976), not dissimilar to those associated with consensus management. If individual responsibility could anywhere be said to exist for the service as a whole, rather than for its separate function/professional groupings, such responsibility was vested only in the person of the Secretary of State. Even at Permanent Secretary level, the situation was complicated by the Chief Medical Officer's status as both a second Permanent Secretary within the Department and as a chief medical adviser to the government as a whole.

During its initial decentralizing phase, Ministers explicitly rejected the notion that each health authority should have a chief executive on the grounds that this 'would not be compatible with the professional independence required' (DHSS 1979a). The medical veto thus remained unchallenged. Four years later, however, a similar proposal from the Griffiths management inquiry was to produce a different response. The Griffiths Report (1983) was published in the form of a 24-page letter to the Secretary of State, indicting the service for 'institutionalized stagnation' and recommending sweeping change.

Criticizing consensus management for delay and 'lowest common denominator' decision-making, the report characterized the service as an organization in which change was difficult to achieve and precise management objectives were rarely set. Its overall assessment of the service was encapsulated in the memorable phrase: 'if Florence Nightingale were carrying her lamp through the corridors of the NHS today, she would almost certainly be searching for the people in charge' (Griffiths 1983: para. 5). Accordingly, the Griffiths' prescription centred on establishing 'a clearly defined general management function at all levels in the service'. At the top, he recommended a Supervisory Board, chaired by the Secretary of State and responsible for the strategic direction of the service. A Management Board within the DHSS and chaired by a Chief Executive, was to be responsible for the execution of that strategy. Outside the Department, consensus management teams were to be replaced by general managers at regional, district and unit levels. These managers were duly appointed on short-term contracts and a system of performance-related pay and individual performance reviews was subsequently introduced. These arrangements were designed, therefore, to link the personal objectives of individual managers with corporate – and ultimately ministerial – objectives for the service as a whole (Wistow 1992).

The management of medicine

No strengthening of the management function in the NHS could be complete without addressing the central role of medical practitioners in determining patterns of resource utilization. One of the most fundamental concepts built into the fabric of the NHS at its inception was that doctors should exercise clinical autonomy, outside the purview of managerial control. With clinicians free to treat patients according to their independent professional judgement, they have determined the place, nature, length and, thus, the cost of individual treatments. As a result, considerable diversity exists in both the pattern and costs of health care as reflected in, for example, significant variations between doctors in referral rates, diagnostic and treatment procedures, lengths of stay and prescribing patterns.

These variations reflect what Klein (1983: 82) described as 'an implicit bargain' struck at the foundation of the NHS between the state and the medical profession, in which the former determined the overall size of the NHS budget and the latter controlled its utilization. The pattern of provision was determined, therefore, less by ministerial objectives than by the aggregation of individual clinical decisions and, thus, the values and interests on which those decisions rested (Haywood and Alaszewski 1980, Wistow 1992). Combined with the absence of hierarchical arrangements for scrutiny and control identified above, clinical autonomy meant that the Ministerial writ did not run very far within the overall parameters set by the service's cash limits.

It was a corollary to the concept of clinical autonomy that the management role was essentially concerned with providing an organizational environment which facilitated clinical practices defined by professionals as being in their patients' best interests (Harrison 1988: 26). This 'supportive' role of management was specifically endorsed in 'Patients First' (DHSS 1979a: 1–2). Moreover, the view of management as wasteful bureaucracy continued up to and beyond the Griffiths management enquiry with criticisms of, for example, the service's 'administrative tail'. Indeed, it was in this context that Margaret Thatcher originally made her best-known statement about the service. Thus, she claimed in 1982 that the NHS 'is safe only with us because this government will see that it is prudently managed and financed, that care is concentrated on the patient rather than the bureaucrat' (quoted in Small 1989: 104). However, in seeking to create a new management culture and hierarchy, her Government began both to raise the status of managers and to weaken their role as the facilitators of medical practice.

Medicine itself was not to be immune from the new management culture. Indeed, Griffiths (1983: para. 8.2) emphasized that the closer involvement of doctors in management was 'critical to effective management at local level . . . They must accept the management responsibility which goes with clinical freedom'. His report made three key recommendations in this respect: more management training for doctors; management budgets for clinicians which would relate workload and service objectives to resource availability; and the strengthening of hospital medical executive committees to increase medical participation in decisions about the use of hospital resources. In fact, management budgets for clinicians had been introduced on four demonstration sites in advance of the publication of the Griffiths Report and another group of pilots was established in 1985. The following year, more development projects were established under the new 'resource management initiative' (RMI). A particular feature of this initiative was the greater emphasis placed on clinical as well as financial data in order to increase incentives for participation by clinicians and thus overcome weaknesses identified in the previous pilots (Pollitt *et al.* 1988).

Alongside these experiments in bringing the activities of clinicians within budgetary disciplines, traditional concepts of clinical autonomy were to be challenged by a number of other developments. First, restrictions on resource growth constituted a most basic constraint on clinicians' capacity to practice as they might wish, ecially at a time of rapid technological development. Second, the introduction of general management resulted in the removal of the medical veto from formal management structures, notwithstanding resistance by the British Medical Association (BMA). Third, performance indicators and the review process have the potential for subjecting the activities of individual doctors to scrutiny since variations between districts or units must ultimately reflect variations between clinicians. Fourth, the introduction in 1984 of restrictions on doctors' freedom to prescribe, together with the absence of the usual pre-consultations with the profession on such matters showed a willingness to challenge medicine at least on the boundaries of territory which had hitherto been regarded as inviolable.

Research evidence suggests however, that the combined effect of these changes was limited, at least in the initial period following their implementation. The further challenges to the traditional concept of clinical autonomy contained within the 1989 White Paper also seem to confirm that the Griffiths and other changes had less impact than hoped. While the style, tone and form of NHS management arrangements undoubtedly changed very substantially over the middle five years of the Thatcher Governments, they should not necessarily be equated with an effective shift in power relationships. Pettigrew *et al.* (1989: 30) concluded that the extent to which managers had been able to exercise 'authority over the medical profession is extremely mixed' (ibid.: 28). Harrison and his colleagues (1989a and 1989b) similarly argued that clinical performance, was 'still regarded as professional territory – or as one (rather pro-Griffiths) consultant put it, "management stops at the consulting room door" ' (1989a: 5). None the less, in suggesting that the managerial hierarchy broke down 'at the point where it should meet the medical profession' they implicitly suggest the existence of hierarchical relationships up to, if not beyond, the interface between management and clinical practice. Indeed, they have argued elsewhere that, while a proactive management style remained more of a vision than a reality, 'Griffiths-model management did seem to have had quite an impact outside the medical domain' (Pollitt *et al.* 1991: 75). Perhaps most significantly they found that resource limitations had enhanced the influence of managers and that the one thing they could do against medical opposition was to close beds (Harrison *et al.* 1989a: 12). Similarly, they reported that managerial agendas were dominated by the concerns of 'central government with fiscal matters and, in particular, with balancing the books' (ibid.: 12; see also Webb, Wistow and Hardy 1986: 222).

An interim conclusion on the combined impact of all the new management initiatives is that new line relationships have been forged from the Department downwards with the consequence that local managers have been shifted strongly towards a principal–agent relationship with the centre. If that relationship had proved effective in ensuring that the service lived within its cash limits, it had proved somewhat less successful in challenging the conseqences for resource utilization of clinical autonomy. On the other hand, Ministers had effectively signalled that cost effectiveness concerns dictated that professional practice could no longer be regarded as sacrosanct from external scrutiny. As Griffiths (1991: 11) has subsequently observed, 'the medical profession saw [my] report correctly as questioning whether their clinical autonomy extended to immunity from being questioned as to how resources are being used'. Bevan's implicit bargain with the profession was clearly under challenge.

Towards a mixed economy? (1989 onwards)

The role of the private health sector became increasingly significant during the 1980s. Between 1979 and 1988, the proportion of the population with private health insurance increased from 5 to about 9 per cent and the number of acute beds in independent hospitals increased by almost 60 per cent over the same period and by 50 per cent in beds in 'for profit' hospitals (Laing 1990: 123 and 98). Also by 1988, spending on acute and non–acute hospital and nursing home care was 12 per cent of UK expenditure on hospital-based care, compared with 7.5 per cent in 1984 (ibid.: 67). The most rapid growth of all independent sector provision, however, was in the field of nursing and residential home care, especially for elderly people. Indeed, the combined private and voluntary sectors overtook the public sector in the middle of the last decade as the largest suppliers of such care. Funding for much of this expansion came not from private insurance or payments by individuals but from the social security system. Support from that source increased from £10m in 1979 to £1,390m in 1990 (House of Commons 1991b: 94). It is likely to exceed £2,000m by 1992. This growth of public funding for independent nursing and residential home care was not only unplanned but proved impervious to government control throughout the last decade (Wistow 1986; Audit Commission 1989; Wistow and Henwood 1989).

By contrast, direct Government support for the expansion of medical care by the independent sector took the more modest form of tax concessions since 1986 on employer-paid medical insurance premiums for people earning less than £8,500 a year and to the encouragement of district health authorities (DHAs) to help reduce waiting lists by contracting out services to the independent sector. An area of more direct government initiative was that of competitive tendering for laundry, domestic and catering services, which authorities were instructed to undertake from September 1983. In the event, 85 per cent of contracts were awarded in-house rather than to the private sector, though apparently at the expense of NHS employment levels: the number of ancillary staff fell by 35 per cent after 1982 (NAHA 1989: paras 9 and 22). Klein (1989: 220–1) suggests that contracting out was 'not so much the product of an ideology of privatisation as . . . [one] of managerial efficiency'. Such an assessment may underestimate the extent of interdependence between such 'ideologies' and particularly the extent to which the latter is to be seen as the product of the former. None the less, by the end of the decade, market forces had been introduced at only the margins of the service. In the final two years of Mrs Thatcher's Government, however, preparations commenced to introduce an internal market to the NHS. This development was accompanied by more initiatives to strengthen further both the managerial hierarchy and the exposure of clinical practice to management values.

Thus, the White Paper, 'Working for Patients' (Secretary of State for Health et al. 1989), proposed changes to the management of the service, the overall effect of which was intended to 'introduce for the first time a clear and effective chain of management command running from districts . . . to the Secretary of State' (para. 2.6). These changes involved the creation: of a Policy Board chaired by the Secretary of State; a National Health Service Management Executive (NHSME) chaired by the Chief Executive; and a line relationship between the NHSME, regions and family practitioner services. Regional and district health authorities were re-constituted as small boards of executive and non-executive directors. The latter were to be appointed by Ministers or regions, thereby terminating any vestigial community representational role and demonstrating that these intermediary bodies were agents of the centre.

The changes at the centre were a response to what Griffiths (1991: 11) has called the 'half-hearted . . . implementation [of his proposals]. Major policy issues were left uncovered. There was no attempt to establish objectives at the centre and no concentration on outcomes'. The first Chief Executive had resigned because of political 'interference' and the chairmanship of the Management Board was taken by the Health Minister. Significantly, the new NHSME is to be relocated in Leeds, a former Regional General Manager has been appointed as Chief Executive, and regional health authorities (RHAs) appear increasingly as the regional arms of the Management Executive. If the distinction between policy and management can be sustained, it has the political advantage of distancing Ministers from detailed operational matters while continuing to control the direction of policy and those responsible for overseeing its execution (and thereby potentially squaring the circle of blame diffusion and central control).

Alongside these developments have been the more controversial initiatives which aim to introduce competition into the NHS through the separation of the purchasing and providing functions. Thus, since 1 April 1991, DHAs have been funded to purchase services from any NHS or independent provider to meet the identified needs of their resident populations. Provider units (hospitals and other health services) will compete for contracts with DHAs. The majority of these units are currently managed at arm's length from their DHA but increasing numbers are expected to become NHS trusts, independent of DHA control, free to set their own terms and conditions of service, to borrow capital and to accumulate surpluses for reinvestment. Fifty-seven such Trusts were established in 1991, amid claims that they were 'opting out' of the NHS, and a further 113 applications were made for the 1992 second wave of trusts of which 99 were successful.

Substantial changes are also being effected in general practice. Not only has this service been the only non-cash limited part of the NHS but it is general practitioner referral patterns which determine much of the workload for hospitals and other health services. Under the reforms and a revised contract, GPs receive indicative prescribing budgets and those which over-prescribe will ultimately be subject to financial penalties. To make GPs more responsive to their users, patients are able to change their doctor more easily and a higher proportion of GP income will come from capitation fees (thereby providing incentives to increase their list sizes after decades of Government incentives to reduce them). Large practices can apply for their own budgets (top-sliced from their DHA) to purchase a range of non-urgent hospital services. Such GP fund holding implies a fragmentation of purchasing power at the district level. The GP's pivotal role is similarly reflected in the need for DHAs to take into account, or seek to modify, GP referral patterns when letting their own contracts.

However, the internal market has direct implications for clinical autonomy. Hospitals will need to compete in terms of costs and outcomes. Thus control over diagnostic and treatment procedures, lengths of stay, readmission rates and other outcomes will be essential to their business planning. Significantly, NHS trusts are to have a medical director and the White Paper proposed additional measures to bring clinical practice into a resource management framework including: a role for managers in consultant appointments and the award of merit payments, with consultant contributions to the management of services being an explicit criterion in both cases; a system of medical audit or peer review; and a much expanded resource management initiative to provide clinicians with comparative data on the costs and outcomes of their practice and that of their colleagues.

In combination, these changes are intended to strengthen control over clinical costs and to reward efficient hospitals (which have hitherto been penalized by a failure to relate funding directly to workload). While not modifying the principles that care should be funded from taxation and free at the point of use, the changes potentially limit access to locally comprehensive services depending on where DHAs place their contracts. However, to operate effectively, the internal market will require, *inter alia*, fuller and more accurate information about costs and outcomes than the NHS has historically possessed. Large investments in information technology and the extended resource management initiatives are designed to meet this need. It remains to be seen, however, whether the pressure arising from the purchaser/provider split will achieve a more ready acceptance and more rapid implementation of such information systems than hitherto.

Resourcing the NHS: inputs and outcomes

Pressures on NHS spending have been a recurrent feature of the last decade. Indeed, it was a number of high profile incidents, allegedly caused by underfunding, which led Mrs Thatcher to establish her NHS review in 1988 and ultimately to adopt the internal market proposals. Opinion poll evidence has consistently suggested widespread satisfaction with the NHS alongside concern about the underfunding of the service and substantial majorities favour increased spending supported by taxation (King's Fund Institute 1988: 9). For its part, the Government has repeatedly argued that the service is better funded and providing a higher level of activity than at any time in its history. As was noted above, the first Thatcher Government more than met its objective of maintaining real spending levels on the NHS. Over the whole period 1979/80 to 1989/90, total current spending on hospital and community health services grew by 7.5 per cent in real terms, measured against changes in NHS pay and price inflation. This represesnted an average annual increase of 0.7 per cent (House of Commons 1991a: 37). (A higher annual figure of 2.4 per cent results if the lower GDP deflator is used but this is a less realistic measure of change in the real purchasing power of NHS resources.)

Increases in input efficiency also influence NHS purchasing power and hence activity levels. The most recent data show that overall activity levels increased by 36 per cent between 1974–75 and 1989–90 compared with expenditure increases (using the NHS inflation index) of 15 per cent, which suggests efficiency gains of some 18 per cent (ibid: 8). Health authorities have formally been expected since 1984 to make what were initially termed efficiency savings – and subsequently 'Cost Improvement Programmes' (CIPs) – to generate at least 1 per cent growth a year from savings within existing budgets. However, two National Audit Office reports (1986, 1987) identified the danger of this initiative concealing cuts in the volume and quality of services. A subsequent study concluded that 'if the figures quoted do not reflect genuine additional sources of finance, they must provide part of the explanation for the severe funding problems faced by many health authorities in recent years' (King's Fund Institute 1989: 33). A further explanation of funding difficulties is that the 'growth dividend' has not been distributed evenly across the country, as a result of a policy of resource equalization (RAWP) which the

Government inherited. Although intended as a levelling-up process, low growth rates have meant that below-target authorities benefit at the expense of cuts in spending by above-target districts (ibid.: 7).

Changes in supply and demand have also created pressures on spending. In 1986, the Minister of Health confirmed that an additional 2 per cent was required annually purely to meet such pressures: one per cent due to the growth in the very elderly population, 0.5 per cent to meet the costs of medical advance and 0.5 per cent to make progress in meeting policy objectives such as improved renal and community care services (House of Commons 1986: para. 12). Using these figures, the Social Services Committee argued that spending growth between 1980/81 and 1985/86 had been only half of the total demanded by the Government's own standards. It calculated that, even after taking full account of cost improvements there had been a cumulative underfunding of £1.3bn. (ibid.) and two years later, the same formula produced a cumulative shortfall of £1.9bn (House of Commons 1988). The Chief Executive of the NHS has since told the Health Committee that the Department has never accepted the 2 per cent figure (House of Commons 1991b: Q572). International comparisons also suggest that the NHS is less well funded than most other countries (King's Fund Institute 1989). However, comparisons in spending as a proportion of GNP make no allowances for variations in efficiency and effectiveness. Traditionally, the lower rate of UK spending has been associated with the low administration costs and other cost control mechanisms inherent in a cash limited system largely funded out of taxation, not charged at the point of delivery and thus incurring minimal transaction costs.

Notwithstanding all the complexity and controversy surrounding NHS funding over the past decade, the following conclusions are apparent. First, aggregate national spending levels have not been cut even using the most demanding (and realistic) higher service specific inflation measure. Rather they increased by an annual average of 0.7 per cent between 1979/80 and 1989/90. Second, that growth rate has been insufficient, according to the standard accepted by the Government in the mid-1980s, to meet supply and demand pressures. Third, modest national growth rates have co-existed with localized cuts as a result of policies for territorial equity. Fourth, however, increases in efficiency have contributed to increased levels of activity over and above those purchased by increased inputs. Fifth, only the Defence and Social Security programmes fared better than the NHS in successive spending rounds.

Much of the debate about resources in the NHS has tended to beg questions about their utilization. In that sense, the Government's insistence on seeking to shift the emphasis from input to activity levels was well justified. However, it was not until the very end of the Thatcher era that the focus of policy further shifted from health service activities (outputs) to health outcomes. Such an approach implies an acceptance that behavioural and environmental factors are more significant influences than personal medicine on improvements in health status (McKeown 1976, Royal Commission 1979). As such, it implies a fundamental challenge to the power of medicine and a policy for health rather than health services co-ordinated across the many Government functions which impact upon health status.

The need for such a broadly based policy was recognized by the Chief Medical Officer's (Acheson) Report on public health but his committee was prevented by its terms of reference from considering it further (DHSS 1988: para. 2.1.6). Patrick Jenkin similarly dismissed such a strategy in his foreword to the Black Report (DHSS 1980) and the Government continued to resist structural explanations or solutions to ill health in favour of an emphasis on changing individual behaviour (Allsopp 1989: 67). The announcement in the autumn of 1990 that a consultative document was being prepared on health strategy appeared to signal a major shift of emphasis. Although its publication falls outside the period under review here, it is notable for recognizing the wide range of bodies with a role in safeguarding and promoting health, together with the need to co-ordinate their contributions within an overall strategy for the 'health of the nation' (Secretary of State for Health 1991).

One of the key issues which a health strategy should address is the distribution of both health services and health status among different social groups. The Black Report (DHSS 1980) identified large differences in mortality and morbidity favouring the higher social classes, a conclusion which has been used to criticize the outcome of health policy and the effectiveness of the NHS. Since then, self-reported morbidity appears to have increased (Le Grand *et al.* 1990: 121–5), though this may reflect changes in the propensity to report illness rather than in its incidence. The same authors have also shown that the lower socioeconomic groups are more likely to visit their GP than the population as a whole, though this reflects the greater distribution of illness among those groups. Standardised for need, their data show that access to GP services are closely related to need. At the same time, Le Grand and his colleagues (1990: 132) have concluded that since the mid 1970s mortality indicators 'suggest that there has been both a steady improvement in the mean level of health and a reduction in inequality in health, at least between individuals'. They also observe, however, that 'the high levels of unemployment and the widening of income inequality that have characterized the 1980s may have an impact on health that is yet to appear' (ibid.). This conclusion is doubly important: first, it underlines the potential contribution to health status of a wider range of policies than those for the NHS; and second, in cautioning against too early an evaluation of Thatcher Government policies for health, as opposed to health services.

Implementation themes and issues

The first Thatcher administration inherited a health service whose organizational arrangements might almost have been designed to frustrate a top-down implementation strategy. Weak vertical linkages between tiers were compounded by apparently no less tenuous horizontal linkages in the shape of consensus management teams. In addition, and most fundamentally, resource utilization at field level was effectively controlled by a profession whose absolute discretion over such matters had been built into the fabric of the service at its inception and whose models of causation and intervention were equally well embedded in the social fabric.

A more robust antidote to hierarchic control would have been difficult to conceive. Indeed, research on the operation of these structures after 1974 shows that the values and interests of medicine were the principal integrating influence in the service (see Wistow 1992). Political influences were largely limited to reorganizing the administrative furniture and seeking to ensure that the service lived within the overall constraints imposed by public expenditure policies (though family practitioner services are still not wholly integrated into the cash limit system some 15 years after its inception). Against this background, the initial objective of the new Government seems at best ill-considered: the targeting of management rather than medicine as the principal area of potential cost savings; and the weakening of such hierarchy as existed at a time when the Deparement needed to be better, rather than less, able to demonstrate its capacity to maximize efficiency and effectiveness in resource utilization.

As we have seen, that approach proved to be short-lived and was replaced by one which, in effect, progressively sought to create the conditions in which a top-down implementation strategy might be sustainable: stronger policy formulation and executive functions at the centre; a general management function to unify all levels of the service; hierarchy and performance review; and steps to limit professional discretion. Indeed, management rather than policy has been the overriding ministerial and departmental preoccupation since the early 1980s. That is to say, their principal purpose has been to create a more effective set of means through which (mostly established) service policies could be better delivered within the resources available. The 'Working for Patients' changes may be seen in much the same light, though they depart from those introduced in the mid-1980s in seeking to combine market forces with managerialism and hierarchy. In so doing, they may also be seen as a recognition of the inadequacy of a top-down implementation model in a context where street-level providers possess significant discretion over resources.

We have argued that the Thatcher Government has been notable for beginning to challenge the principle of clinical autonomy, an issue which had hitherto been kept off the policy agenda through a process of 'non-decision making' (Bachrach and Baratz 1970). Indeed, this Government was no different from its predecessors in this respect as is illustrated by its view in 1979 that the creation of chief executive posts in health authorities would be incompatible with professional freedom. Since then, the notion that the management process exists largely to facilitate clinical practice has been replaced at the level of policy intent by one which emphasizes the resource management responsibilities which flow from the exercise of clinical autonomy. In policy outcome terms, however, there appears to have been significantly less progress in bringing clinical practice within the management process, at least until the implementation of the current

Like the previous Labour administration, it saw nuclear power as the cheap means of meeting demand – which was in line with the beliefs of the Central Electricity Generating Board (CEGB) and the nuclear construction industry. However, there were also political reasons for the nuclear programme; it is clear that Thatcher saw an expanded nuclear programme as a way of undercutting the power of the miners.

Despite growing parliamentary disquiet about the economic case for nuclear power and environmentalists' concerns about nuclear power in general, the Government pressed ahead with plans for the first pressurized water reactors (PWRs) at Sizewell in Suffolk, the preliminary hearings of the public enquiry being held in June 1982. In March 1987, after a protracted public enquiry, the go ahead for the building of the Sizewell PWR was given (O'Riordan et al. 1988). The Government planned to build up to four more PWRs by the year 2000, starting with Hinkley Point in Somerset.

The Government's general energy programme betrayed remarkably little broad environmental awareness, although electoral pressures sometimes caused it to back down, as in the case of disposal of nuclear waste. Although grants for home insulation were introduced, total expenditure on energy conservation was relatively low. A 1982 report of the Commons Select Committee on Energy put the figure at £149 million annually, which compares rather unfavourably with the £550 million subsidy to the coal industry, £218 million for nuclear research by the UK Atomic Energy Authority, or £218 million for heating allowances for pensioners and those on social security (Williams 1985: 282). A central rhetorical plank of the Government in this period was the introduction of competition into the energy sector, which was seen as heavily monopolized by public corporations. In practice this meant steep increases in prices, particularly for gas but also for electricity. These increases were justified in terms of the reduction of market distortions and a belief that higher prices would automatically lead to significant energy saving, along the lines of the market's response to the oil price shocks of the 1970s. In fact, the inelasticity of energy demand among domestic consumers made this unrealistic. Moreover the Government openly used British Gas profits to cut the public spending borrowing requirement (PSBR).

The successful privatization of British Gas was followed by the privatization of the electricity industry in two stages; the distribution side was sold in 1990 and the generation side in 1991. These sales proved to be the key development in the politics of energy in the 1980s, for it led to the demise of the Government's nuclear plans while further reinforcing the bias against conservation and renewable energy.

As originally drafted, the Electricity Bill further extended the Government's nuclear commitment: National Power was to take on all the nuclear power stations in England and Wales giving it a 70 per cent market share, while the 12 area electricity boards, to be privatized as distribution companies, were to take 20 per cent of their supplies from non-fossil fuel sources, that is nuclear power, a 4 per cent increase over the pre-privatization figure.

In the light of the comparatively poor economic record of nuclear power in Britain, as finally publicly disclosed by the CEGB at the Sizewell and Hinkley Point public enquiries, there was great scepticism about the economic case for nuclear power – especially among institutional investors. One commonly accepted figure is that British nuclear electricity costs 40 per cent more than best practice coal-produced electricity. The Government's decision to legislate in favour of nuclear power was seen as a 'nuclear tax' on consumers and investors, despite the possibility of importing cheaper French nuclear generated power. In order to sugar the nuclear pill for investors, the Government initially set aside £2.5 billion for waste disposal and the decommissioning of existing plants, including the ageing first generation Magnox reactors, the Advanced Gas Cooled Reactors and the Sizewell PWR. Subsequently, it withdrew the Magnox reactors from the privatization and promised to bear the full costs of waste disposal. Finally, the Government completely withdrew all nuclear reactors from the privatization and shelved its plans to build further PWRs after the completion of the Sizewell reactor. In the short to medium term, at least, electricity privatization spelled the end of the expansion of the British nuclear programme.

While some other EC countries took wave, wind, geothermal and solar power very seriously in the 1980s, the British Government's research funding for these technologies was always minuscule. Following a report by the Advisory Council for Research and Development, the Government cut funding for research on renewable sources of energy in 1982/83, effectively killing British wave power research (Williams 1985: 281–2). The Government refused to write in specific targets on energy conservation, renewables, and emission control into the Electricity Bill, although it did place a very general environmental duty on the Office of Electricity Regulation – the new competition watch-dog for the privatized industry. This failure, together with the further reduction of the already minuscule energy conservation promotion budget in 1989, were extensively criticized by the Opposition, the Commons Select Committee on Energy, environmental pressure groups and the energy conservation industry. The energy conservation lobby argued that conservation supplemented by some expansion of renewables and more efficient energy burning systems such as combined heat and power, is the least costly and most environmentally friendly way of reducing pollution. However, the Government's argument continued to be that market forces would promote conservation, while carbon dioxide and sulphur dioxide emissions from electricity generation will be further reduced by the operation of market forces as the privatized generating companies switch from burning coal to gas.

The experience of other countries suggests that energy conservation can best be achieved by combining information programmes with positive incentives for energy conservation. The Government's proposals on energy conservation in its 1990 Environment White Paper go nothing like this far, although there is a belated recognition of the need to provide consumers with adequate information via an enhanced Office of Energy Efficiency. Electricity prices to the consumer, already increased by 9 per cent in the year 1987–88 as privatization loomed, may increase at well beyond the rate of inflation, hitting poorer consumers and further reducing many families' ability to invest in conservation. Carbon-dioxide emissions from road transport, which already account for around 16 per cent of the total in Britain, are highly unlikely to be contained under the Government's planning targets for growth in traffic announced in the 1989 White Paper *Roads to Prosperity*, even under optimistic technological assumptions (Grubb 1990: 200–9). In the light of the lack of concern for energy conservation and the lack of will to control road traffic, it is difficult to see how the Government's target – which is modest compared to some of its EC partners – of containing carbon dioxide emissions at their current level by the year 2005 can be attained.

Electricity privatization will not disturb the major actors within the energy policy network. Leaving aside Scotland and Northern Ireland, where a straightforward privatization of existing vertically integrated generation/ distribution companies is proposed, and the abolition of the Electricity Council (always a weak body relative to the CEGB), the major change is the splitting of the CEGB into two companies, National Power and Power Generation. National Power and Power Generation are likely to inherit CEGB modes of thinking, investment plans and forecasting methodologies, along with its plant. Privately owned electricity supply and distribution systems, notably in the USA, have placed emphasis upon conservation, renewable and new fossil fuel burning technologies, with conservation often being regarded as more profitable than building new plants (e.g. Lovins 1990). This might suggest that the CEGB's successors could make money by selling conservation rather than extra electricity. However, it will take time, and probably some pushing by the Government, to change attitudes in the industry. Moreover, extra electricity sales may appeal to newly privatized companies looking for short-term profits in order to appeal to investors. In this way, low cost contracts offered to large industrial users by National Power and Power Generation may encourage a switch to electricity from more energy-efficient direct burning of fossil fuels.

The control of emissions may also be made more difficult by privatization. The CEGB's plans for a 40 per cent reduction in nitrous oxide emissions over the next ten years by fitting low nitrous oxide burners will probably be carried over. However, Christopher Patten's desire to comply with EC legislation committing Britain to the reduction of sulphur dioxide emissions by 40 per cent by 1998 and by 60 per cent by 2003 led to conflict with the Energy Secretary, John Wakeham. Patten was worried that, unless £2 billion was spent on fitting sulphur-dioxide scrubbers, Britain would not comply with the EC legislation, while Wakeham was mindful of the impact of such costs on the immanent privatization of the electricity industry. In the end, a compromise was struck committing the electricity industry to £1.2 billion expenditure, while further reducing emissions through importing low sulphur coal and building gas-fired power stations. Critics argued that electricity privatization was once again placed above environmental considerations. Recent delays and cost overruns in fitting sulphur-dioxide scrubbers suggest that, in the absence of financial penalties, privatized producers will be loath to proceed with them and that EC standards will not be met (Milne 1989). The defeat of Christopher Patten's proposals for a fossil fuel tax will make the meeting of these targets all the more difficult, especially given the Government's lack of will to control private motoring.

Transboundary pollution problems: depletion of the ozone layer

The major environmental concerns of our time – global warming, acid rain, the depletion of the ozone layer, marine pollution – are transboundary and, thus, need international collective action which immediately raises the problem of free-riding in which nation states pursue their own economic and political interests and refuse to co-operate (O. Young 1989). Britain has moved away from the intransigent position of the USA on global warming and EC pressure has forced concessions on acid rain and North Sea pollution. However, Thatcher's Governments were not at the forefront of the groping efforts to construct new international arrangements in these areas (Tuchman-Mathews 1991). While Britain's position on CFCs moved further and faster than on other issues, Thatcher's claims to world leadership lacked substance, even though they had some public appeal in Britain.

CFCs have become a mainstay of modern industrial life since their development 50 years ago. As long ago as the early 1970s, halogenated CFCs were implicated in the destruction of stratospheric ozone. Since then, a scientific consensus has clearly emerged that CFCs destroy stratospheric ozone at a faster rate than it is regenerated. This trend has implications for increases in rates of skin cancer, lower agricultural yields and, crucially, the destruction of oceanic phytoplankton – the very basis of the oceanic food chain and an important pollution sink for the greenhouse gas carbon dioxide. Furthermore, CFCs are greenhouse gases in their own right making a significant contribution to global warming – possibly one-third the amount from carbon dioxide.

In 1980, the United Nations Environment Programme (UNEP) asked governments to reduce production and consumption of CFCs, but it was not until 1985 that the Vienna Convention for the Protection of the Ozone Layer was adopted by 21 states and the EC. However, the Vienna Convention only dealt with international co-operation and research: it contained no specific controls. Within the EC, strict CFC controls were only supported by a handful of nations, including Denmark, West Germany and the Netherlands. Other countries, most notably Britain, France and Italy seemed more responsive to the wishes of their chemical manufacturers for a 'go-slow' approach.

Increasing international pressure, particularly from the USA, led to the signing of the Montreal Protocol in September 1987 by the Vienna Convention countries and six other states. The protocol treated the production and consumption of CFCs separately. Based on 1986 levels, the protocol called for a freeze in consumption by 1989, followed by a 20 per cent reduction by 1994 and a further 50 per cent reduction by 1999. However, production was to be allowed to increase by 10 per cent up to 1990 but was required to fall to 90 per cent of 1986 levels by 1994 and to 65 per cent by 1999. This difference between production and consumption was allowed since it was felt that it was only fair to allow developing countries, who had benefited little from CFCs, to increase their consumption up to a ceiling of 0.3 kg per capita. Twenty-seven countries, including Britain, signed the Montreal Protocol.

However, almost immediately after the protocol had been signed, a major scientific expedition returned from the Antarctic with the message that ozone depletion was much worse than had been expected. Furthermore, in February 1989 the Meteorological Office reported that levels of chlorine over the Arctic were 50 times higher than had been theoretically predicted. Most experts now believe that the Montreal Protocol would be totally inadequate to protect the ozone layer, even if it were fully implemented.

The British Government's stance on the limitation of CFC consumption and production has not developed purely as a result of concern over the depletion of the ozone layer. Indeed, the Government has been strongly influenced by the powerful lobby of ICI, Europe's largest producer of CFCs, with a market share estimated to be worth around £100 million annually (Johnston 1987). It is true that during the 1987 negotiations Britain supported a 40–50 per cent CFC cut-back. However, even this revised position contained the proviso that the timescale of implementation should be long enough to accommodate ICI's development of CFC alternatives – an area in which ICI has basic research strengths which require time to exploit. As recently as the end of 1989, the Government was still protecting ICI's interests by blocking international efforts to ban ethyl chloroform – discovered to contribute to about 16 per cent of ozone depletion.

Although the pace of change in the British Government's position has been much affected by ICI's interests, it now claims a leading role in the ozone protection debate. This claim is questionable. In March 1989, a few days before Mrs Thatcher's hastily convened 'Saving the Ozone Layer' conference, it was pressure from European Environment Ministers which led to Britain accepting a 100 per cent ban on CFCs by the year 2000. It is also significant that, in line with Mrs Thatcher's free market philosophy, the Department of the Environment has constantly dismissed calls for domestic legislation, preferring instead a voluntary reduction in the use of CFCs, facilitated by consumer pressure for products which do not use CFCs.

It has been estimated that if just four nations with growing populations, China, India, Indonesia and Brazil, were to increase their consumption *within* the limits laid down by the Montreal Protocol (which, as we noted above, makes special allowance for developing countries), worldwide production and consumption of CFCs based on 1986 levels would double. Many developing countries are loath to switch to the expensive, more ozone friendly alternatives, which are exclusively manufactured and patented by developed countries. On grounds of social justice, Third World delegates to the London ozone conference stressed the need for Western aid to implement alternative CFC technologies, China and India refusing to ratify the Montreal Protocol without such aid. At the first official meeting of the signatories of the Montreal Protocol at Helsinki in May 1989 signatories agreed that some form of financial aid was required to encourage developing nations to take up the ozone friendly, but costly technologies. However, the notion of an international funding mechanism was blocked by a number of industrialized countries, principally the USA and Britain, who argued for the disbursement of aid bilaterally and through existing multilateral institutions such as the World Bank. It is likely that this type of arrangement is favoured by Britain since it would ensure that British aid largely benefits British manufacturers like ICI. This sort of arrangement is likely to hinder the transition to a post-CFC world.

Conclusion

Our analysis here suggests three major conclusions. First, although there have been changes in environmental policy there has been no transformation, even in the most recent period. In addition, there is little prospect of major change in the future. Second, in so far as change occurs it will continue to result from international forces rather than Conservative Government initiatives. Third, environmental policy is marked by continuity in large part because of the continued importance of a series of policy networks.

Change, past, present and future

The White Paper, *This Common Inheritance*, launched with a major publicity fanfare in September 1990, was supposed to set the agenda for environmental policy until the end of the century. However, it bears the clear marks of Christopher Patten's widely reported failure to win Cabinet battles with other Departments. Although Patten and his new adviser, Professor David Pearce, had been keen to introduce 'green taxes' on fossil fuels, along with the other measures to manipulate market incentives, these were ruled out by the opposition of the Treasury, which sees them as inflationary, and DTI, which sees them as damaging to business interests. In addition, while the White Paper does refer to the idea that building roads encourages car use, Cecil Parkinson ensured that it contained no commitment to limiting motoring. Similarly, no new substantive commitments on countryside conservation were made, probably because of MAFF opposition. The White Paper does contain significant new thinking on energy efficiency, recycling of household waste, and 'green labelling' of consumer products. Nevertheless, much of it is either a reiteration of existing policy or involves minor incremental policy change.

As part of the John Major's 'social market' rhetoric, we can expect rather more consideration to be given to the environment and, perhaps, increased backing for regulatory agencies. One important administrative change already brought into operation is a structure, with a Cabinet Committee at its apex, to co-ordinate policy-making over all Government Departments so as to ensure that environmental considerations enter at the very beginning of the policy-making process rather than as an afterthought (*The Times*, 17 December 1990). There are also some signs that the Government wishes to see a tougher regulatory line. This shift has been most visible in relation to water pollution, which became highly politicized because of the very effective campaign fought by environmental groups in the privatization process. Although Nicholas Ridley's original intention had been to transfer regulatory functions to the privatized regional water authorities, in the event the new National Rivers Authority (NRA) will be responsible for the quality of rivers, while HM's Inspectorate of Pollution will monitor drinking water quality. This separation of regulatory powers was pushed for by environmental groups and by large industrial polluters who did not wish to be regulated by private-sector concerns. Nevertheless, this change owed much to the fact that the most significant factor was probably that the initial proposal violated EC competition policy.

Given that the NRA was created by fusing the regulatory functions of the old water authorities, some suspected that it would take a similar, relatively easy-going line. However, there are indications that the NRA is trying to establish a tougher reputation. For instance, by the end of 1990 the NRA had either brought prosecutions, or had prosecutions pending, against all ten privatized water companies (*Environment Digest*, October 1990) and demonstration prosecutions of large industrial concerns – notably Shell UK – have taken place. Nevertheless, just like other regulatory agencies discussed in this chapter, the NRA is chronically short of money and manpower, which reduces the chances of a tough line being feasible. Moreover, Major's Government has further weakened the conservation watch-dogs by setting up a lay committee of appeal in Scotland which can override decisions made by the new Scottish conservation agency discussed above (*The Times*, 2 July 1991).

Of course a change of Government might lead to a policy shift. Certainly the Labour Party's policy document on the environment, published in September 1990 in an attempt to pre-empt the impact of the Government's White Paper, proposes stronger measures to control carbon dioxide emissions. However, although Labour appears more committed to renewable sources of energy, support for countryside conservation, public transport, and opening up environmental regulation, it is no more willing than the Conservatives to contemplate fundamental change which would inevitably result in slower growth or loss of jobs.

The importance of international pressure

The major forces propelling changes in environmental policy in Britain in the short to medium term will probably remain international. Because of the link made by the EC between environmental regulation and competition policy, the likelihood is that Britain, along with other more backward members, will converge upon the standards of EC members with tougher legislation and better implementation and toe something closer to the EC line on transboundary pollution. Once again, though, the overall pace of change in the EC and its other member states is unlikely to be that rapid given the continued importance of conventional definitions of economic growth to the political process.

Continuity and policy networks

As we saw in the section on energy, in relation to CFCs, and in relation to the debates behind the 1990 Environment White Paper, British Governments cannot ignore the adverse reactions of powerful corporations and financial institutions to the loading of the costs of environmental clean-up onto industry. By extension, while economic growth continues to be so important electorally, it is highly unlikely that major changes will occur in environmental policy in the face of likely adverse business reaction to redefinitions of the major parameters of a growth-oriented society. While these effects may have been especially important given the economic goals of the Thatcher Governments and their orientation to finance capital, they will continue to be significant. As we have also shown in this chapter, the older policy networks persisted through the decade of Thatcherism, albeit with minor boundary adjustments and some shaping and trimming to current circumstances. At least in the short term, they will continue to be a major barrier to change in the particular areas of policy with which they are concerned. What the last decade illustrates, though, is that deregulation, even pursued in the somewhat patchy, covert manner of Thatcher's first two terms in office, is probably too politically costly to contemplate. In contrast, the politics of symbolic reassurance has distinct electoral benefits. If there is a distinct Thatcherite policy legacy on the environment it is probably the discovery of how little actually needs to be done to satisfy public demand.

9

CAP and agricultural policy

Martin J. Smith

In 1979 agricultural policy was costly in terms of public expenditure. It violated the principles of the free market and it pandered to the demands of special interests. Yet even by 1990 these three non–Thatcherite principles appeared to remain dominant in Britain's agricultural policy. Agriculture clearly demonstrates the difficulties of national governments implementing radical policy changes. First, there was a very closed, national policy community; second, with British membership of the European Community (EC), agricultural policy-making became supra-national, making it difficult for the Government to implement the reforms it wanted; and, third, policy changes, as Marsh and Rhodes suggest (see pp. 4, 176–7), often had unintended consequences. The implementation of a Thatcherite agricultural policy has faced problems not at a single point but at a number of stages over the past 11 years. This chapter will examine the objectives of the Thatcher Government's agricultural policy, how these objectives have changed and how successfully the various reforms have been implemented.

Phase I: maintaining the traditional agenda

Throughout the postwar period successive governments were prepared to provide farmers with high levels of agricultural support in order to encourage the expansion of agricultural production. The reasons for this support were partly economic and partly political. It was believed that increasing agricultural production was a means of improving Britain's balance-of-payments deficit. This belief was reinforced by the existence of an agricultural policy community. Agricultural policy was made within a closed group including Ministry of Agriculture Fisheries and Food (MAFF) officials and the leaders of the National Farmers' Union (NFU) who accepted the consensus that agriculture should be supported and production increased (Smith 1990). Groups which might challenge this consensus were excluded. Once Britain joined the EC in 1973 farmers were given the added protection of the Common Agricultural Policy (CAP). Under CAP the market price of agricultural produce is artificially raised through import levies and intervention buying. Farmers were effectively provided with a substantial subsidy and so encouraged to increase production.

Therefore when the Conservative Government came to power in 1979, agricultural policy was based on a high level of support through the CAP and the institutionalization of a special interest group into the policy-making process. Initially the new Conservative Government did not challenge this policy but had two contrary objectives. The first was to maintain the expansion of British agricultural production and the second was to limit the costs of the Common Agricultural Policy. As Hugh Clayton (1979) noted, 'The Government has placed farming in the same category as defence as one of the activities it intends to stimulate and which it intends to exempt from spending cuts.' 'Agriculture has long occupied a special place in the pantheon of traditional tory values . . .' and the Conservative party always had close ties with rural areas (Cox *et al.* 1989a: 129). Consequently, the Government was not immediately prepared to take on agricultural interests in the same confrontational manner used against trade unions.

Nevertheless, the Government still wanted to restrain the CAP. The Chancellor of the Exchequer, Sir Geoffrey Howe, said that in fixing farm prices, agricultural Ministers should bear in mind the need to control public spending, to fight inflation and to reduce the share of the EC budget taken by the CAP (*The Times*, 17 February 1981). The CAP was already in a state of overproduction and so the British Government was calling for reform and price restraint.

Of these contradictory goals, the Ministry of Agriculture continued to support increased prices and production for British farmers. Even as late as 1981, the British Minister of Agriculture, Peter Walker, was in Europe arguing against a revaluation of the green pound (which would have cut prices to British farmers) and he went so far as to reject the European Commission's price package, which called for a modest increase, on the grounds that British farmers would have no increase at all (*The Times*, 12 March 1981). The final price agreement was an increase of 9.5 per cent which with green currency changes was actually closer to 15 per cent (*The Times*, 2 April 1981). Mr Walker was proud to announce that the British Government had won almost everything it wanted and that he had achieved the substantial price increase necessary to prevent falls in production (*The Times*, 27 July 1981).

So the first few years of the Conservative administration saw the Minister attempting to increase production. Peter Walker used the Labour Government's 1979 White Paper, which called for a considerable expansion of British agricultural production (MAFF 1979: 1–2), as the basis of policy. He was also prepared to increase prices to British farmers to achieve this goal despite the already apparent budgetary and supply problems of the CAP. Yet, as we saw above, the Government was also committed to the reform of the CAP and restrictions on price increases. What accounts for the discrepancy between these two policies and for the lack of the development of a coherent Thatcherite agricultural policy?

Of major importance was the departmental nature of the British Government and the continued existence of the agricultural policy community. The contradictory policy arose from conflict between the Treasury calling for the reform of the CAP and the Ministry of Agriculture which wanted price increases for British farmers. Agricultural policy was made within a small community committed to increasing production and prices. In addition the Ministry had an advocate in Walker who was prepared to support the farmers' case in Cabinet and who believed that the farmers' need was greater than the consumers' (*The Times*, 23 February 1981). The policy community continued to dominate policy-making in agriculture and so could ensure that increasing production and maintaining farmers' income were central to agricultural policy. There was a clear difference between the objectives of the Government as a whole and the Ministry of Agriculture.

Perhaps the key to this continued agricultural domination was the fact that the community was afforded the protection of the European Community. When Britain joined the EC, final decisions on agricultural prices were transferred to the Council of Agricultural Ministers. As a consequence the Treasury lost any real input that it had into agricultural policy-making and the Minister of Agriculture had more or less complete autonomy within Europe. The policy community was able to ensure that policy-making continued within the well-established standard operating procedures.

The established policy community was in some part able to continue the old policy because the Treasury and the Prime Minister also had inconsistent objectives. They were not completely opposed to price and production increases for British farmers. Britain had a deficit in terms of its contribution to the EC budget and increasing agricultural production and prices was a means of ensuring that more of the CAP money flowed to Britain. In addition, the logic of the negotiation within the Council of Ministers is to argue for protection of national causes. The CAP has great difficulty reforming itself because no country will accept measures that increase its share of the cost of reform. Instead of countries making a sacrifice in order to see CAP reformed, the tendency is for countries to swap concessions. Britain fought hard to maintain its suckler cow premium and its headage payment for sheep but the cost was that it could not force other countries to accept price cuts.

This demonstrates the way in which the paradoxes within Thatcherism of supporting both the free market and nationalism have affected agricultural policy (Marquand 1988). Initially the Government's position was to call for the reform of CAP whilst protecting the interests of British farmers. This position was viable whilst Britain could devalue the green pound and had the potential to increase domestic production but as costs and production rose within the CAP it was a position that was increasingly untenable.

Phase II: support for agricultural reform

Despite the Thatcher Government's initial tolerance of the agricultural policy community and its agenda, by 1983/84 attitudes and objectives were beginning to change. The new agricultural Minister, Michael Jopling, told the Conservative Party conference in 1983, 'The CAP has grown obese and needs slimming . . . we cannot go on producing more and more food which we cannot either eat or sell' (*The Times*, 17 February 1981). Two Government Ministers, John McGregor and Nicholas Edwards, announced that 'a support system that continued to ensure greater and greater surpluses, regardless of the market was no longer acceptable' (*The Times*, 11 June 1984). Reportedly Margaret Thatcher ordered a review of policies for protecting the countryside in order to 'replace the policy of expanding food production – which had dominated the British countryside for forty years – with one that emphasises conservation of the countryside' (Lean 1984). The Government questioned the tenets of the agricultural agenda – the levels of prices and production. So in principle at least, farmers' support was no longer sacrosanct. Since this change in policy the Government's line in negotiation was to achieve price restraint and the Minister of Agriculture called for a price freeze or even price cuts for products in surplus (House of Lords 1985b). The Government's goal, explicitly stated, was to create a more market orientated agricultural policy.

In addition, the Government proposed non-market measures to deal with overproduction and to help farmers through the transition to a new policy. Jopling proposed to the Commission that farmers be paid to take cereal producing land out of production and the Government announced a scheme to be introduced for British farmers by December 1987 (UK Government 1986). MAFF also announced proposals for alternative land use which included schemes to encourage woodlands, Environmentally Sensitive Areas (ESA), forestry, grants for diversification and reduction in planning controls so that some agricultural land could be used for building. The Government drastically cut capital grants so that there are no more grants for measures which increase production. Hence at the national level the Government has been prepared to cut subsidies. In 1984 capital grants were cut by £40 million (*Farmers Weekly*, 16 November 1984) and the Government cut spending on agricultural research by £50 million over three years (*Farmers Weekly*, 25 January 1985). In addition the Government promised to pay increased attention to the environment and to provide grants for conservation (Lean 1984; *The Times*, 12 December 1984). What led to these changes in policy?

Pressures for change

The reasons for change in Conservative policy came from within Britain, the EC and from the rest of the world. They were not, on the whole, part of

Table 9.1 Farm price guarantee spending, 1975–85

	Farm price spending in ECU 000s	% increase over previous year
1975	4327	28
1976	5710	32
1977	6512	14
1978	8679	33
1979	10387	20
1980	11292	9
1981	10952	-3
1982	12294	12
1983	14040	14
1984	18331	30
1985	19955	9

Source: Huhne (1986).

Conservative ideology. The main cause of change was that the CAP finally reached crisis point. Britain's goal of increasing production was feasible whilst the EC had to import certain foodstuffs but by 1984 most major products were in surplus (House of Lords 1984a). By 1987 the stores held 1⅓ million tonnes of butter, one million tonnes of skimmed milk powder, 600,000 tonnes of beef and 13 to 14 million tonnes of grain (BBC 1987).

The overproduction was partly the result of the high prices offered to farmers through the CAP. The high prices sent the costs of CAP up as the surpluses had to be bought through intervention buying and then stored or exported with the use of subsidies. In particular, the cost of the CAP increased rapidly between 1982 and 1984 due to the fall in the value of the dollar and a general world crisis in agriculture (Goodman and Redclift 1989) (see Table 9.1). Spending increased much faster than inflation and CAP spending was rising faster than the VAT resources of the CAP. By 1986 the CAP was, on paper, bankrupt (BBC 1986a).

The increasing costs of the CAP and the rising level of surpluses made it very difficult for the Government to maintain the line that whilst CAP should be reformed, British agriculture should be allowed to expand. It became clear that reform would not be achieved on that basis and that it was no longer viable for Britain to increase production. In addition there was increasing domestic pressure for a change in policy. The right of the Conservative Party became increasingly critical of the CAP and the anomalies between the Thatcherite position and agricultural policy became increasingly apparent (Body 1982 and 1984). The right and Mrs Thatcher used the issue of agricultural policy as a means of attacking the EC and its profligacy. It was after the crisis became severe that ideology became important in determining the direction of agricultural policy.

However, whilst the right had long been critical of agricultural subsidies and the EC, in the mid-1980s criticism extended much further in the party. Since the 1970s there had been a change in the composition of the Conservative Party. The number of Members of Parliament from agricultural constituencies and with agricultural backgrounds was declining and there were fewer MPs sympathetic to the NFU and rural affairs (BBC 1986b). With this change and the obvious crisis within the CAP there was a general acceptance that agricultural policy had to be reformed. In addition, certain Conservative MPs were becoming increasingly concerned with the environmental impact of the highly intensive agriculture that the CAP was encouraging and proposed that this required the reform of policy (Carlisle 1983; Bow Group 1984).

There also seemed to be increasing unease amongst the general public over an agricultural policy which produced food at very high cost, often to be sold cheaply to 'the enemy' (at that time the Soviet Union) when events like Live Aid were highlighting starvation in other parts of the world. Concern with food has changed from one of quantity to questions of food quality, safety and the environmental impact (M.J. Smith 1991). As *The Times* (23 February 1983) remarked: 'The continuing willingness of a largely urban nation to be taxed directly, or indirectly by Whitehall, or Brussels, to preserve the evident wealth of farmers cannot be relied on.'

This general dissatisfaction led to increased criticism from both consumer groups, and food producers and retailers (CECG 1984: NCC 1988). Consumer groups maintained that agricultural policy was developed regardless of the 'cost to the consumer' (CECG 1984: 10). They were highly critical of the mechanism of support and the fact that the prices paid to farmers increased despite overproduction. The force of consumer criticism was heightened by food producers and retailers' concern over the impact that the CAP was having on food prices and their access to world markets for food supplies. They argued that the high prices of the CAP could not be passed on to the consumer without demand falling and so they supported a market economy to regulate the food economy (Marsh 1979; *Europe*, 28 August 1980).

Pressure for change also came from environmental groups. In the 1980s bodies like the Council for the Protection of Rural England, Friends of the Earth and the Royal Society for the Protection of Birds became more active in the agricultural arena. The media highlighted the environmental degradation resulting from intensive agriculture and it is claimed that *The Observer*'s 'Save Our Countryside' campaign had a major effect on Government policy (Thomas 1984). Cox *et al.* (1986) believe that the environmental policy network has mushroomed in the last twenty years and 'that this has been the most serious challenge to the privileges of the farmers'. Even the farmers, seeing the pressures for reform building up, realized that if they tried to maintain the old policy line they would be left out of the reform process (Smith 1992). Consequently, they accepted the need for policy change. The NFU in 1984 explicitly recognized the need to reduce production and even developed its own reform alternatives.

The change in the Government's attitude towards agricultural policy was, therefore, a combination of structural and political pressures which could activate an ideology opposed to the type of support system that existed within the agricultural arena. The political pressures highlighted and were encouraged by the severe problems which were becoming apparent within the CAP. This did not, however, force a dramatic change in Government policy. The Government had always demanded the reform of the CAP but in practice made protection of national agriculture more of a priority. From 1983/84 Prime Ministerial and Treasury pressure, combined with the appointment of a new Minister of Agriculture, led to the emphasis being placed firmly on reforming CAP. To what extent then was this policy successful?

Implementing CAP reforms

If the British Government was to change its agricultural policy, it first had to convince the European Commission of the need for reform. In fact, the European Commission had been forced by the crisis of the CAP to recognize that some action was necessary. In its Green Paper, *Perspectives for the Common Agricultural Policy* (European Commission 1985), the Commission stated that the CAP had to take account of markets, international realities and financial constraints. It asserted the need to 'give market price a greater role in supply and demand', to take more account of the 'demands of the consumer . . . (and) to the requirements of the food industry', and to consider 'the role of agriculture as the protector of the environment' (European Commission 1985: ii–vii). Consequently, the Commission proposed a restrictive pricing policy and called for measures to balance supply with demand.

More importantly, the Council of Agricultural Ministers which actually makes the final policy decisions on agricultural policy (and which was, and is, strongly pro-farmer) also appeared to accept the need for reform. In 1984 after years of debate over methods to control milk production they accepted milk quotas. They also recognized that wider reform of CAP was necessary and so introduced guarantee thresholds (where farmers would not receive support for production over a certain level), price reductions and the need to keep agricultural spending within budgetary limits (House of Lords 1985a: vii, ix and xv). In 1986 they introduced further sweeping changes by tightening beef intervention buying and reducing the milk quota by 9.5 per cent. In June 1987 intervention buying for butter was suspended and this marked the end of guaranteed markets for all that was produced (*The Independent*, 8 June 1987). In July 1987 intervention standards for cereals were tightened up which was equivalent to a 10 per cent cut in cereal prices (*Green Europe*, 2 July 1987). Due to the critical state of CAP and the fact that Heads of Government at the Fontainebleau and Brussels summits had insisted on CAP reform, even the Council of Ministers had been forced into accepting the necessity of change.

So did these changes result in the Government achieving its goal of reforming the CAP? In order to make an assessment it is necessary to

Table 9.2 Average rates of change in agricultural price support, 1980/81–1988/89

	In ECU	In national currencies
1980/81	4.8	5.7
1981/82	9.2	10.9
1982/83	10.4	12.2
1983/84	4.2	6.9
1984/85	0.4	4.1
1985/86	1.8	1.8
1986/87	−0.3	2.2
1987/88	−0.2	2.6
1988/89	–	1.6

Source: Caspari and Neville Rolfe (1989: 5).

look at how these reforms were implemented at the domestic and European level.

The Commission proposed, and the Council of Ministers accepted, real cuts in agricultural prices. However, it is equally apparent that these cuts have not had the intended effect. First, whilst Ministers have accepted the need to cut prices they have also devalued green currencies which effectively increases the prices farmers receive (see Table 9.2). Even the British Minister, despite all the calls for reform, obtained a large devaluation in 1987 (*The Guardian*, 26 May 1987).

Second, the disposing of stocks through export subsidies was very expensive and so added to the CAP budget – an unintended consequence of reform. Third, the Council of Ministers was slow in adopting measures necessary to reinforce the freezing of prices. Finally, the fall in the value of the dollar resulted in higher export subsidies due to lower world prices (Caspari and Neville Rolfe 1989: 4). So despite these reforms the cost of CAP between 1986 and 1988 continued to increase (see Table 9.3).

The case of milk quotas demonstrates the problems of implementation which occur within the EC. Initially, the quota was set so high that there was still 9 per cent overproduction and, despite the surplus, milk prices were increased to compensate farmers for their introduction. The situation was such

Table 9.3 CAP expenditure, 1986–89

	ECU mn
1986	22.193
1987	13.176
1988	28.795
1989	28.303

Source: Caspari and Neville Rolfe (1989: 6).

that by October 1986 there was a possibility that dairy farmers could increase their profitability by 20 per cent (*Farmers Weekly*, 31 October 1986). According to Gardner (1987: 168) by 1987:

> the community's milk production is again little less than it was in 1983, expenditure has not only increased by 33 per cent but threatens to increase by a further 30 per cent annually . . . The reason, as the EEC Commission revealed, is that EEC ministers have consistently cheated in the application of the milk quota legislation so as to completely subvert its spirit and intention.

A report by the EC Court of Auditors indicated that milk quotas failed to live up to the scale of the problem because individual countries did not implement them properly. In addition to the quota being set too high, member states allocated farmers quota above the national quota, whilst in others the levy payable on overproduction was diluted. Italy did not even adopt the quotas (Court of Auditors 1987: 6–10).

In terms of environmental goals, there was little sign of substantial change. At both the European and national level measures to help the environment were adopted but there was no wholesale move to an environmentally sensitive agriculture. The policies that have been introduced are relatively expensive and have only been applied to marginal producers. They have largely been schemes for alternative land use rather than for changing farming methods. As Cox *et al.* (1989b and 1989c) argue,

> The alternative land use debate by shifting attention from food surpluses and their fundamental cause to questions of farm diversifiation and novel uses for rural land, has helped to reinstate a productionist and innovative image for the agricultural industry. (p. 183)

The view of the Government was that the majority of farming should remain intensive (Shoard 1990), and indeed, only 1 per cent of UK farms were organic by 1990 (*The Guardian*, 3 July 1990).

Consequently, despite the apparent radical reforms and the intentions of the British Government, the European Commission and the Council of Agricultural Ministers, the key features of CAP were still in place at the end of 1987. The cost of CAP was increasing and the level of production had not been brought under control. Basically a system of high support for intensive agriculture remained. Why was reform not implemented?

Despite the attempts by national leaders and finance Ministers to change the CAP, segmented policy-making meant the parameters for agricultural policy continued to be set by the policy community. In both Britain and the EC faith in the CAP still existed. The British Minister of Agriculture, although desiring the reform of CAP, actually wanted the control of CAP spending not the overhaul of the policy. Jopling did not want the complete elimination of surpluses and he maintained that 'CAP has provided a satisfactory framework for British farming in the ten years or so since we joined the community'

(House of Lords 1985b: 2; House of Lords 1986: 5–6). Within Europe there was still a strong belief in the CAP and although the Commission wanted to reform CAP it continued to respect 'the basic principles' (*Europe*, 29 January 1982).

More importantly, it was still the Council of Ministers which was responsible for developing and implementing reform. They, again, had conflicting objectives. The need to reform the CAP was often overwhelmed by concern for protecting their own national interests. German agricultural Ministers continually resisted cuts in cereal prices and in 1985 the Commission backed down from demanding price cuts for the Germans (*The Guardian*, 17 May 1985). The French have called for increases in exports rather than cuts in production and most nations have been more concerned with farm incomes rather than reducing costs (*The Guardian*, 26 March 1986). Britain has also played the national game arguing for the maintenance of subsidies for sheep and for devaluations of the green pound. Despite the attacks on farmers and subsidies, devaluation of the green pound in 1985/86 wiped out the impact of the 1986 price cuts and farm income increased by £245 million in 1985 and remained buoyant in 1986 (*The Guardian*, 29 October 1987). Gardner (1987: 178) believes, 'British agricultural ministers [were] as committed to resisting substantive reform as their French or Irish colleagues.'

The policy changes also had unintended consequences. Milk quotas, instead of undermining the policy community and exposing farmers to the harsh winds of the market, actually protected them to a greater degree. Cox *et al.* (1989b) have suggested that the introduction of milk quotas has increased corporatization in the dairy sector by giving responsibility to the administration of dairy quotas to the Milk Marketing Board. In addition, those with milk quotas have a secure market and guaranteed income whilst making it very difficult for new entrants to join the dairy sector. In fact they can only enter if some producer leaves thus freeing a quota. So milk quotas have created a well-protected market governed by a corporate authority.

As well as unintended consequences, there were failures of implementation. National governments are responsible for implementing policy and are able to avoid its consequences. The implementation of reform has also been bypassed by increases in national support to replace that lost at the EC level. Other policies have not had the expected effect. 'Set-aside', which was a means of reducing land in production, has only had a minimal impact. In most countries, well under 1 per cent of arable land has been set-aside (Caspari and Neville Rolfe 1989: 10). In addition, set-aside attracts mainly marginal producers and there is a tendency for farmers to set-aside their worst land whilst increasing production on the rest. Consequently, its impact on production is minimal (*The Times*, 10 August 1989).

Finally, the effect of the reforms proposed within the policy community is to dissipate pressure for radical change. The policy community has been quick to realize that if it did not introduce some reform, radical change would be forced on it. Therefore, the community has been careful to introduce

Table 9.4 Changes in real support and farmgate prices, 1984–87

	1984	1985	1986	1987
Cereals:				
support	–3.2	–5.6	–8.9	–9.6
farmgate	–7.3	–9.6	–2.8	–7.8
Oilseeds:				
support	–4.5	–5.87	–2.5	–13.6
farmgate	–4.6	–8.2	–5.0	–13.9
Sugar:				
support	–2.2	–2.5	–1.9	–2.7
Milk:				
support	–2.3	–2.1	–1.9	–4.9
Beef:				
support	–3.3	–3.8	–2.0	–12.8
farmgate	–6.5	–4.7	–6.7	–4.2
Sheepmeat:				
support	–3.6	–3.4	–2.1	0.9
farmgate	–5.1	–4.6	–4.8	–5.9

Source: Caspari and Neville Rolfe (1989: 9).

reforms which limit production but have a limited impact on farm incomes and do not replace CAP with a market system (Smith 1992). In the area of environmental policy farmers have argued that through voluntary agreement and special programmes they can preserve the countryside. Hence, they have prevented external regulation and deflected the arguments of environmentalists calling for a complete overhaul of agricultural policy (Cox *et al.* 1989c: 9). By responding to external pressure the policy community has managed to contain the pressure for change.

This is not to say that in the period from 1983 to 1987 there was no change in policy. Clearly there were changes in intention and these did have some impact. Milk quotas limited milk production and both dairy and other stocks declined. Between 1987 and 1988 butter stocks fell from 1,106,000 tonnes to 183,000 tonnes, skimmed milk powder from 708,000 to 13,000 tonnes and wheat from 5,152,000 to 3,847,000 tonnes (*The Economist*, 17 December 1988). From 1984 to 1987 there was a real fall in support and farmgate prices of commodities with cereal and oilseeds in particular seeing substantial falls (see Table 9.4). Moreover, where the Government did have control, over research funding and a few national grants, there were substantial cuts.

At the same time the system of support remained more or less intact and neither agricultural spending nor production had been reduced. If anything they were continuing to rise. Hence a third stage of reform was initiated in 1987/88.

Phase III: the 1988 reforms

By 1987 it was clear that the budgetary discipline which was initiated at
Fontainebleau with milk quotas and a restrictive pricing policy had not
worked. According to Moyser and Josling (1990: 79):

> Agricultural spending in the subsequent period had increased by more
> than 18 per cent per year, depsite the two per cent limit allowed under
> the Fontainebleau formula. The growth of agricultural spending had
> prevented other community programmes from developing and had ex-
> hausted all available revenues. Indeed, the budget shortfall for 1987 was
> estimated at 4–5 billion ECU . . . The commission estimated that, by
> 1987, the Community had accumulated net liabilities of 17 billion ECU,
> with a rapid upward trend. Things could not continue without signifi-
> cant change.

By 1987 the financial and over-supply crisis was again so severe that the
agricultural Ministers had no choice but to reform other agricultural markets.
Even so it took nearly a year and a failed heads of government summit to get
agreement (see Moyser and Josling 1990). The final agreement produced stabilizers for all produce whereby if production was above a certain level there
would be automatic price cuts. Initially, the Commission proposed limits of 155
million tonnes for cereals but after French and German intransigence the final
agreement was 160 million tonnes (Smith 1992). With the agreement on budgetary discipline at the Brussels summit in 1988 and the reforms announced by the
Council of Ministers, the CAP was in theory subject to strict controls with:

1 legal instruments to limit increases in expenditure;
2 no exceptional circumstances provision;
3 agreement that the Commission would accept limits on price proposals and
  any proposals outside these limits to be referred to a joint meeting of finance
  and agricultural Ministers;
4 monthly monitoring of the budget of each regime;
5 a range of stabilizers;
6 systems for dealing with stocks (House of Lords 1988: 20).

With these new controls it is supposed to be impossible for member states to
breach budgetary discipline (Treasury and Civil Service Committee 1988: vii).
It is too early to assess the long-term impact of these reforms. Undoubtedly, the severity of the financial crisis has forced the Council of Ministers to
take some harsh measures. Following the reforms, cereal and beef prices have
been reduced substantially and 1989/90 saw a big fall in the level of intervention stocks. Since 1986 support levels for cereals have been reduced by 10 per
cent and 15 per cent for livestock (House of Lords 1990: 7). Moreover, CAP
spending has stayed within budgetary limits with the 1990 budget being about
£2,775 million below the agricultural guideline (House of Lords 1990: 17). As
the agricultural committee (Agricultural Committee 1990: 3) reported in 1990:

At a national level considerable success has been achieved in securing controls over Community expenditure on the CAP. Stabilisers are in place for most commodities. In 1989–90 they are estimated to have saved the EC over 1 billion ECU.

The last few years has seen the income of British farmers fall by 25 per cent (*The Times*, 15 February 1989). The real income of dairy farms in 1990 was only 60 per cent of their 1982/83 value whilst those for cereal producers fell to 20 per cent (*The Independent on Sunday*, 5 May 1991). Within Britain the Government's agricultural spending which rose by 23 per cent between 1979 and 1987 fell between 1987 and 1990 with a projected fall of 5.5 per cent for 1991 (HM Treasury 1990; *The Guardian*, 9 November 1990). At the national level farmers are beginning to feel the effect of agricultural reform and the Government is reducing the level of its spending.

However, there is evidence to suggest that the implementation of 1988 reforms might not have such a dramatic effect in the long term. The improvement in the situation in 1989 was not in fact due to EC reforms but the result of drought in the United States of America. With the drought US wheat production was cut by 30 per cent with a subsequent increase in world prices. As a result the EC could export to third countries with the cost of export subsidies falling by 60 per cent (Gardner 1990). Gardner (1990: 26) maintains that:

> The Community's agricultural surpluses have not gone away, but have been hidden from public view by fortuitous circumstances on international markets. Instead of piling up grain bins and cold stores they have been exported to third countries.

Moreover, the main features of the CAP remain. Producers continue to receive artificially high prices in order to maintain production. The level for cereal production at which price penalties came into play was higher than the level of cereal production at the time. The Commission failed to use the opportunity of high world prices in 1988/89 to cut dramatically institutional prices (House of Lords 1990: 7). Prices are still double world prices, the cost of export refunds remain high and production is well above demand (House of Lords 1989; 1990). As a consequence, the food stocks which disappeared in 1989 returned. In 1990 there was a tripling of the beef stocks, the store of skimmed milk powder rose from 5,000 tonnes to 333,000 tonnes, the butter stock increased by 450 per cent and there were increased cereal stocks (*The European*, 9–11 November 1990). The cost of the CAP in 1991 is expected to be 31.5 billion ECU which will mean that spending will again break through the legally binding guideline (*The Independent on Sunday*, 5 May 1991).

The failure to implement radical reform reflects both the nature of the CAP and the continued maintenance of national interest. Even after the 1988 reforms the British Minister of Agriculture, John McGregor, called for 'further cuts in EEC financial support for agriculture, which was still too high in spite of cost cutting measures' (*The Times*, 23 February 1989). Yet the following

Table 9.5   Expenditure of Ministry of Agriculture, 1979/80–1990/91

1979–80	1,007	1985–86	2,436
1980–81	1,347	1986–87	1,757
1981–82	1,378	1987–88	2,060
1982–83	1,748	1988–89	2,047
1983–84	2,032	1989–90★	2,086★
1984–85	1,999	1990–91	2,357†

Notes: ★ estimated out-turn;
         † planned expenditure.
Source: Various public expenditure white papers.

month, the Minister was proudly proclaiming to have won a £155 million increase in the incomes of British farmers by obtaining a significant devaluation of the green pound. In July 1989 McGregor fought against the Commission's plans to cut financial support for the sheep industry because Britain receives a third of the £1,120 million sheep subsidy (*The Times*, 24 July 1989). Even at the 1990 Conservative conference, John Gummer, the agriculture Minister said, 'We're not going to lay waste to British farming in order to allow the midwest to take over our markets.' He insisted: 'I have stood up for British interests and I will stand up for British interests and I am standing up again here. In fact when I am in Brussels sitting down, I'm standing up for British interests' (*The Guardian*, 11 October 1990).

The French and German Ministers merely followed the same logic when negotiating reforms in 1988. They realized that there had to be reform but ensured a package that would do the least possible damage to their farmers. The final package had to provide a 'balance between the members in the benefits awarded and the sacrifices required' (Moyser and Josling 1990: 100). Consequently, the problem remains that the CAP was still setting prices too high because it was meeting the social demands of France and Germany to keep inefficient farmers in production (Gardner 1990).

Undoubtedly, the situation has changed in ten years. The attitude of the Government toward agriculture has become harsher, the income of farmers has declined and the level of price support has been reduced. Yet the CAP with high support prices, intervention and import levies still controls the agricultural market. The Government has to some extent reduced agricultural spending (see Table 9.5) but Mrs Thatcher's Governments were not able to achieve a fundamental reform of CAP. The policy is a long way from a free market in agriculture with, if anything, greater controls introduced in an attempt to reduce costs. Farmers continue to be paid well above world prices for producing too much. In addition the agricultural policy community remains strong. The reform of the policy has been within the closed world of national agricultural Ministries, national farm groups, the Commission and the Council of Agricultural Ministers. As Moyser and Josling (1990: 100) remind us, in the reform process, individual nations, with the exception of the UK and the Netherlands, represented agricultural interest almost to the exclusion of all other interests. No public group mobilized demanding that other interests should be given priority over agricultural ones.

Conclusion

The case of agriculture demonstrates both the limited impact that Thatcherism has had on certain policy areas and the difficulties that exist in implementing policy change. Much of the Thatcher Government's agricultural policy was not determined by ideology but by exogenous factors. Initially the Government was prepared to accept the policy of the Labour Government. However, the Government's objectives changed because of the crisis of the CAP, the international farm crises and the continual pressure of groups within and outside of the Conservative Party.

Once the need for reform was accepted the objectives were often contradictory. The Treasury's main concern was reform in order to reduce costs. The Ministry of Agriculture wanted reform that did not adversely affect British farmers. Moreover, the Government was uncertain whether the goal of reform was to introduce market mechanisms, provide alternative but cheaper forms of support, to make agriculture more environmentally sensitive or even to force general reform of the European Community.

In addition the Government faced great difficulties in implementation. Agricultural policy was made within a closed policy community both at the national and European level. This has made it very difficult for outsiders to reform the CAP. They lacked both the access and expertise either to initiate reform or to ensure its viability. Summits of Government leaders and Finance Ministers failed to force more radical change because they lacked knowledge on the detail of agricultural policy-making (Moyser and Josling 1990). More importantly, national leaders have been prepared to leave agricultural reform to the policy community and consequently the goal of reform has been to ensure the maintenance of CAP and the policy community, not their destruction. National governments, which were responsible for the implementation of reform, were not enthusiastic about putting the policy into practice.

Further problems arose because of the complexity of agricultural support. Set-aside and environmental policies and even price cuts were unable to tackle the severe problems of the CAP. Consequently, as Marsh and Rhodes point out (see p. 180), much policy change has been dealing with policy failure or the unintended consequences of previous policy. To a great extent, the 1988 reforms were a result of the failure of the 1984 measures. Although the Thatcher Governments wanted to reduce the costs of the CAP, they were unable to control the process of reform, the groups involved, the implementation of reform and the consequences of new policies.

10

The European Community

John Peterson

A study of the implementation of Thatcherite policies and the European Community (EC) immediately encounters problems of scope, purpose, and definition of what 'EC policy' means. The EC quite often has been a matter of 'high politics' for British international diplomacy. As for foreign policy generally, '[s]ome of its outputs are declaratory, some [like defence] preventative, some entirely symbolic . . . Much of its implementation is a matter of behaviour, attitudes and exhortation rather than clearly identifiable outputs' (Wallace and Wallace 1990: 86–7).

This book consciously avoids the obsession of previous studies with the 'heroic', symbolic politics of Thatcherism. But style, values, and ideology cannot be ignored in assessing Thatcherite EC policy. Style in diplomatic negotiations generally and at the level of the EC's Council of Ministers particularly mightily determines which negotiators hold the most sway over others. The often hyperbolic, muscle-bound approach of the Thatcher government toward the EC – what Lord Carrington labelled 'megaphone diplomacy' (quoted in Byrd 1988: 6) – had far-reaching implications for actual policy outcomes.

At a separate level of analysis, EC legislation now encroaches on a rapidly expanding array of domestic policy areas. Gregory (1983: 82) argues, 'It is nearly impossible for a government to present a comprehensive EC policy to Parliament. The EC covers too many diverse policy areas.'

It is similarly difficult to present a succinct survey of domestic EC policy implementation in the United Kingdom. Nearly every pattern of policy-making and implementation described in this volume applies to some area of

'EC policy implementation'. It includes the installation of tachographs in British commercial vehicles and issuing small, flexible, maroon 'European' passports instead of large, stiff, blue, British ones. But the mere presentation and defence of the UK's point of view in EC negotiations is also a form of policy implementation. Establishing a British position routinely involves consulting multiple government departments, and often sub-central governments and private actors. The UK's approach to the EC as a matter of 'high politics' is thus uniquely informed by the 'low politics' of existing patterns of domestic policy implementation. Any meaningful discussion of the UK in the EC must acknowledge that EC policy is a two-way street.

EC law may be 'superior' to domestic law in legalistic terms. But since legal bases for EC policies are international treaties, 'their implementation is often as much a matter for negotiation and bargaining as their initial formulation' (Wallace and Wallace 1990: 86). The process is by nature more complex and politicized than the implementation of policies which result from simple Acts of Parliament.

Yet, this chapter attempts to ensure consistency of purpose with the present volume's focus on the impacts of centrally determined policy objectives. At the most general level, there were four central elements of the Thatcherite project as applied to the EC. First, the Thatcher Government sought a better deal for the UK in budgetary terms. Second, they strove to instil the EC with the principles of market liberalism: free and open markets, deregulation, minimal and efficient administration, and reduced subsidies – especially to agriculture. Third, the Thatcher Government fought to preserve the paramount American role in European defence through NATO. Finally, they sought to block any attempts toward further political integration at the EC level. As De Gaulle, Thatcher wanted a *Europe des patries*.

In EC policy perhaps more than in any other sector covered in this collection, official objectives appeared to be essentially the Thatcher Government's actual objectives. This stemmed from the unprecedented centralization of authority for foreign policy generally and EC policy, particularly at 10 Downing Street. For the most part, 'British foreign policy was presented as the policies of one woman, so that in many respects this method became the message' (Bulpitt 1988: 194).

But EC policy has always been very diffuse and difficult to control from the centre. George (1990a: 7) has argued, 'it is not a single discrete policy issue, but a congeries of issues, only some of which will have a high political profile at any one time'. In many respects, the UK's approach to the EC has remained relatively consistent since 1973. What changed was the debate throughout Europe about how the EC should properly evolve, the higher stakes involved for the UK, and the increased saliency of European issues in British domestic politics.

This chapter proceeds in four sections. First, the changing foreign and domestic political environments within which EC policy was formulated and implemented in the 1980s are considered. Second, the administrative setting is assessed to determine the effect on British EC policy of changes within the Cabinet Office, civil service, and European Commission. Third, specific policy sectors are disaggregated so that the Thatcher Government's approach to EC policy can be considered alongside actual policy outcomes. The conclusion provides an audit of how much has changed in the realm of EC policy, by how much, and why.

The shifting political landscape for EC policy-making

Concern for preserving national sovereignty in the face of European integration is not a new feature of British political life. The tendency of the Thatcher Government to speak of national sovereignty in terms of 'Hobbesian indivisibility' (Pinder 1985: 483) was broadly consistent with all postwar British Governments. But the traditional inability of the British political class to distinguish between national *sovereignty* and national *autonomy* in foreign affairs became far more costly in the 1980s.

National sovereignty implies the formal ability of nations to act independently, as opposed to under the instructions of other nations. By contrast, national autonomy is the ability of nations to achieve goals through unilateral action (Cooper 1985: 1229). While the UK's national sovereignty remained essentially intact through the postwar period, its autonomy in foreign affairs diminished to the point of near non-existence.

Following Cooper, William Wallace (1986) has argued that postwar British foreign policy has been schizophrenic in drawing a line between preservation of national autonomy and promotion of interdependence. The UK's political, economic, and military dependence on the United States was largely accepted. Integration into a wider European framework was not. Writing in 1986, Wallace observed:

> The eventual acceptance of British membership in the European Community by all British political parties and the relative decline of the 'Community' issue as a divisive theme within British politics reflect a widespread assumption that the transfer of sovereignty involved has proved to be limited and controllable . . . yet the ground has continued to shift underneath this apparently stable structure. (Wallace 1986: 375)

By the mid-1980s, European governments had begun to focus political energies on the relaunch of the EC, which eventually culminated in the Single European Act (SEA). Political consensus on the need to implement the SEA and 'kick-start' the Community emerged as a response to lack of investment in Europe, the slow recovery from the 1979 recession, and a growing technological gap, especially *vis-à-vis* Japan. But the SEA was also a response to the widespread perception that the Reagan administration cared little about the effect on European economies of its domestic macroeconomic policies, which induced global recession, high interest rates, capital flight, and severe trade imbalances in the early 1980s. For the UK, as Smith observed (1988: 26),

Despite the ideological similiarity between Thatcherism and 'Reaga-nomics,' the development of the economic policy in Reagan's America came to constitute one of the most worrying and least tractable problems facing the British economy.

In this context, the Thatcher Government was forced to consider the declining utility of its 'special relationship' with the US. By the mid-1980s, the UK, as all EC states, had become far more dependent on international trade than the US. Germany had begun to surpass the US as the most important British trading partner. Western Europe as a whole accounted for close to 60 per cent of total British trade and the EC itself nearly half. In short, the fate of the British economy had become inextricably linked with that of the EC as a whole (see Table 10.1).

The new Eurocentrism of British foreign policy by the mid-1980s was reflected in the intense diplomatic interaction of the UK with its major EC partners. Besides thrice-annual European Council summits, the British Prime Minister regularly met with other EC leaders at annual Western economic summits, less regular NATO summits, and scheduled annual bilateral meetings with France, Italy and Germany. As Foreign Secretary, Geoffrey Howe claimed that he often saw his opposite numbers from other large EC states more often than his colleagues in British Cabinet (Tugendhat and Wallace 1988: 26). British ability to formulate domestic economic policy autonomously of a wider European framework progressively diminished in the 1980s. In international econom-ic diplomacy, Allen (1988: 49) argues, 'there has been little pretence that Britain can do anything other than co-operate with its Community partners'.

The UK's political influence at the EC level has always been constrained by the institutionalized strength of bilateral Franco-German ties. But British political leverage with other EC states is more fundamentally limited by the fact that the UK is the most important trading partner of no EC country besides Ireland. As debates about the Community's development took on added urgency in the mid-1980s, the Thatcher Government realized that it was 'no one's first bilateral priority' (Wallace 1984: 18).

Moreover, British public opinion shifted markedly toward general sup-port for British EC membership in the mid-1980s after the effects of the

Table 10.1   UK trade with the European Community (%)

	1973	1986
British exports to the EC		
per cent of UK GDP	6.1	9.3
per cent of UK total exports	32.3	47.9
British imports from the EC		
per cent of UK GDP	7.7	11.6
per cent of UK total imports	32.8	51.7

Source: CEC *European Economy* (1987): 129, 131; Harrop (1989: 56).

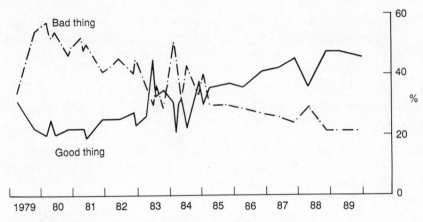

Figure 10.1 British attitudes toward EC membership
Source: Eurobarometer in *The Economist*, 17 February 1990. Reproduced with permission.

recession began to fade and the SEA captured public attention (see Figure 10.1). Dalton and Eichenberg (1990: 12) use pooled, cross-sectional time series data to show that British public support for EC membership increased faster than support in any other member state between 1983–89. To be sure, the British public remained more sceptical of the EC than any European people save the Danes or Greeks. But this secular shift provided an opening for the Labour Party in its effort to become a credible opposition after the disastrous election of 1983.

Labour party conferences voted by huge majorities in 1980 (71 per cent) and 1981 (85 per cent) to make withdrawal from the EC party policy (Gregory 1983: 202). But the experience of the French Socialist Government in 1981–82 impressed upon the British Labour leadership that national economic strategies could no longer work unless they were supported by a positive approach to international co-ordination within Europe. Under the leadership of former anti-marketeer Neil Kinnock, Labour Party support for EC membership began to cohere in the mid-1980s, and by 1988 official party documents referred to the need to stay in Europe.

Meanwhile, debates about the relaunch of the EC increasingly highlighted divisions within both Thatcher's Cabinet and the Conservative Party. No Thatcherite Cabinet was ever dominated by strongly committed anti-marketeers. By 1986 Howe, Chancellor Nigel Lawson, and even Brian Griffiths, a committed monetarist in charge of the Prime Minister's Policy Unit, were all clearly on record in favour of early British entry into full membership of the European Monetary System (EMS) (Johnson 1986: 174). Within the Tory Party, 'only a minority of the radicals of the new right retained their earlier suspicions of the European continent' (Wallace and Wallace 1990: 98). By 1989, Norton (1990: 22) concluded that close to 20 per cent of all Tory Members of Parliament were firm EC supporters, and that a much higher number took a pragmatic, if more cautious line on the EC.

By this time, the UK's approach to the EC had become a key domestic issue when open conflict developed within Cabinet over Thatcher's refusal to take sterling into the exchange rate mechanism (ERM) of the EMS. The controversy contributed both to Labour's best electoral performance in a decade in the June European Parliament (EP) elections and Lawson's resignation as Chancellor in the autumn. Crucially, as the EC became the most important, broad 'state of the nation' issue for British foreign policy in the late 1980s, Margaret Thatcher found she could no longer make policy on her own with Cabinet and Parliament falling dutifully into line.

The administrative setting for EC policy

The administrative setting in which British EC policy was implemented changed as much as did the regional and domestic political settings in which it was made in the 1980s. After British accession in 1973, responsibility for EC policy was parcelled out according to pre-existing departmental divisions in Whitehall. Yet, the Foreign and Commonwealth Office (FCO) was given the task of centrally co-ordinating British policy, and its general policy profile was significantly expanded in the process.

Thatcher was the first British Prime Minister elected since Neville Chamberlain with no previous ministerial experience in any external Government department. In her first major foreign policy test, the FCO appeared to 'out-vote' her on the Rhodesia question in 1979–80. Afterwards, the Prime Minister's determination to impose her own views on EC policy clearly increased (Bruce-Gardyne 1984: 39). Viewing the FCO as a 'nest of dovish Europeans and professional compromisers' (Wallace and Wallace 1990: 93), Thatcher acted to substantially centralize authority for EC policy in the Cabinet Office.

The Cabinet Secretariat was reorganized and sub-divided in 1979, with a new European Secretariat (ES) given substantial authority to co-ordinate Government EC positions independently of the FCO (Seldon 1990: 107–8). The head of the ES personally briefed the Prime Minister for every European Council summit, and attended all summits, meetings of the EC's Council of Ministers and Cabinet meetings when EC affairs were discussed. While the FCO traditionally had acted as a 'barrister' between the views of different departments (Wallace 1984: 49), the ES tended to 'tak[e] the initiative itself, rather than awaiting Whitehall departments to proffer instructions' (Seldon 1990: 109). It took the policy lead on the UK budgetary dispute (with the Treasury), the accession of Spain and Portugal, and negotiations on the SEA.

The FCO was represented in the ES by only one official in low-level position. But due to its small size, the ES remained dependent on the FCO to help co-ordinate policy and provide day-to-day back-up support. More importantly, with only eight administrative staff recruited from outside Departments on two-year secondments, the ES by nature had 'too little time in which to do any forward thinking on policy' (Gregory 1983: 130). The FCO view occasionally was decisive in debates about broad, long-term strategies. But British EC policy generally remained short-term in focus and ad hoc in style.

At the Cabinet level, time was allotted to EC affairs in full Cabinet meetings only 'to report rather than to stimulate discussion' (Gregory 1983: 129). Most EC matters requiring active Cabinet attention were referred to a committee chaired by the Foreign Secretary. But key policy decisions often were made by the Prime Minister herself, especially when British position diverged from those of other major EC states, such as on the Strategic Defence Initiative, research and development (R&D) policy or the US bombing of Libya (George 1990b: 200; Keliher 1990: 80; Wallace and Wallace 1990: 99).

Parliament's role in EC policy-making has always been minimal, and it remained so during the Thatcher years. Most EC legislation is given effect in UK by statutory instruments which generate little political controversy or opportunities for back bench influence (Gregory 1983: 82). Only on major EC matters, such as the budget, is legislation needed to be placed on the parliamentary timetable.

At the parliamentary committee level, scrutiny of EC legislation is performed by the European Communities Committee in the Lords and European Legislation Committee (ELC) in the Commons. The Lords is truly one of the only arenas within British Government for strategic, long-term thinking on EC policy. But there is little indication that it held much sway over policy-making during the Thatcher years. The ELC in the Commons is empowered to review most documents and legislation which are submitted to the EC Council of Ministers. Theoretically no UK Minister can approve EC legislation in the Council before the ELC has decided whether it merits full Commons debate (Wilson 1985: 237). But the ELC must scrutinize an avalanche of documents. It sees many proposals only after they have already gone to the Council and does not issue opinions. In practice, it worked closely with the Cabinet Office throughout the Thatcher years in determining which issues to 'flag' for Commons debates.

When full debates do occur, they are usually thinly attended and dominated by a cross-party coalition of 'anti-Euros'. Such debates have the potential to stir wider public debate, but parliamentary influence in this setting, when there is any, is usually a force for policy inertia. Wallace and Wallace (1990: 87) argue the effect is to

> inhibit governments in attempting to override entrenched interests. Where ministers and officials assess the cost of parliamentary rows and public response as higher than the benefits a policy change would achieve, they act effectively as a veto group.

A central problem for parliament in trying to influence EC policy is ministerial accountability. There is no clear method for the Commons to hold Ministers accountable after the House has presented a view, as British positions often change in negotiations, especially with the wider use of majority voting mandated by the SEA. Put simply,

> the processing of an EC legislative proposal seems to increase the opportunities for the exercise of ministerial and official power and influence,

and the opportunities for non-parliamentary pressure-group influence. (Gregory 1983: 26)

While the dominance of ministerial and official power in EC policy-making is not unique to the UK, no other EC member state divides so sharply between political Ministers and non-political officials. Most continental Ministers involved in EC policy rely heavily on their *cabinets*, or political State Secretaries, to engage in the sort of strategic reflection required to place day-to-day EC business in the context of long-term policy goals (Wallace 1984: 60). If, as Mrs Thatcher has suggested, other EC leaders regularly emit bold vague visions of how the EC should develop from 'cloud-cuckoo land', at least they have the in-house 'think tanks' necessary to take the initiative in such debates. For the UK in the EC, as Sir John Hoskyns has suggested, 'for practical purposes, strategy . . . can be defined as the "thinking we should have done three years ago, but don't have time to do today" ' (quoted in Wallace 1984: 77). Lacking their own *cabinets* and with minimal official support, it is little wonder that British Ministers had difficulty thinking beyond the short-term or resisting the ES's power to prioritize the needs and wishes of different departments during the 1980s.

Intuitively, the general administrative culture of the British civil service – insular, conservative, pragmatic – would seem closely compatible with the political stance of the Thatcher Governments in EC negotiations. In this context, the Thatcherite pursuit of 'new managerialism' in the civil service and the reassertion of ministerial autonomy was reflected in the government's refusal to substantially expand the number of domestic officials dealing with EC policy (H. Wallace 1986: 589). Moreover, the UK Permanent Representation (UKREP), the office of the UK Ambassador to the EC, which is responsible for negotiating many low-profile, non-controversial issues, is kept on a tighter rein by London than are other member states' 'Perm-Reps' by their governments. Gregory (1983: 130) argues that the UKREP 'unlike its counterparts in Brussels, is closely integrated into the Whitehall decision-making system'.

Yet, a point crucial to any discussion of the implementation of EC legislation in the UK is that the administrative culture of the British civil service clearly 'spills over' into the approach of British negotiators on a political level (Butt-Philip *et al.* 1988; George 1990b: 210–11). The UK has long had the best record in the EC in avoiding 'unexecuted judgments' handed down by the European Court of Justice against states which fail to enforce or properly implement EC legislation. The UK's credibility is high on harmonization of its national laws to fit EC legislation (Twitchett 1981: 23). There is evidence that the UK has substantially influenced the Commission to avoid proposals which skirt the boundaries of the Treaty of Rome or undermine the essential goals of national provisions (Plaskitt 1981).

Officials who brief Ministers before Council negotiations often advise them to vote against draft legislation if there are doubts about whether it may be smoothly implemented in the UK. One UKREP spokesman claims, 'We don't shrug our shoulders and say "well, okay then" if we think compliance or implementation of EC legislation will be difficult or impossible as much as other representations do' (interview in Brussels, September 1990). The British Civil Service likes to see itself as a force for efficiency and effectiveness within the EC. The seemingly nationalistic approach of the UK on the Council thus may be partly a product of civil service influence.

Against this image of EC British officials must be set the gradual development of a true 'EC cadre' of Britons in both the domestic civil service and the European Commission during the Thatcher era. Gregory (1983: 160) is struck by the 'outward-looking stance' of UK civil servants in the mainstream of EC business. The advice given to ministers in briefings has become far more informed by an overview of the interests of other member states than in years past. The general inexperience of the British political class with coalition government and deal-making of the sort that dominates at the EC level has accentuated the civil service's gradual adaptation to the politics of compromise and consensus.

The Commission saw its own independent powers and influence significantly expanded during the 1980s both by the SEA and the forceful leadership of Jacques Delors. At the same time, British representation in the Commission increased exponentially. The UK Civil Service took 'no significant interest in British postings until about 1977–78' (Gregory 1983: 160), when an inter-departmental 'Euro-staff committee' began to actively seek placement of British candidates. The UK also secured more short-term appointments of administrative 'experts' to the Commission than any other member state through the early 1980s.

The goal was to maximize British influence in the Commission. But the practical result was to expand the number of Britons who naturally are compelled to consider British national interests in the context of a more general 'European interest' at the EC level. Cases of British appointees 'going native' in this way at the highest level of the Commission are notorious: Lord Cockfield's proposals for value-added tax harmonization, Leon Brittan's hard-line stance on the sale of the Rover group to British Aerospace, and David Williamson's upbeat pronouncements on agricultural reform (see Allen 1988: 51) all contrasted sharply with Mrs Thatcher's repeated use of the term 'our Commissioners'. Other member governments thus began to view British obstinacy at the EC level more as a product of Thatcherism than of a general British national mindset.

To sum, several key changes in the administrative setting of the 1980s emerged unambiguously. First, the greatly expanded role of the Cabinet Office in EC policy-making added to the centralization of authority for British EC policy at the highest political level. It is not reckless to conclude that the problem of conflicting signals sent to British negotiators at the EC level from different government departments in London – particularly the Treasury and FCO – has largely subsided. The UK now has a highly developed and co-ordinated machinery for instructing its negotiators with the

European Secretariat of the Cabinet Office at the centre and the FCO in a subsidiary role.

Second, the Thatcherite defence of British parliamentary sovereignty as a pretext for resisting institutional reform of the EC was a ruse. It also damaged British credibility at the EC level. The weakness of parliamentary control over British EC policy was widely understood by other EC leaders, who resented the style as much as the content of Mrs Thatcher's 'one woman' EC policy-making. In their view,

> the paradox emerges, therefore, that the British governments 'principled' defence of British parliamentary sovereignty curtails the democratization of the EC decision-making process and so ensures that British ministers effectively escape both national and supranational democratic control. (Judge 1986: 326)

Third, the civil service influence on EC policy-making has evolved considerably. The British Civil Service is now far more 'Europeanized' than it has ever been. Its ethos is that attention to the nuts-and-bolts details of EC business helps prevent legislation from being adopted that cannot be implemented to achieve its intended effect. In this respect, civil service influence on British EC policy reinforced the pragmatic, sceptical political stance of Thatcherite Governments *vis-à-vis* the EC. But the development of a sophisticated, cosmopolitan British EC cadre in the Civil Service and Commission – concerned more with ensuring that the UK has a voice in debates about the EC's development than 'attachment to an 18th century concept of sovereignty' (*The Economist*, 7 October 1989) – produced perceptible optimism in Brussels about the prospects for a far more constructive British presence in the EC in the post-Thatcher era.

The policy setting

The UK's contribution to the *EC budget* has been the single most important issue for the EC policies of all post-1973 British Governments. Repeated British demands for more favourable budgetary terms have posed considerable difficulties for other EC states, who have been asked to contribute more themselves as well as alter existing budgetary conventions. Germany always has been the key member state. In 1975, the Wilson Government accepted a rebate formula designed largely by the German Finance Ministry, and then exaggerated its benefits in the campaign to ensure a 'yes' vote on the British referendum on continued EC membership. The Callaghan Government vigorously committed itself to renegotiation, but ended up with a very modest short-term agreement after much German resistance in 1978 (Gregory 1983: 188).

Thatcher, much as Callaghan before her, chose to make the EC budget controversy into a major domestic issue in the context of the UK's economic problems. At the 1980 Dublin European Council, Thatcher made her infamous pledge to 'get our money back'. But she eventually settled for another short-term agreement on rebates for 1980–83, which was only secured after major British concessions on agriculture and the common fisheries policy (Gregory 1983: 190). As Wilson had done, Thatcher sold the deal to a sceptical public, of whom nearly half thought she was 'not tough enough' in the negotiations (Gallup poll cited in Rutherford 1981: 19).

What set the budget row of the 1980s apart from those previous was Thatcher's negotiating style and the linking of the issue with debates about the EC's long-term future. Wallace and Wallace (1990: 92) observed that while Mrs Thatcher faced tough negotiations, 'she chose to add a strident style'. Bruce-Gardyne (1984: 48) concluded, 'She had broken all the rules of international negotiation. She had alienated all sympathy for the British case.'

As part of Thatcher's first budget deal, other states agreed to launch a comprehensive evaluation of all of the EC's policies, especially the CAP and budget. Such a broad critique was long overdue, but the report had the unintended consequence of helping to generate political consensus on the need to relaunch the EC. After 1984, especially as Mediterranean enlargement loomed, British concerns about growth in the EC budget began to be shared by the French and Germans, who were both net contributors by the mid-1980s (de La Serre 1987: 208–12; Allen 1988: 42; Levy 1990: 191). The linking of the budget issue with other concerns by the UK inspired both the Germans and French to use calls for political unity to pressure Thatcher to accept compromise on the budgetary settlement.

The French became convinced that the budgetary issue required a permanent solution as they took over the EC's presidency in January 1984. At the Brussels summit in March, François Mitterrand proposed that the UK should receive a 1.1 billion ECU rebate. Thatcher insisted on a minimum of 1.25 billion, which particularly angered German Chancellor Helmut Kohl, and the summit ended in acrimony over a minuscule amount of money. The French, with tacit German support, then began to hint that the UK might be excluded from discussions on new initiatives related to the SEA. The British cabinet subsequently discussed the (probably illegal) idea of holding back payments to the EC. Taylor (1989: 4–5) suggests this represented the lowest point ever in relations between the UK and the Nine.

The deal agreed at the Fountainebleu summit in June was only marginally different from that discussed in Brussels. But the British attitude had changed dramatically. At Fountainebleu, the UK delegation presented a decidedly upbeat discussion paper entitled 'Europe – the Future' (HMSO 1984), in which the freeing of the internal market was featured prominently. Allen (1988: 41) and Helen Wallace (1986: 590) agree that the paper put the UK in a position to have a significant and positive impact on the evolution of EC's agenda for the first time ever.

At Fountainebleu, general agreement on limiting the growth of the EC's budget showed that Mrs Thatcher successfully had made budgetary control a key issue for the EC as a whole. Moreover, the landmark reform of the CAP's intervention system in 1988 was directly inspired by a 1983 British proposal to limit the future rate of CAP growth to a level below the rate of increase of the EC budget (see Howe 1984: 189). Yet, damping down the cost of the CAP freed resources for new interventionist EC policies, such as collaborative R&D programmes and more regional spending. The Thatcher Government resisted fiercely the links drawn by other member states between the internal market and more spending on these and other policies. Thatcher's strident style returned as the UK voted with Greece at the 1985 Milan summit against launching the intergovernmental conference to negotiate the SEA.

Mrs Thatcher herself became 'extremely bad-tempered', showing 'anger and frustration', and even 'undisguised fury' (quoted in Taylor 1989: 9). Even the eventual agreement on CAP reform came only after she had generated much ill will by insisting that progress in areas such as technological collaboration had to be linked to CAP reform (Riddell 1983: 211–15).

Yet, once the conference was underway the UK took the negotiations seriously and 'in the event probably contributed far more to [the SEA's] eventual success than many of the countries that had most enthusiastically argued for it in principle' (Allen 1988: 51). The SEA contained many concessions to British positions, such as its provisions for majority voting *only* on legislation related to the internal market (H. Wallace 1986: 591). Even on institutional reform, the new co-operation procedure with the EP left states with veto power. Procedures for the liberalization of banking and insurance laws cut out the EP altogether, but were still made subject to majority voting so that other member states could not slow progress on a process that stood to benefit the UK more than any other member state (Taylor 1989: 12–13).

But substantial British concessions in 1988–89 – on agricultural reform, doubling the EC's structural funds, and the launch of an intergovernmental conference on Economic and Monetary Union (EMU) – were in part a consequence of outrage, both within Mrs Thatcher's Cabinet and on the part of other member states, at Mrs Thatcher's behaviour from 1979–86. Other EC members – particularly the Germans and French – had talked openly of the possibility of a 'two-tier Europe' in which the UK would be unable to influence initiatives launched without her. UK negotiators were forced to focus their energies on merely 'staying in the game' (Taylor 1989: 3) and avoiding total British isolation on these issues, as well as ensuring that UK would not lose some or all of its rebate or concessions gained on budgetary discipline in 1987–88. Mrs Thatcher's 'one woman' diplomacy thus became tempered by concerns within her government and the civil service that her uncompromising approach might leave the UK without influence in crucial debates about where the EC was heading.

A key factor which pushed the Thatcher Government toward compromise was its commitment to the *European Political Cooperation* (EPC) mechanism. EPC was created in the early 1970s as an intergovernmental forum for the co-ordination of national foreign policies. All post-accession UK governments viewed EPC as an opportunity for the UK to retain influence in foreign affairs despite the decline of its international stature. The mechanism had transformed British foreign policy-making by the mid-1980s. As Douglas Hurd observed, 'in some areas of diplomacy our policy is formed wholly within a European context; and in no area is the European influence completely absent' (quoted in Allen 1988: 48).

The Thatcher Government, at least initially, contributed much to the institutional development of EPC. It took a lead role in creating the 'troika' system in 1980, which linked the administrative structures of successive EPC Presidencies to ensure continuity in EPC initiatives. The high point of the 1981 British Presidency of the EC was the signature of the London Report committing member states to intensify exchange of information and positions within EPC. The UK also lobbied for more effective crisis management provisions after six weeks were needed before a common EPC position on the invasion of Afghanistan could be agreed in 1979 (H. Wallace 1986; Allen 1988: 47).

These initiatives paid dividends when the Thatcher Government successfully engineered an EC-wide trade and arms embargo of Argentina within a few days of the invasion of the Falkland Islands in 1982. Yet, the Thatcher Government seemed incapable of comprehending the difficulties faced by other EC countries in supporting the UK. Argentina was an important arms customer for France and retained close cultural ties with Italy. Mrs Thatcher paid for her apparent lack of interest in negotiating a diplomatic solution to the Falklands crisis in subsequent negotiations on the British rebate and especially CAP price-fixing. When the UK threatened to veto a 1982 farm pricing compromise, the package was approved by an unprecedented majority vote, in a clear case of high-level revenge.

Moreover, other EC member states used British enthusiasm for EPC as a lever to secure acceptance of the SEA and moves toward institutional reform. By early 1985, the internal market, EPC, and institutional reform were all linked in negotiations on the SEA (Taylor 1989: 8). The prospect of a 'two-tier' Europe led to fears that the British role within EPC might be fundamentally weakened. The Thatcher Government was thus hung on its own petard:

> [The UK] tended to push on enthusiastically with the development of EPC without regard for the soundness of the foundations . . . All this only goes beyond common sense into hypocrisy if a government operates on the basis of an *à la carte* approach while strongly preaching the virtues of progress towards a truly common policy. (Hill 1983: 25–6)

Indeed, the Thatcher Government, through its approach to *security and defence* policy, encouraged interest in a more formalized structure for EPC and, by extension, a truly common European foreign policy. In the early 1980s the Irish, Greeks, and Danes all eventually were persuaded, largely due to British pressure, that EPC should discuss security matters. The idea was then taken up in 1983 by Germany and Italy in the Genscher–Colombo proposals for European Union, which provided crucial political momentum to the relaunch of the EC.

British Governments had encouraged collaboration in security and defence policy by founding the Eurogroup of NATO in the late 1960s and championing the Independent European Programme Group (IEPG) to rationalize European arms production in the early 1980s (Allen 1988: 49). The UK responded to the signing of the Franco-German bilateral defence treaty of 1982 by participating in the first-ever tripartite meeting of Defence Ministers. A substantially increased Franco-British dialogue on defence was launched in 1987–88, leading to exchange and co-ordination on nuclear defence strategies.

Yet, the connection between these actions and an independent European presence within NATO was resisted by Mrs Thatcher, despite clear interest within the FCO and Ministry of Defence in developing the connection. The French proposal to revive the West European Union, a loose framework for EC members to discuss defence policies, was welcomed by Howe. But Mrs Thatcher criticized the development of 'sub-structures' within NATO and their potential for 'undermining links across the Atlantic' (quoted in George 1990b: 202) and appeared uninterested 'in participating in any fundamaental changes in the European security system' (Allen 1988: 50). The Westland affair and the UK's continued reliance on the US for major weapons systems reinforced the impression that the Thatcher Government was unwilling to sacrifice short-term savings for the long-term development of a stronger, independent European defence capability.

Lack of concern for the British technological dependence on American defence industries carried over into Mrs Thatcher's positions on the Strategic Defence Initiative (SDI) and the EC's new *collaborative R&D programmes*. While other EC states shunned SDI, Thatcher welcomed the offer of contracts to European firms. Meanwhile, Mrs Thatcher almost single-handedly blocked approval of the budget for the EC's new R&D Framework programme for nine months in 1986–87, despite having previously accepted the SEA's provisions for increased spending on R&D (Sharp 1989: 215; George 1990b: 200).

Yet, the Thatcher Government's minimalist approach to collaborative R&D was tempered by the development of a transnational European information technology (IT) policy network, which included ICL, Plessey, and GEC. These firms first pushed the Government to fund the ambitious British Alvey project in the early 1980s (Keliher 1990), then the expanded Esprit programme contained in the Commission's Framework proposal. They were also instrumental in securing British support for the French-led, intergovernmental Eureka initiative (Peterson 1989). Still, as Wallace and Wallace (1990: 91) argue, the Thatcher Government seemed to decide on ideological grounds that '[t]rade and industrial policy were to be determined by domestic priorities, not by the international context. Even more than the FCO, DTI [the Department of Trade and Industry] was a bureaucracy to be tamed.'

The Thatcher Government's mission to 'tame' the DTI also was evident in its approach to EC *regional policy*. DTI funds for regional economic and industrial development were steadily reduced after 1979 as the Government espoused market solutions to encourage the 'natural adjustment' of labour markets (Anderson 1990: 239). Party political considerations inspired the move away from distributing grants on objective needs-based criteria in 1984 and the abolishment of automatic grants altogether in 1988. Labour strongholds in the rapidly deindustrializing north of England and Scotland thus no longer automatically qualified for aid.

Yet, the development of EC regional policy to some extent forced the Thatcher Government to continue extending national aid to the most disadvantaged British regions. Prior to 1984, 95 per cent of the European Regional Development Fund (ERDF) was allotted according to strict national quotas on a project-by-project basis. The UK thus received nearly one-quarter of all ERDF funds, more than any member state besides Italy, with few strings attached. After 1984, national quotas were replaced by 'indicative ranges' (Armstrong 1989: 177). Henceforth, if the UK wished to secure more than the 'bottom end' figure in its indicative range, it had to justify its claim to the Commission and other member states on the ERDF's Management Committee. The expansion of non-quota funds – for regions designated by the EC as disadvantaged – forced all states to develop specific programmes for combining national aid with EC funds.

Moreover, as the British Manpower Services Commission's funds for training and employment were squeezed in the 1980s, British local and regional authorities scrambled to secure benefits from the EC's European Social Fund (ESF), which has a strong regional bias and no national quotas. Many authorities appointed EC Liaison Officers or implemented other institutional changes to attract ESF funds (Harrop 1989: 125; Teague 1989: 49–51). The expansion of the EC's regional policy generally was the key to the Labour Party's gradual evolution towards a pro-EC line, which emerged at the local government level before it solidified within the party's leadership (Grahl and Teague 1988: 83–4).

In *agricultural policy*, Mrs Thatcher's efforts to reform the CAP met with stiff resistance from a tightly integrated domestic policy network. The Conservative Party, the National Farmers Union, and the MAFF had 'if anything become closer allies since (EC) entry' (Gregory 1983: 138). Mrs Thatcher's assault on the CAP was first delayed and then watered-down by the strength of the alliance. MAFF regularly pursued EC policies at odds with the Government's position on the CAP until well into the second Thatcher administration (Bulpitt 1988: 192).

Finally, the EMS controversy showed that in *monetary policy*, as in regional policy, the UK eventually was forced to co-operate in a European context against the strong ideological predisposition of the Prime Minister. Mrs Thatcher's enthusiasm for the internal market in the mid-1980s was undermined by her apparent willingness to accept severe fluctuations in the pound, especially compared with currencies in the ERM, and the consequent disincentives for increased British trade with the continent. Chancellor Lawson's policy of 'managed money', or shadowing the Deutsche Mark, was an alternative to his preferred solution of placing sterling in the ERM. But the UK's inflation rate remained the highest in the EC and its trade deficit steadily worsened. By 1989, the development of the internal market made reducing the UK's inflation and current account deficit without a full domestic recession nearly impossible.

Moreover, Nigel Lawson and others within the Cabinet became convinced that the UK could not influence the EC toward liberal, free market principles as long as it remained outside the ERM. Mrs Thatcher herself remarked that by the mid-1980s she saw herself as 'leader of Opposition within her own cabinet' on the EMS issue (Johnson 1986: 175). Her intransigence long after a majority of her Cabinet favoured full EMS entry cost her much political capital and contributed to her downfall.

The EMS also mattered symbolically. For other EC states, no other issue more exemplified the UK's lack of commitment to European unity. The ability of the EC to engage in global economic management was severely constrained by the absence of sterling in the ERM. Many, including Lawson, believed that the full benefits of the internal market could not be realized without EMU, and that it in turn required strengthening both the framework of EC law and representative government at the EC level (Pinder 1989: 56). In short, Mrs Thatcher's position on EMS was the single most important cause of the UK's eventual isolation in debates about the EC's political development.

Conclusion

An audit of Thatcherite EC policy must emphasize the gap between central objectives and actual outcomes. Thatcher secured a marginally better deal than did her predecessors on the UK's budgetary contribution. But she inadvertently encouraged linkage of the issue to institutional reform of the EC. Thatcher's own free-market principles inspired the 1992 initiative, but the SEA led to much that was anathemic to her. Partial success was achieved in reforming the CAP, but far less than was hoped for, and reduced agricultural spending meant more funds for the EC's collaborative R&D and regional programmes. The UK contributed significantly to EPC's empowerment, but this in turn generated political momentum for political union and an independent European defence capability. Mrs Thatcher's obstinacy on the EMS issue was a key factor leading other member states to push for the early development of EMU. By her own criteria, Mrs Thatcher failed miserably to get what she wanted from the EC.

There are many striking continuities to British EC policy since 1973. Edward Heath was strongly *communautaire* in rhetoric but equally resistant to new, common energy and monetary policies (Bruce-Gardyne 1984: 47, 118). James Callaghan accepted a smaller Regional Fund rather than agree to plans to allot more power to the EP in 1978 (Gregory 1983: 191). The style of the Thatcherite Government within the EC also appears less exceptional when compared to previous governments. In 1975, Wilson turned renegotiations on the UK's budgetary contribution into a Brussels-bashing exercise for domestic political consumption (George 1990b: 87). Callaghan's key EC Ministers severely alienated other EC states with baldly partisan positions on agricultural pricing and collaborative R&D programmes during the British presidency of the EC in 1977 (Gregory 1983: 145).

What made Thatcherite EC policy different were three broad changes which fundamentally altered the UK's approach to the EC in the 1980s. First, authority for EC policy-making was centralized at the highest political level to an extent previously unseen. Mrs Thatcher's one-woman diplomacy acted to *personalize* British EC policy far more than ever before. Howe, Lawson, and the British Civil Service (if not Nicholas Ridley!) were all viewed as potentially constructive forces in the building of a New Europe. For the UK's EC partners – as for the British Tories by November 1990 – the problem was Mrs Thatcher herself.

The second broad change was the economic and political revival of the EC in the mid-1980s. Domestic economic policy became progressively more constrained by the UK's dependence on trade with the EC. The EC moved toward creating a truly common market – not just a customs union – and became a potential framework for political, economic, and monetary union. Prior to 1979, the UK had both less to lose from alienating its EC partners and less to gain from cooperating with them. By the late 1980s, the potential costs of political isolation within a 'two-tier' Europe had become daunting.

Third, the EC's impact on a wide range of domestic British policy sectors was heightened considerably. Attempts by the Thatcher Governments to centrally and unilaterally impose purely domestic goals in foreign, regional, and technology policies were fundamentally constrained by new common policies agreed at the EC level. Domestic policy networks with important supranational elements – the European information technology producer network, the alliance between the Commission and British local authorities, and the MAFF-led agricultural cabal – limited the Thatcher Government's ability to direct policy from the top down.

Finally, a survey of EC policy during the Thatcher era must acknowledge the Government's failure to nurture domestic consensus within the British polity or public at large in support of its approach to the EC. The Government's 1984 discussion paper, *Europe – the Future*, urged other member states 'to make actions undertaken within the Community relevant to the lives of our people . . . encourage the learning of other Community languages', and 'heighten the consciousness among our citizens of what unites us' (HMSO 1984: 74–5, 81). The Thatcher Government did almost nothing to promote these high-minded goals. To the extent the progressive Europeanization of British foreign and domestic policies was embraced in the 1980s, it occurred because there was either no alternative, or because 'within the complex network of Community institutions a British government could obscure responsibility and hide from awkward domestic forces' (Bulpitt 1988: 199).

By 1990, an apparently solid majority of the British public appeared to support British EC membership, even if its image of the EC was informed as much by tabloid journalistic clichés as reasoned public debate. Only at the margins of party political debate were calls for British withdrawal still espoused. Against this backdrop, Mrs Thatcher's approach to the EC ultimately contributed to her isolation within her Cabinet and her party, as well as the EC, by November 1990. Perhaps the lesson is that British politics places more limits on the ability of a Government to impose its own will in the face of contrary Cabinet, parliamentary and popular impulses than ever could have been appreciated at the height of the Thatcher era.

Acknowledgements

The author is grateful to Neil Carter, Andrew Dunsire, Stephen George, Martin Smith, Hugh Ward, and the editors for helpful comments on earlier drafts.

11

The implementation gap: explaining policy change and continuity

David Marsh and R.A.W. Rhodes

In the introduction we posed three key questions which we now return to. How much policy change occurred during the Thatcher years? To what extent did this change result from a distinct policy agenda and legislative programme which was pursued by the Thatcher Governments? Why did more change occur in some policy areas than in others and, in particular, why was there less change than might have been expected? We shall deal with each of these questions in turn.

How much change?

This volume suggests that a great deal of legislation was introduced during the Thatcher years, much of it very radical. Certainly in terms of legislation, many policy areas were characterized by change rather than continuity. Some of the policies pursued by the Conservatives built upon what existed before but even then, the way in which such policies were developed represented a substantial change. In addition, this legislative change often involved changes in the political/administrative institutions through which policy was implemented. However, as far as outcomes are concerned much less changed. The Thatcher Government may have had more radical objectives than previous governments, but they were probably no better at achieving those objectives.

Legislative change

A great deal of legislation has been introduced and passed in many of the areas reviewed in this book. In fact, this reflects the general pattern revealed by

Burton and Drewry (1990: 92); more legislation was introduced by the Thatcher Government than previously. In addition, much of this legislation has been very radical in intent. There is little doubt that in some areas a major transformation was attempted by the Thatcher Government. Few of these policy initiatives were new but they were pursued with a vigour which represented a break with the past. However, the Government's policy initiatives were concentrated in a limited number of policy areas.

Obviously, economic policy was the core of the supposed Thatcher 'revolution'. Here, as Jackson (Chapter 2) shows, the Government identified the control of inflation as the primary target of economic policy. This aim represented a break with the postwar Keynesian consensus, although it had been clearly presaged in the policies pursued by the previous Labour administration after 1975. The Conservatives thought that the role of government in relation to the economy should be restricted. Government should create the climate within which the market could function effectively by pursuing sound monetary policies to reduce inflation; creating incentives through lower taxation; and reducing the power of the unions to constrain the market by reforming industrial relations law. The Government attempted to carry out such a policy. It introduced the medium-term financial strategy (MTFS), reformed the tax system and pushed through radical trade union reform. There is no doubt that all this represented an important change. The individual policies had been pursued before, but not with such vigour and not together. A great deal of legislation was introduced in the four policy areas identified by Savage and Robins (1990: 245) as being marked by radical change in the Thatcher era: local government; industrial relations; housing; and privatization. For example, there were more than 40 Acts passed which affected local government during the 1980s. Similarly, five major pieces of legislation restructuring industrial relations law were introduced between 1980 and 1990. In the housing area four key Acts were passed, while each sale of nationalized assets was initiated by an Act of Parliament.

In each of these fields, the legislation introduced involved a major transformation of the existing order. The industrial relations legislation had seven major elements. The blanket immunity enjoyed by unions, as distinct from unionists, was removed by the Employment Act 1982. The definition of a legitimate trade dispute was successively narrowed so as to reduce the immunities enjoyed by unionists (and now unions). The legal basis of the closed shop was first restricted, and then removed in the Employment Acts of 1988 and 1990. Under the Trade Union Act 1984, unions are required to hold secret ballots for the election of officers and this legislation also requires unions to conduct political fund ballots. The 1988 Employment Act gave individual unionists a series of rights *vis-à-vis* their unions. Finally, the 1990 Employment Act made unions responsible for unofficial strike action unless they specifically opposed it. These changes are major. Certainly, the combined effect of the legislation is more radical than that of the 1971 Industrial Relations Act.

The housing legislation was also radical. The 1980 Housing Act gave sitting council tenants a statutory right to buy their house or flat at significantly below the market price. The legislation required councils to sell and the initial, limited, resistance of some councils was quickly dealt with by the courts. The 1986 Housing and Planning Act, the 1988 Housing Act and the 1989 Local Government and Housing Acts were together designed to produce a fundamental reform in rented housing. The 1986 Act allowed councils to transfer their houses to Housing Associations or private landlords. The 1988 Act contained a 'tenants' choice' provision which gave council tenants the right to transfer their tenancy to other landlords. The Act also allowed approved landlords to bid for most local authority housing. In order to prevent this occurring, more than 50 per cent of the council tenants affected must vote against the transfer. The 1989 Act prevented councils subsidizing council house rents.

The Government introduced three major pieces of legislation designed to control local government finance. In addition, there was other legislation which significantly altered central–local relations: for example the 1985 Local Government Act abolished the Greater London Council and the Metropolitan County Councils; the 1988 Local Government Act compels councils to put refuse collection, street cleaning, cleaning of buildings, ground maintenance and vehicle maintenance out to tender; six Acts reduced the local authorities' role in relation to housing; and six Education Acts changed their role in education.

As far as privatization policy was concerned, the legislation was designed, among other things, to: transfer a wide variety of state assets to the private sector; liberalize markets and remove entry barriers in bus and coach services, telecommunications, oil, gas and electricity supply, financial markets and the private rented housing market; encourage the private provision of public services; and reduce subsidies and increase charges, particularly in the welfare sector (Marsh 1991).

It is difficult to over-emphasize the scale of these putative changes. In no field was there a total break with the past, for in each area elements of the policy pursued by the Thatcher Government had been present previously. For example, previous governments had attempted to restrict the immunities enjoyed by trade unions, while many previous governments had attempted to achieve more control over local government expenditure. Nevertheless, the scale and scope of the policy and legislative initiatives in these four areas makes it easy to see why they were highlighted by Savage and Robins.

Elsewhere there has been less legislative activity, although the pattern varies significantly between policy areas. Some other areas have witnessed major policy initiatives which, however, fall short of the changes in the areas already discussed. For example: as Wistow (Chapter 7) shows, there was a significant growth in legislation affecting the NHS, particularly towards the end of the 1980s, much of it radical. In particular, the Government made some attempt to restrict the clinical autonomy of doctors and to introduce market mechanism into the health service. Other areas were intended to have major overhauls but are still marked predominantly by continuity. Thus Bradshaw

(Chapter 6) demonstrates that social security expenditure increased rapidly, largely as a by-product of the Government's economic policies, and the attempt to reform the social security programme came to nought; this policy area is deeply impervious to change.

There were areas where very little change has occurred. In the field of agricultural policy, as Smith (Chapter 9) indicates, there have been very few policy initiatives. Such inertia is surprising given the Government's market rhetoric which clashed noticeably with the policy of high production and high subsidies pursued by Governments since the 1930s. As Peterson (Chapter 10) argues, Thatcherite policies towards Europe were broadly consistent with those of all postwar governments, although they were pressed more overtly and more vigorously. Finally, in environmental policy, Ward and Samways (Chapter 8) suggest that the Government was strong on rhetoric but showed little interest in legislation. They argue that the Government was indulging in 'symbolic politics'. They talked a lot about change and protecting the environment but essentially continued with a policy based on regulation by consent.

Institutional change

Much of the legislation introduced by the Conservative Government resulted in change in the institutions and administrative structures which implemented policy. It has been argued that Margaret Thatcher was people-centred in her decision-making; that she had a minimal interest in the structure of government (King 1985: 122). In fact, in the fields examined in this volume, there has been important, if not radical, organizational change.

In the local government policy area, not only has the whole basis of local government finance been transformed, but also the metropolitan authorities were abolished and the powers and responsibilities of other local authorities were significantly reduced. At the same time, privatization meant the demise of a considerable number of nationalized industries which had been important institutions upon the political and economic scene. In addition, there have been important institutional changes in the health field, with, as Wistow (Chapter 7) shows, the abolition of Area Health Authorities. In the environment policy area, new organizations were established which were responsible for nature conservancy and an Inspectorate of Pollution was created. In the social security field, the Department of Health and Social Security (DHSS) was split into two separate departments and five new Agencies were created in addition to the constant small changes in structure noted by Bradshaw (Chapter 6). The civil service was not spared. The Civil Service Department and the Central Policy Review Staff were abolished and the Efficiency Unit's (1988) call for agencies heralded an era of substantial institutional reform. Finally, as Peterson (Chapter 10) shows, there were important changes in the administrative setting within which British EC policy was implemented, and crucial institutional changes at the EC level, which influenced British policy-making on a broad front. Institutional change became a prominent feature of the landscape of the Thatcher Government.

Of course, even radical institutional changes do not always have a commensurate effect on policy or implementation. Indeed, Bradshaw argues that the constant changes in social security structure have had little effect on policy outcomes. Similarly, Ward and Samways (Chapter 8) suggest that the establishment of the Pollution Inspectorate has not undermined the basic policy of regulation by consent. In other areas, however, these institutional changes have had more significance. So, for example, the institutional changes brought about by the privatization of nationalized industries have had a crucial effect on the balance between the private and public sectors, and will provide a key element of the institutional framework within which future economic policy is developed and implemented.

Changes in policy outcomes: the achievement of objectives

A government may introduce major new policies which are enacted without difficulty. In general terms, the Conservative Party passed a great deal of new legislation in a whole variety of fields. However, such legislative change may not achieve a particular government's objectives. In fact, the Thatcher Government, like its predecessors, failed to achieve many of the aims it set itself. In addition, as is always the case, the policies pursued sometimes had unintended consequences which undermined the effect of the policy or the achievement of some other policy objective.

Obviously, the picture is more complex than this summary suggests. Certainly, policy areas have to be disaggregated. However, it is noticeable that even in those areas which the Government regarded as most important, and in those areas where many observers have identified a substantial degree of change, the Government's achievements have been much less substantial than is often claimed.

As Jackson (Chapter 2) shows, any claim that the Thatcher Government transformed the economy or economic performance is, at best, highly questionable. Annual growth in the Thatcher years was slower than in previous comparable periods. The volume of imports increased and the balance-of-payments position deteriorated. Exports as a percentage of GDP showed very little change. Perhaps most importantly, the Government failed to bring inflation under control, although that was the main aim of its economic policy. Inflation fell from over 10 per cent in 1979 to 3 per cent in 1986, in part as a result of significant falls in import prices. However, subsequently it rose again to reach 8 per cent in 1990; a rise which owed something to other Government policies which led to a consumer boom and massive rises in house prices. Indeed, many observers suggest that the only significant achievement of the Government's policy to encourage economic restructuring was the improvement in productivity which occurred and which may have a lasting effect. Even here, there is considerable dispute as to the extent and cause of these improvements. Overall, while there were significant changes in economic policy in the Thatcher years most observers suggest that few of the Government's objectives were achieved.

Even in the four areas marked by radical change, the pattern is mixed and the Government had difficulty in achieving its objectives. Its greatest 'success' was in the relatively narrow field of housing policy, while it had particular difficulty in changing outcomes in the area of local government finance.

Kemp (Chapter 5) shows that, for housing policy, the Conservatives achieved four of their five aims. They significantly increased owner-occupation, reduced local authority housing provision, reduced public expenditure on housing and gained electoral advantage. However, even here they failed to expand the private rented sector. In the industrial relations area they achieved two of their three aims. They reduced the unions' role in the policy-making process and passed legislation which was used by employers and complied with by unions thus establishing Government authority in relation to the unions and creating an image of governing competence. However, they have not succeeded in transforming shopfloor industrial relations in a way which significantly favours management.

A similar pattern emerges as far as privatization is concerned although this area is not dealt with in this volume. However, Marsh (1991) argues that the Government's privatization policy achieved five of its seven aims. It certainly reduced both Government involvement in industry and the Public Sector Borrowing Requirement (PSBR). It also encouraged employee share ownership and wider share ownership. In addition, the process clearly benefited the Conservatives politically. However, it is more doubtful that the policy achieved its aim of improving the efficiency of the public sector or even of the newly privatized companies. Similarly, there is limited evidence that the policy eased problems in public sector wage bargaining by weakening public sector unions.

The Thatcher Government achieved even less success with its local government policy. It achieved only one of its four objectives. They failed to control local government expenditure and had limited success in strengthening accountability by introducing a clear link between the provision of services and paying for them. The poll tax débâcle clearly lost them electoral support. In this field, their one success was to introduce competition into service provision.

None of these points justify the conclusion that the Government in question had no success. No government will achieve everything it sets out to do and, indeed, it could be argued that no government expects to achieve more than a proportion of its objectives. The Thatcher Government could be content with what it achieved. Be that as it may, it is in the five areas so far considered that claims of a transformation are most often made on the strength of, at best, ambiguous evidence. Elsewhere even less has changed.

Wistow (Chapter 7) indicates that spending on the National Health Service was not cut, although it did not keep pace with demand or need. He also argues that the basic principles of the NHS have remained intact despite their apparent incompatibility with the ideology of the Thatcher Governments. More specifically, while the attack on the clinical autonomy of doctors had limited effect, the move towards an internal market in the health service is a threat to the principle of access to a comprehensive range of local services.

As Bradshaw (Chapter 6) shows, the Thatcher Government did attempt major changes in the social security system and it did make greater use of incomes-related/means-tested benefits; a success in their terms. In particular, there were changes which significantly cut the benefits available to the unemployed and young people; in the Government's view changes necessary to price them back into jobs (and to contain the increase in expenditure). However, the major objective in social policy during the Thatcher era was to cut public expenditure. In fact, social security expenditure increased in absolute terms, real terms and, for most of the period, as a proportion of GNP.

Smith's (Chapter 9) analysis of agriculture policy also indicates that, although the policy of high subsidies and high production has been subject to increasing criticism, this area has been marked by continuity rather than change. When Mrs Thatcher resigned, agriculture policy was still based upon three non-Thatcherite principles. It remained costly in terms of public expenditure, it violated the principles of the free market and it reflected the demands of a powerful special interest, the farmers.

As far as policy towards Europe is concerned, Peterson (Chapter 10) shows that, although the Conservatives did better than did their predecessors on the UK's budgetary contributions and in relation to CAP reform, these 'successes' were marginal. Of the policy areas examined in this volume, environmental policy appears to have experienced least change in the Thatcher era. Certainly, Ward and Samways (Chapter 8) argue that Thatcherism had little intererst in environmental policies except to ensure that they did not lose out electorally from failing to address green issues. In their view, the great success of the Conservative Governments was to recognize just how little needed to be done to satisfy public demand.

Overall, although the Thatcher Governments did attempt to transform a number of areas of policy by introducing a great deal of legislation, they proved less successful in achieving their objectives. Even in those areas in which they concentrated their efforts, less was achieved than they hoped or than many observers have claimed. Elsewhere, they attempted less and achieved little. However, one other point needs some consideration. Many of the policies pursued had unintended consequences which undermined government objectives both inside and outside the area concerned.

Unintended consequences

Some Thatcherite policies had spectacular unintended consequences which undermined other policies. Housing policies presented a particularly good example. The emphasis on home ownership, together with the expansion of mortgage tax relief, had an inflationary impact. Property prices rose sharply and the equity tied up in this seemingly ever-increasing asset encouraged private landlords to realize their assets and helped to fuel a credit boom and growing consumer expenditure which sucked in imports. This outcome was not anticipated and, coupled with tax cuts, it helped to undermine the Government's economic strategy.

At the same time, the problem of homelessness became increasingly acute. So, for example, the number of homeless households accepted for re-housing by English local authorities more than doubled; from 57,000 in 1979 to 127,000 in 1989. In addition, the number of households in arrears on their mortgages increased from 30,000 in 1983 to 130,000 in 1990. Repossessions of mortgaged properties grew from 5,000 in 1981 to an estimated 40,000 for 1991. These trends had important knock-on effects on social security expenditure. Once again, the Government did not appear to have anticipated the developments which resulted in part from its housing policy.

Government economic policy also had an important unintended consequence. The Conservatives gave priority to controlling inflation and, in large part, as a consequence unemployment rose sharply. As far as the Goverment was concerned, this rise should have led to a fall in wages as people priced themselves back into a job. In fact, the rise in unemployment led to a large increase in social security payment which helped undermine the Government's objective of cutting public expenditure. Between 1978/79 and 1989/90 expenditure in real terms on benefits for the unemployed increased by 46 per cent. In addition, as Bradshaw (Chapter 6) shows, growing unemployment has also led to greater expenditure on family credit, housing benefit and income support. Clearly the attempt to achieve one objective of economic policy, lower inflation, indirectly made it more difficult to achieve another objective, lower public expenditure.

Peterson's (Chapter 10) review of policy towards Europe offers another excellent example of how the pursuit of one policy objective can undermine another one in the same policy area. While the Conservatives' aggressive campaign led to marginal reductions in the British budgetary contribution, it was at the cost of accelerating the momentum for political union; an outcome which was unintended, at odds with the Conservatives' aims, and divisive within the party.

Why change?

In some policy areas at least, the Thatcher Governments set out to transform policy and initiated a great deal of legislation. At the same time, the Government was more successful in pushing through its legislative initiatives than in achieving policy objectives. However, it is still possible that those changes which occurred owed less to Thatcherite policies than is claimed. After all, correlation is not cause so that, for example, any weakening of the trade unions since 1979 may owe as much to changes in the economic structure as to the Conservatives' industrial relations legislation. In this section, we explore the origins of policy and of legislation, focusing on two related questions. Was policy innovation a product of the Thatcher Government's distinctive ideology and policy agenda? To what extent were the actual changes a product of that ideology and agenda?

Origins of policy and legislation

What role did New Right ideology play in the development of Conservative policy and manifesto commitments? What influence did manifesto commitments have upon the legislation which was introduced?

This book is not the place to discuss either the content of New Right ideology or the role it played more generally in the development of the Conservatives' policy agenda (see King 1987). However, it is clear that, although New Right ideology played some role in relation to most of the policy areas considered in this volume, it was by no means the only, or even the most important, influence. Certainly, the Thatcher Government entered office committed to such New Right tenets as reducing the role of the State and the size of the public sector; strengthening the operation of market forces; and transforming the postwar consensus. There is little doubt that such intentions helped shape specific policy agenda. The Government's economic policy, with the initial emphasis on monetary policy, was designed to reduce inflation even at the expense of higher unemployment; reversing the priorities of the Keynesian consensus. Subsequently the switch to privatization as a major tool of economic policy reflected a desire to reduce the public sector, to stimulate the operation of market forces and reduce the public sector borrowing requirement (PSBR). Similarly, the Thatcher Government's industrial relations legislation aimed in large part to reduce the trade unions' capacity to restrict the operation of the market, while the attempt to control local government finance rested in part on the perceived need to control public expenditure and the PSBR. In addition, New Right ideology also influenced the move to introduce market forces into the NHS and the attempt to increase the use of means-tested social security benefits.

However, it would be misleading to characterize the Thatcher Government as ideological. It may be true that they pursued an ideological position more thoroughly than previous British Governments, although even here comparisons with the Attlee Labour Government are instructive. After all, his Government played the key role in establishing the postwar consensus. Nevertheless, in a number of policy areas, the Thatcher Government proved unwilling to pursue its ideological hares when such a pursuit might have damaged them politically or electorally. Bradshaw (Chapter 6), Ward and Samways (Chapter 8) and Wistow (Chapter 7) all provide examples of the effect of electoral pressure on ideological commitments. However, the privatization case probably illustrates the point best. The failure to introduce more competition into the initial privatizations of the nationalized industry owed a great deal to the Government's belief that greater competition would reduce the attractiveness of and financial gain from the share issues to small investors and thus the putative electoral advantage to the Conservatives (see Marsh 1991).

In most of the areas examined in this volume, the Thatcher Government fulfilled its manifesto commitments. So, in the industrial relations field 12 of the 14 pledges the Government made in its three manifestos were enacted. Most legislation was passed as introduced; not surprisingly given that, if anything, executive dominance over the legislature grew during the 1980s (Marsh and Tant 1991). Once again, this reflects a general pattern; the Thatcher Government placed great stress upon the fulfilment of manifesto commitments.

Of course, the Government did not fulfil all its commitments. Even in the field of industrial relations, it failed to enact two pledges. In particular, Marsh (Chapter 3) shows how trade union opposition and strategic political judgements led the Government at the time to withdraw its commitment to reintroduce 'contracting in' to the political fund.

More important, party programmes/manifesto pledges were not the only source of legislation. For the policy areas examined in this volume, demographic changes, economic changes and political considerations provided important stimuli to the introduction of legislation. So, Bradshaw (Chapter 6) argues that, as far as social security policy was concerned, demographic trends had most influence on legislation and expenditure patterns. For health, Wistow (Chapter 7) shows that the combination of demographic trends and developments in medical technology exercised a continuous upward pressure on expenditure. For economic policy, the shift from monetarism to privatization during the second term was not informed by Conservative programmes or ideology but rather resulted from the failure of monetarism to reduce inflation and the political benefits which resulted from the limited experiment with privatization in the first term (Marsh 1991).

Of course, Mrs Thatcher herself was seen as a major source of policy innovation in the 1980s. King (1985: 98) describes her as 'unique among 20th-century prime ministers in having a policy agenda'. The list of policies with which she is associated range from football hooliganism and litter on the one hand to the community charge and EMU on the other. The ability to get policy items on the agenda, however, and, the capacity to put those policies into practice do not necessarily go together. Strong leadership and ineffective policies can co-exist. Doig and Hargrove (1987: 8), in a survey of leadership and innovation in American Government, argue that 'innovative programs are important, but strategies of implementation are at least equally critical'. In a more pessimistic vein, March (1984: 33) argues that

> When an organizational system is working well, variations in outcomes will be due largely to variables unrelated to variations in the attributes of top leaders. Where leadership affects variations in outcomes, the system is probably not functioning well.

In short, identifying leadership as a source of innovation tells us very little about the effectiveness of either the implementation of policies or the overall performance of government. Common sense may associate leadership and effectiveness, but in the study of policy-making a far wider range of factors has to be considered.

Policy was also its own cause. The Government introduced new policy initiatives and legislation to remedy some of the problems their own previous legislation had caused. This pattern is most clear in the area of local government finance where, although the desire to control local expenditure was a key Conservative manifesto commitment, the later legislation introduced was, for the most part, a reaction to the previous failure. As Rhodes (Chapter 4) argues, not surprisingly this repetitive legislation produced a policy mess.

It is often suggested that, after 1979, there was little role for interest groups in the creation of policy; that consultation became a thing of the past. This generalization is true of the policy areas examined here. Certainly, the representative organizations of local government were not consulted during the saga of the reform of local government finance. Nor were the trade unions consulted about the content of most of the Thatcher Government's industrial relations legislation; at 'best' they were called in to be told what the Government of the day intended.

Of course, there were exceptions. Indeed, McCormick (1991) has argued that the 'greening' of the Thatcher legislation is a direct result of the increased importance and influence of environmental pressure groups. However, Ward and Samways (Chapter 8) are highly sceptical both of the extent of the greening and of the influence of the environmental groups. Elsewhere, this volume does offer some examples of pressure group influence. Marsh (Chapter 3) shows that consultations between the Government and the unions led to the removal of an important clause from the 1984 Trade Union Act. Similarly, and perhaps more significantly, denationalization was not associated with increased competition, because the putative managements of the privatized companies successfully opposed Government attempts to liberalize the industries (see Marsh 1991: 467).

Two other institutions also influenced the shape of Government policy in some areas. First, EC policy had an increasing influence in the environment, agriculture and particularly economic policy areas. Second, in health, the Government's move to strengthen accountability within the NHS after 1982, which as Wistow (Chapter 7) shows represented a change in policy, came about in large part as a result of parliamentary pressure, more specifically, in response to criticisms of Government policy from the Social Services Select Committee.

It is clear that party ideology and manifesto commitments were only one source of policy change. Indeed, there are some areas in which policy change has little, if anything, to do with such factors. This is most noticeable in the field of foreign affairs and defence. Policy in these two areas has changed a great deal in the recent past but such changes are clearly related to international events. The Falklands War, the Gulf Crisis and, particularly, the collapse of the Eastern Bloc and the end of the Cold War have proved decisive influences at different periods and these factors had nothing to do with Thatcherite ideology or policy commitments.

Influencing policy outcomes

The policy pursued by the Thatcher Government and the legislative initiatives taken were not the only factors which affected policy outcomes. Other factors included, for example, economic instability and implementation problems. These factors helped prevent the Government from achieving its policy objectives; they are the subject of the next section. However, on occasions, such factors had a positive effect on Government policy. Consequently, it is often difficult to assess the relative importance of Government legislation in the achievement of policy objectives. The industrial relations case study clearly illustrates this problem. Many observers have argued that changes in the economic structure and processes – deindustrialization, rising unemployment, inflation – had more influence than the legislation on the declining position of trade unions. As Marsh argues, it is difficult to resolve this question; both sets of factors seem important. Clearly, we must be careful about assigning 'Thatcherism' a causal influence in every case where change in policy outcomes have occurred.

Why continuity? Problems of implementation

The Thatcher Government certainly set out to transform outcomes in a significant number of policy areas. Change was greater in some policy areas than in others. The aim of this section is to explain why there was a greater Thatcher effect in some policy areas than in others and, more generally, why the Thatcher effect was limited.

The evidence from our case studies suggests that the major cause of the Thatcher Government's failure to deliver more radical policy change, and more specifically greater change in policy outcomes, is the 'implementation gap'. The Government experienced major implementation problems. Some of these problems are common to all governments: conflicting objectives, insufficient information or limited resources. However, some problems were clearly exacerbated by the Thatcher Government's approach to policy-making. In particular, their rejection of consultation and negotiation almost inevitably led to implementation problems, because those groups/agencies affected by the policy, and who were not consulted, failed to co-operate, or comply, with the administration of policy.

As we indicated in the introduction, Sabatier (1986) suggests that change is more likely to the extent that the Government has:

1 clear, and consistent, objectives;
2 adequate causal theory or sufficient information about the problem and its causes;
3 appropriate policy tools and sufficient resources to implement the policy;
4 control over implementing officials;
5 the support of, or compliance from, the interest groups/agencies affected by the policy;
6 stable socioeconomic contexts which do not undermine political support.

Our case studies indicate that the Conservatives rarely enjoyed the luxury of all the information, competence and support and stability that this list implies. In other words, on different occasions and in relation to different policies, there were shortfalls throughout the policy process. The rest of this section will examine these shortfalls, though it will not examine implementation theory. Our concern here is to explain the implementation gaps in Thatcherite policy-making.

Clear and multiple objectives

The initial point to emphasize is that the achievement of objectives implies the setting of objectives. As we saw earlier, the Thatcher Government did concentrate its reforming zeal in a restricted number of areas. In other fields, like Northern Ireland, law and order, foreign affairs and defence they emphasized continuity rather than change. If a government is not committed to change, then such change is unlikely, although by no means impossible, as indicated by the changes in foreign affairs and defence policy.

Change is most likely to the extent that a government has clear, non-contradictory objectives. Housing policy provides the best example in the Thatcher era. The Government transformed the pattern of housing tenure and, in doing so, obtained considerable political advantage. There were few problems involved in the implementation of the 'right-to-buy' policy because the Government had one major aim, it had a clear idea about how that objective could be attained and those whom the policy affected either had no effective means of resisting (Labour local authorities) or whole-heartedly endorsed it (Conservative local authorities and council tenants). In this case, the policy-making process did operate in a top-down manner with little or no resistance to Government policy. Moreover, as Rhodes (1988: 393–4) has argued targeting, or a limited, focused policy intervention, is an effective strategy. It is exemplified by the right-to-buy policy. While it is clear that objectives should not be multiple and conflicting they should also be limited. However, even in the housing field, the Government's subsidiary aim of increasing the private rented sector was unsuccessful, in part at least because it conflicted with the primary aim of extending home ownership.

Elsewhere, the Thatcher Government was less successful in achieving its aims because it had multiple and conflicting objectives. For example, while privatization policy transformed the balance between the private and the public sector, it failed significantly to increase competition or efficiency. In large part, this outcome was a result of the successful pressure exerted by the potential mangement of the emerging privatized companies which prevented the Government breaking up the monopolies. The Government decided it needed the co-operation of the companies and their managements if privatization was to be successful. In effect, the Government, like others before it, put its political objectives first. It stood to gain politically, and particularly electorally, from a successful privatization; it needed the putative managements' support to help ensure success. At the same time, allowing the newly privatized companies to retain a monopoly, or near-monopoly, position made the offer of the shares more attractive, more successful and electorally advantageous to the Conservatives (Marsh 1991).

The Thatcher Government was frequently viewed as an ideological or conviction government and, therefore, different from its postwar predecessors. However, electoral considerations frequently undermined the Government's ideological predispositions. Two examples from the case studies presented here should suffice. In the environmental policy area, Ward and Samways (Chapter 8) argue that, while the Thatcher Government's ideological position pointed towards deregulation, public opinion supported more regulatory controls on polluters. Faced with this situation the Government compromised its ideology; it persisted with the existing policy of voluntary regulation or regulation by consent. Similarly, Wistow (Chapter 7) argues strongly that the Government was dissuaded from a more broad-based attempt to introduce market forces into the NHS because it feared the electoral consequences of such a policy.

Information, tools and resources

Governments rarely have perfect information about a problem. They may often have an incorrect assessment of its causes. Their choice of policy instruments may be inappropriate or they may use existing policy instruments inappropriately. The Government may not have the resources, financially or otherwise, to achieve its objectives. Each of these points is amply illustrated by our case studies.

The wrong model

If a government is operating with an inadequate theory or, more specifically, an inaccurate explanation of a problem, then, even if it introduces radical policies, they will not prove successful. Jackson (Chapter 2) presents the Thatcher Government's economic policy in this light. Their emphasis upon the expansion of the money supply as the cause of inflation was inadequate and inaccurate; in consequence, the policy they initially pursued, with its emphasis upon the control of the money supply and the establishment of a MTFS, was misguided and, indeed, damaging. In fact, Jackson (Chapter 2) goes as far as to claim that one of the main achievements of the Thatcher era was to provide an experiment for economists which indicated that the monetarists were wrong! On a less heroic note, Rhodes (Chapter 4) points out that the theory of accountability which underlined the community charge was defective in a number of respects. In particular, in so far as there was evidence, it showed that, throughout the postwar era, rate increases had affected local election results.

Inappropriate tools

Rhodes (Chapter 4) argues strongly that one of the major reasons for the 'policy mess' in the field of local government was the Thatcher Government's failure to use appropriate tools. The Conservatives did not have the policy instruments necessary to implement control over local budgets – they would have needed something like a system of prefects to supervise local authorities – nor did they create them. At the same time, they used existing policy instruments inappropriately. In particular, they failed to use the grant system to place local authorities under significant fiscal pressure. As a result, local authorities found it relatively easy to avoid the impact of the Government's policy.

In a number of other fields the Government's use of policy instruments was inconsistent, especially in the case of economic policy. Initially, the money supply was targeted and the MTFS was the major instrument through which control of the money supply was to be achieved and inflation reduced. By the second parliament, however, monetarism was on the wane, the MTFS had faded into the background and the use of interest rates to regulate the balance-of-payments and the exchange rate had become the chief instruments of economic policy. Privatization, which had barely featured in the first term, also became a key instrument. Allied to a tendency to create pre-election booms, such inconsistencies in economic policy did not increase business confidence or convince observers that the Government had the 'solution' to Britain's economic problems.

Resources

It is as well to bear in mind that governments are not omnipotent. In particular, in many policy areas they can only set the legislative, and perhaps the ideological, frameworks within which other actors interact. This sign–posting strategy (Rhodes 1988: 384) is exemplified by industrial relations. Here, major legislative change was achieved with little difficulty and the problem of compliance was bypassed by placing the initiative with managements, not Government. The experience of the Heath Government was not repeated. The Thatcher Government significantly reduced the political role of the unions which had relatively little influence over the evolution or administration of policy. However, there was no transformation in shopfloor industrial relations, a key objective of the Conservatives, because they are only indirectly influenced by government policy. Here, managements in most cases choose not to use Government legislation as a means of significantly undermining the position of unions on the shopfloor. Marsh (Chapter 3) explains this outcome but the key point is that, in some fields, a government can only, at best, have an indirect influence on a key policy outcome.

Control over street-level bureaucrats

The British administrative system is not designed to give the centre hands-on control over local officials. In a number of fields this non–executant tradition presented Thatcher's Conservative Government with problems. We have already touched upon them in relation to local government finance. As Rhodes (Chapter 4) shows, local government found ways to circumvent central government controls over local expenditure. The 1984 Rates Act gave the Secretary of State for the Environment power to determine an 'over-spending' council's maximum rate. In response, Treasurers in non-capped authorities advised their Councils to put up their rates as an insurance against future rate-capping. Given that any future rate-capping would be based on current rate levels, it was logical that local Treasurers would want to ensure that any cutting would be from a high base. As a result, local government expenditure rose rather than falling.

The health policy area reveals a number of similar examples. Indeed, Wistow (Chapter 7) argues that the NHS organizationl arrangements were almost designed to frustrate a top-down implementation strategy. Initially, the management structure was decentralized with weak vertical control and ten-uous horizontal linkage based upon consensus management teams. After 1982, the Government tried to move towards more hierarchical control with more sophisticated management structures. Nevertheless, the key constraint upon central control of implementation remained the brute fact that resource utiliza-tion in the NHS was, and is, effectively controlled by the medical profession which has almost absolute control over such matters. As Wistow (Chapter 7) shows, the profession consistently and trenchantly defended its autonomy and was unwilling to act as an agent of Thatcherite policy.

The power of interests

We have identified a number of important constraints upon the effective implementation of the Thatcher Government's policy. Nevertheless, it seems clear to us that, despite the Government's expressed desire to centralize power and authority and particularly to reduce the role of interest groups, it is the continued existence and power of policy networks which has acted as the greatest constraint on the development and implementation of radical policy (Rhodes 1988; Marsh and Rhodes 1992).

Most of the case studies in this book point to the continued importance of policy networks. Ward and Samways (Chapter 8) emphasize that British Governments cannot ignore the adverse reaction of powerful corporations and financial institutions to 'the polluter pays' approach of loading the costs of an environmental clean-up onto capital. Hence, they persist with an ineffective policy of voluntary regulation. Overall, Ward and Samways (Chapter 8) argue that the older policy networks persisted with only minor boundary adjustments and some trimming to current circumstances. They will continue to be a major barrier to change for the foreseeable future. Smith (Chapter 9) reaches a similar conclusion in the agriculture policy area. He suggests that little change occurred, despite the fact that existing agriculture policy was at odds with Thatcherite market ideology. This continuity resulted from the continuing importance of the agriculture policy community, supported and reinforced, as it was over the past decade, by the EC agriculture policy. This view is echoed by Peterson's (Chapter 10) analysis of EC policy, although he extends the point in two ways. First, he offers a number of other examples of policy networks which constrained the Thatcher Government's policy initiatives. Second, he points out that the influence of such groups and networks have been strengthened by their European level connections. He argues that domestic policy networks with important supra-national elements – for example the European Information Technology producer networks – limited the Thatcher Government's ability to direct policy from the top down.

In all these cases, continuity has been preserved, in part, because of the ability of the policy network to prevent radical policies being brought forward. Elsewhere in these case studies, we have examples of policy networks, or at least strong individual interests, preventing the successful implementation of policies once they were introduced. Once again, local government finance offers the best example, although Wistow's (Chapter 7) analysis of health policy suggests a similar pattern. Rhodes (Chapter 4) emphasizes that policy networks were an 'important brake on the Government's ambitions'. Specifically, he argues that the decision to downgrade the role of the Consultative Council on local government finance isolated the Treasury at the very time when the Government in question was introducing hands-on controls of local expenditure. It no longer had any point of contact with local authorities. The price for not consulting was high. Here, the Government tried to bypass the policy network at the policy formation stage, but the implementation of the policy was constrained by the actions of the members of that network.

A stable socioeconomic situation

In essence, we dealt with this point earlier. Demographic and socioeconomic changes clearly undermined the Thatcher Government's ability to fulfil its policy objectives. For example, it was impossible for the Government to cut social security expenditure with unemployment rising rapidly. However, in at least one major policy area – industrial relations – socioeconomic changes actually made it easier for the Government to achieve its ends. Here, rising unemployment and deindustrialization clearly reinforced the effect of legislation in reducing union power.

Conclusion

This volume suggests that much of the previous literature on policy change since 1979 tends to overestimate the Thatcher effect. Indeed, it was only in the area of housing that her Government achieved its policy and political aims. In the other three areas of fundamental change – industrial relations, privatization and local government – a great deal changed in terms of legislation but much less changed in terms of outcomes. If we take industrial relations as an example; the legislation severely reduced the immunities which unions and unionists enjoy but it did *not* transform shopfloor industrial relations which was, of course, the crucial area, given that a key aim of

Thatcherite policy was to change the balance between unions and employers in favour of the latter.

In fact, much of the previous literature overestimates the degree of change because they concentrate on legislative change rather than policy outcomes; the Conservatives had major implementation problems in areas like local government, industrial relations, privatization and health. In addition, most observers fail to recognize one of the great ironies of the Thatcher years. Obsessed with the need for strong government, an obsession which was reinforced by the widespread belief that its image of governing competence was a major reason for its electoral success, the Thatcher Government tried to end consultation with interest groups. However, there were reasons for such consultation; it did not merely reflect a weak government. It also meant a more informed government and one which had fewer problems of compliance from the interests affected by legislation because they had been consulted. By ending consultation, the Thatcher Government ensured it would have implementation problems. In effect, its style of policy-making helped render its policies less effective, one might say much less effective. The Thatcherite revolution is more a product of rhetoric than of the reality of policy impact.

References and bibliography

Adams, W. (1984). *The Effectiveness of the Wildlife and Countryside Act*. Oxford, British Association of Nature Conservation.

Agriculture Committee (1990). *The Public Expenditure White Paper*, HC 330. London, HMSO.

Allen, D. (1988). 'British foreign policy and West European cooperation', in P. Byrd (ed.) *British Foreign Policy Under Thatcher*. New York, St Martin's Press, pp. 35–53.

Allsopp, J. (1989). 'Health', in M. McCarthy (ed.) *The New Politics of Welfare*. London, Macmillan, pp. 53–81.

Alt, J.E. (1985). 'It may be a good way to run an oil company, but . . . Oil and the political economy of Thatcherism'. Mimeo.

Anderson, J.J. (1990). 'When markets and territory collide: Thatcherism and the politics of regional decline', *West European Politics,* 13(2), 234–57.

Argyris, C. (1962). *Interpersonal Competence and Organizational Effectiveness*. Homewood, Ill, Irwin.

Armstrong, H. (1989). 'Community regional policy', in J. Lodge (ed.) *The European Community and the Challenge of the Future*. London, Pinter, pp. 167–85.

Atkinson, A. and Micklewright, J. (1989). 'Turning the screw: benefits for the unemployed, 1979–1988', in A. Dilnot and I. Walker (eds) *The Economics of Social Security*. Oxford, Oxford University Press, pp. 17–51.

Audit Commission (for Local Authorities in England and Wales) (1984). *The Impact on Local Authorities' Economy, Efficiency and Effectiveness of the Block Grant Distribution System*. London, HMSO.

Audit Commission (1989). *Developing Community Care for Adults with a Mental Handicap*, Occasional Paper No. 9. London, HMSO.

Auerbach, S. (1987). 'Legal restraint of picketing: new trends; new tensions', *Industrial Law Journal,* 18, 227–44.

Bachelor, R.A. (1983). 'British economic policy under Margaret Thatcher, a mid term examination: a comment on Darby and Lothian', *Carnegie Rochester Conference Series on Public Policy*, 18, 208–20.

Bachrach, P. and Baratz, M.S. (1970). *Power and Poverty: Theory and Practice*. London, Oxford University Press.

Bacon, R. and Eltis, W. (1978). *Britain's Economic Problem: Too Few Producers*. London, Macmillan.

Ball, M. (1983). *Housing Policy and Economic Power*. London, Methuen.

Bardach, E. (1977). *The Implementation Game*. London, MIT Press.

Barnett, R.R., Barrow, M. and Smith, P. (1991). 'Representation without taxation: an empirical assessment of the validity of the accountability argument underlying the reform of local government finance in England', *Fiscal Studies*, 12(3), 30–46.

Barnett, R.R., Levaggi, R. and Smith, P. (1990). 'An assessment of the regional impact of the introduction of a community charge (or poll tax) in England', *Regional Studies*, 24, 289–97.

Barr, N. and Coulter, F. (1990). 'Social security: solutions or problems?', in J. Hills (ed.) *The State of Welfare*. Oxford, Clarendon, pp. 274–337.

Barrett, S. and Fudge, C. (1981). 'Examining the policy–action relationship', in S. Barrett and C. Fudge (eds) *Policy and Action*. London, Methuen, pp. 3–22.

Bassett, P. (1987). *Strike Free: New Industrial Relations in Britain*. Basingstoke, Macmillan.

Bassett, P. (1988). 'Non-unionisms' growing ranks', *Personnel Management*, March, 44–7.

BBC (1986a). *Analysis*. Radio 4, 13 January.

BBC (1986b). *On Your Farm*. Radio 4, 17 February.

BBC (1987). *Analysis*. Radio 4, 11 March.

Bean, C. (1987). 'The impact of North Sea oil', in R. Dornbush and R. Layard (eds) *The Performance of the British Economy*. Oxford, Oxford University Press, pp. 171–89.

Bean, C. and Gavosto, A. (1989). 'Outsiders, capacity shortages and unemployment in the United Kingdom', in J. Dreze, C. Bean and R. Layard (eds) *Europe's Unemployment Problem*. Cambridge, MA, MIT Press, pp. 86–102.

Bean, C. and Symons, J. (1989). 'Ten years of Mrs T', *NBER Macroeconomics Annual*. Cambridge, MA, MIT Press, pp. 13–60.

Beaumont, P. (1987). *The Decline of Trade Union Organisation*. London, Croom Helm.

Beechy, V. and Perkins, T. (1987). *A Matter of Hours*. Cambridge, Polity Press.

Bell, D.S. (ed.) (1985). *The Conservative Government, 1979–84: An Interim Report*. London, Croom Helm.

Berthoud, R. and Kempson, E. (1990). *Credit and Debt: First Findings*. London, Policy Studies Institute.

Beynon, J. (1989). 'Ten years of Thatcherism', *Social Studies Review*, 4(5), 170–8.

Biddiss, M. (1987). 'Thatcherism: concept and interpretation', in K. Minogue and M. Biddiss (eds) *Thatcherism: Personality and Politics*. London, Macmillan, pp. 1–20.

Blowers, A. (1987). 'Transition or transformation: environmental policy under Thatcher', *Public Administration*, 65, 227–95.

Blunden, J. and Curry, N. (1988). *A Future for Our Countryside*. Oxford, Blackwell.

Body, R. (1982). *Agriculture: the Triumph and the Shame*. London, Maurice Temple Smith.

Body, R. (1984). *Farming in the Clouds*. London, Maurice Temple Smith.

Booth, A. (1989). 'The bargaining structure of British establishments', *British Journal of Industrial Relations*, 27, 225–34.

Booth, P. and Crook, A.D.H. (eds) (1986). *Low Cost Home Ownership*. Aldershot, Gower.

Bow Group (1984). *Conservation and the Conservatives*. London, Bow Group.

Bradbeer, J. (1990). 'Environmental policy', in S.P. Savage and L. Robins (eds) *Public Policy Under Thatcher*. London, Macmillan, pp. 75–88.

Bradshaw, J. (1990). *Child Poverty and Deprivation in the UK*. London, National Children's Bureau.

Bradshaw, J. and Holmes, H. (1989). *Living on the Edge*. London, Tyneside Child Poverty Action Group.

Bramley, G. (1987). 'Horizontal disparities and equalization: a critique of "paying for local government" ', *Local Government Studies*, 13(1), 69–89.

Bramley, G., Le Grand, J. and Low, W. (1989). 'How far is the poll tax a "community charge": the implications of service usage evidence', *Policy and Politics*, 17, 187–205.

Bramley, G. and Stewart, M. (1981). 'Implementing public expenditure cuts', in S. Barrett and C. Fudge (eds) *Policy and Action*. London, Methuen, pp. 39–63.

Brittan, S. (1988). *A Restatement of Economic Liberalism*. London, Macmillan.

Brittan, S. (1989). 'The Thatcher Government's economic policy', in D. Kavanagh and S. Seldon (eds) *The Thatcher Effect*. Oxford, Oxford University Press, pp. 1–37.

Brown, W. and Wadhwani, S. (1990). 'The economic effects of industrial relations legislation since 1979', *National Institute of Economic Review*, February, 57–70.

Bruce-Gardyne, J. (1984). *Mrs Thatcher's First Administration*. London, Macmillan.

Buiter, W. and Miller, M. (1981). 'The Thatcher experiment: the first two years', *Brooking Papers on Economic Activity*, 2, 315–79.

Buiter, W. and Miller, M. (1983). 'Changing the rules: economic consequences of the Thatcher regime', *Brooking Papers on Economic Activity*, 2, 305–65.

Buiter, W. and Tobin, J. (1980). 'Fiscal and monetary policies, capital formation, and economic activity', in G.M. von Furstenberg (ed.) *The Government and Capital Formation*. Cambridge, MA, Ballinger, pp. 286–98.

Bulpitt, J.G. (1983). *Territory and Power in the United Kingdom*. Manchester, Manchester University Press.

Bulpitt, J. (1986). 'The discipline of the new democracy: Mrs Thatcher's domestic statescraft', *Political Studies*, 34, 19–39.

Bulpitt, J. (1988). 'Rational politicians and conservative statecraft in the open policy', in P. Byrd (ed.) *British Foreign Policy Under Thatcher*. Oxford, Philip Allan, pp. 180–205.

Burgess, T. and Travers, T. (1980). *Ten Billion Pounds: Whitehall's Takeover of the Town Halls*. London, Grant McIntyre.

Burns, T. (1988). 'The UK government's financial strategy', in W. Eltis and P. Sinclair (eds) *Keynes and Economic Policy: The Relevance of the General Theory after Fifty Years*. London, Macmillan, pp. 145–62.

Burton, I. and Drewry, G. (1990). 'Public legislation: a survey of the sessions 1983/1984 and 1984/1985', *Parliamentary Affairs*, 41, pp. 92–128.

Butt-Philip, A. and Baron, C. (1988). 'United Kingdom' in H. Siedentopf and J. Ziller (eds) *Making European Policies Work: The Implementation of Community Legislation in the Member States – II. National Reports*. Brussels and London, Sage, ch. 10.

Byrd, P. (1988). 'Introduction', in P. Byrd (ed.) *British Foreign Policy Under Thatcher.* Oxford, Philip Allan, pp. 1–7.

Cairncross, A.K. (1980). 'Evidence presented to Treasury and Civil Service Committee', *Memoranda on Monetary Policy,* HC 720. London, HMSO.

Carlisle, K. (1983). *Conserving the Countryside.* London, Conservative Political Centre.

Carter, N. (1991). 'Learning to measure performance: the use of indicators in organisation', *Public Administration,* 69, 85–102.

Caspari, C. and Neville Rolfe, E. (1989). *The Future of European Agriculture.* London, Economist Intelligence Unit.

Central Statistical Office (1990a). *Economic Trends,* No. 439. London, Her Majesty's Stationery Office (HMSO).

Central Statistical Office (1990b). *Family Expenditure Survey.* London, HMSO.

Chartered Institute of Public Finance and Accountancy (1989). *Local Government Trends 1989.* London, CIPFA.

Chartered Institute of Public Finance and Accountancy (1990). *Finance and General Statistics 1989/90.* London, CIPFA.

Child Poverty Action Group (CPAG). *Poverty: The Facts.* London, Child Poverty Action Group.

Clapham, D., Kemp, P. and Smith, S.J. (1990). *Housing and Social Policy.* London, Macmillan.

Claydon, T. (1989). 'Union deregulation in the 1980s', *British Journal of Industrial Relations,* 27, 214–24.

Clayton, H. (1979). 'Quiet revolution in food policy', *The Daily Telegraph,* 3 December.

Coates, D. (1989). *The Crisis of Labour.* Oxford, Philip Allan.

Cockburn, C. (1983). *Brothers.* London, Pluto.

Cockburn, C. (1985). *Machinery of Dominance.* London, Pluto.

Cole, J. (1987). *The Thatcher Years.* London, BBC Books.

Coleman, D.A. (1989). 'The new housing policy – a critique', *Housing Studies.* 4, 44–57.

Commission of the European Community (1987). *European Economy.* Brussels, Commission of the European Communities.

Committee of Public Accounts (1985). *Operation of the Rate Support Grant System.* 7th Report, Session 1985–86, HC 47. London, HMSO.

Conservative Party (1979). *The Conservative Manifesto.* London, Conservative Party Central Office.

Conservative Party (1983). *The Conservative Manifesto.* London, Conservative Central Office.

Conservative Party (1987). *The Conservative Manifesto: The Next Moves Forward.* London, Conservative Central Office.

Consumers in the European Community Group (1984). *Enough is Enough.* London, Consumers in the European Community Group.

Conway, J. and Kemp, P.A. (1985). *Bed and Breakfast: Slum Housing of the Eighties.* London, SHAC.

Cooke, A. (1989). *The Revival of Britain: Mrs Thatcher's Speeches 1975–1988.* London, Arum Press.

Cooper, R.N. (1985). 'Economic interdependence and coordination of economic policies', in R.W. Jones and P.B. Kenen (eds) *Handbook of International Economics,* vol. 2. Amsterdam, Elsevier, pp. 1225–43.

Court of Auditors (1987). 'Special Report No. 2/87 on quota/additional levy system in the milk sector accompanied by the replies of the commission', *Official Journal of the European Communities,* C266, 5 October.

Coutts, K. and Godley, W. (1989). 'The British economy under Thatcher', *The Political Quarterly,* 60, 137–51.

Coutts, K., Godley, W. *et al.* (1990). *Britain's Economic Problems and Policies in the 1990s,* Economic Study No. 6. London, Institute for Public Policy Research.

Cox, G., Lowe, P. and Winter, M. (1986). 'Agriculture and conservation in Britain: a Policy Community Under Siege', in G. Cox, P. Lowe and M. Winter (eds) *Agriculture: People and Policies.* London, Allen & Unwin, pp. 169–98.

Cox, G., Lowe, P. and Winter, M. (1989a). 'The farm crisis in Britain', in D. Goodman and M. Redclift (eds) *The International Farm Crisis.* London, Macmillan, pp. 113–34.

Cox, G., Lowe, P. and Winter, M. (1989b). 'Agriculture regulation and the politics of milk production', in C. Crouch and R. Dore (eds) *Corporatism and Accountability: Organised Interests in British Politics.* Oxford, Clarendon Press, pp. 169–98.

Cox, G., Lowe, P. and Winter, H. (1989c). 'Agriculture and the state: must the dismantling of productivism compromise corporatism?'. *Paper presented to ESRC Conference on Corporatism and Accountability,* 29–31 March. Newnham College, Cambridge.

Crafts, N. (1988). 'British economic growth before and after 1979: a review of the evidence', *Centre for Economic Policy Review Discussion Paper,* no. 292.

Crewe, I. (1988). 'Has the electorate become Thatcherite?', in R. Skidelsky (ed.) *Thatcherism.* London, Chatto & Windus, pp. 25–49.

Crewe, I. and Searing, D. (1988). 'Ideological change in the British Conservative Party', *American Political Science Review,* 82, 361–84.

Crook, A.D.H. (1986). 'Privatisation of housing and the impact of the Conservative government's initiatives on low cost home ownership and private renting between 1979 and 1984 in England and Wales. Part 4: Private Renting', *Environment and Planning A,* 18, 1029–37.

Crook, A.D.H. *et al.* (1991). *Rented Housing and the Business Expansion Schemes.* York, Joseph Rowntree Foundation.

Crouch, C. (1986). 'Conservative industrial relations policy: towards labour exclusion', in O. Jacobi *et al. Economic Crisis, Trade Unions and the State.* London, Croom Helm, pp. 131–58.

Curwen, P.J. (1986). *Public Enterprise: A Modern Approach.* Brighton, Wheatsheaf.

Dalton, R.J. and Eichenberg, R. (1990). 'Europeans and the European Community: the dynamics of public support for European integration'. *Paper presented at the Annual Meeting of the American Political Science Association,* August. San Francisco.

de La Serre, F. (1987). *La Grande-Bretagne et al Communaute Europeenne.* Paris, Press Universitaires de France, Coll, Perspectives Internationales.

Department of the Environment (1987). *Housing: The Government's Proposals,* Cm 214. London, HMSO.

Department of the Environment (1990). *Housing and Construction Statistics 1979 to 1989.* London, HMSO.

Department of the Environment (1991). *Annual Report 1991.* London, HMSO.

Department of Health and Social Security (1971). *Better Services for the Mentally Handicapped,* Cmnd 4683. London, HMSO.

Department of Health and Social Security (1976a). *Better Services for Mentally Ill*, Cmnd 6233. London, HMSO.

Department of Health and Social Security (1976b). *Priorities for Health and Personal Social Services in England*. London, HMSO.

Department of Health and Social Security (1977). *The Way Forward*. London, HMSO.

Department of Health and Social Security (1979a). *Patients First*. London, HMSO.

Department of Health and Social Security (1979b). *Local Management, Not Centralised Bureaucracy: Mr Patrick Jenkin Identifies the Needs of the NHS*. Press Release No. 79/133, 30 May.

Department of Health and Social Security (1979c). *The NHS and the Future*. Press Release No. 79/153, 20 June.

Department of Health and Social Security (1980). *Inequalities in Health: Report of a Research Working Group Chaired by Sir Douglas Black*. London, HMSO.

Department of Health and Social Security (1981). *Care in Action*. London, HMSO.

Department of Health and Social Security (1985). *The Reform of Social Security: Programme for Action*, Cmnd 9691. London, HMSO.

Department of Health and Social Security (1988). *Public Health in England*, Cm 289. London, HMSO.

Department of Social Security (1990a). *Children Come First*, Cm 1264. London, HMSO.

Department of Social Security (1990b). *The Way Ahead*, Cm 917. London, HMSO.

Department of Social Security (1991). *The Government's Expenditure Plans 1991–92 to 1993–94*, Cm 1514. London, HMSO.

Dex, S. (1987). *Women's Occupational Mobility*. London, Macmillan.

Disney, R. (1990). 'Explanation of the decline in trade union density in Britain: an appraisal', *British Journal of Industrial Relations*, 28, 165–78.

Doig, J.W. and Hargrove, E.C. (1987). 'Leadership and political analysis', in J.W. Drewry and E.C. Hargrove (eds) *Leadership and Innovation*. Baltimore, Johns Hopkins Press, pp. 1–23.

Dornbusch, R., Blanchard, D. and Layard, R. (1986). *Restoring Europe's Prosperity*. Cambridge, MA, MIT Press.

Dudley, G. (1983). 'The road lobby: a declining force?', in D. Marsh (ed.) *Pressure Politics*. London, Junction Books, pp. 104–28.

Dunleavy, P., Gamble, A. and Peele, G. (eds) (1990). *Developments in British Politics 3*. London, Macmillan.

Dunn, S. and Gennard, J. (1984). *The Closed Shop in British Industry*. Basingstoke, Macmillan.

East, R., Power, H. and Thomas, P. (1985). 'The death of mass picketing', *Journal of Law and Society*, 12, 305–19.

The Economist (1989) 'Did someone say go', *The Economist*, 7 October, pp. 15–16.

Edwards, C. and Heery, E. (1989). 'Recession in the public sector: industrial relations in freightliner, 1981–1985', *British Journal of Industrial Relations*, 27, 57–71.

Efficiency Unit (1988). *Improving Management in Government: The Next Steps*. London, HMSO.

Elmore, R. (1978). 'Organisational Models of Social Program Implementation', *Public Policy*, 28, 185–228.

Elmore, R. (1982). 'Backward mapping', in W. Williams (ed.) *Studying Implementation*. Chatham, NJ, Chatham House, pp. 18–35.

Esam, P. and Oppenheim, C. (1989). *A Charge on the Community*. London, Child Poverty Action Group/Local Government Information Unit.

European Commission (1985). *Perspectives for the Common Agricultural Policy*. Com (85) 333, Brussels, Commission of the EEC.

Evans, S. (1985). 'The use of injunctions in industrial disputes', *British Journal of Industrial Relations*, 23, 131–7.

Evans, S. (1988). 'The use of injunctions in industrial disputes 1984–April 1987', *The British Journal of Industrial Relations*, 26, 419–35.

Finer, S.E. (1987). 'Thatcherism and British political history', in K. Minogue and M. Biddiss (eds) *Thatcherism: Personality and Politics*. London, Macmillan, pp. 127–40.

Flynn, N., Leach, S. and Vielba, C. (1985). *Abolition or Reform: The GLC and the Metropolitan County Councils*. London, Allen & Unwin.

Forrest, R. and Murie, A. (1986). 'Marginalisation and subsidised individualism', *International Journal of Urban and Regional Research*, 10, 46–65.

Forrest, R. and Murie, A. (1988). *Selling the Welfare State*. London, Routledge.

Forrest, R., Murie, A. and Williams, P. (1990). *Home Ownership*. London, Methuen.

Forrester, A., Stewart, L. and Pauley, R. (1985). *Beyond Our Ken: A Guide to the Battle for London*. London, Fourth Estate.

Foster, C.D. (1986). 'Reforming local government finance', *Public Money*, 6(2), 17–22.

Frankel, J. (1985). 'Portfolio crowding-out empirically estimated', *Quarterly Journal of Economics*, 100, 1041–65.

Freeman, R. and Pelletier, J. (1990). 'The impact of industrial relations legislation on British Union density', *British Journal of Industrial Relations*, 28, 141–64.

Friedman, M. (1969). *A Programme for Monetary Stability*. New York, Fordham University Press.

Friends of the Earth (eds) (1990). *How Green is Britain: The Government's Environmental Record*. London, Hutchinson.

Gamble, A. (1988). *The Free Economy and the Strong State: The Politics of Thatcherism*. London, Macmillan.

Gardner, B. (1987). 'The common agricultural policy: the political obstacles to reform', *The Political Quarterly*, 58, 167–79.

Gardner, B. (1990). 'The cap that does not fit', *The Guardian*, 26 September.

George, S. (1990a). 'Commentary: Britain and the European Community', *European Access*, 6, December, 7–9.

George, S. (1990b). *An Awkward Partner: Britain in the European Community*. Oxford, Oxford University Press.

Glendinning, C. and Millar, J. (eds) (1987). *Women and Poverty in Britain*. Brighton, Wheatsheaf.

Gibson, J. (1985). 'Why block grant failed', in S. Ranson, G. Jones and K. Walsh (eds) *Between Centre and Locality*. London, Allen & Unwin, pp. 58–80.

Gibson, J. (1990). *The Politics and Economics of the Poll Tax: Mrs Thatcher's Downfall*. Warley, West Midlands, EMAS Ltd.

Godley, W.A.H. (1989). 'The British economy during the Thatcher era', *Economics*, Winter, 158–62.

Goldsmith, E. and Hilyard, N. (eds) (1986). *Green Britain or Industrial Wasteland*. Cambridge, Polity.

Goodhart, C.A.E. (1984). *Monetary Theory and Practice – The UK Experience*. London, Macmillan.

Goodman, D. and Redclift, M. (1989). 'Introduction: the international farm crisis', in D. Goodman and M. Redclift (eds) *The International Farm Crisis*. London, Macmillan, pp. 1–22.

Grahl, J. and Teague, P. (1988). 'The British Labour Party and the European Community', *The Political Quarterly*, 59, 72–85.

Grant, D. (1987). 'Unions and the political fund ballots', *Parliamentary Affairs*, 40, 57–72.

Green, F. (ed.) (1989). *The Reconstruction of the UK Economy*. Hemel Hempstead, Harvester Wheatsheaf.

Gregory, F.E.C. (1983). *Dilemmas of Government: Britain and the European Community*. Oxford, Martin Robertson.

Gregory, M., Lobban, P. and Thomson, A. (1985). 'Wage settlements in manufacturing 1979–84: evidence form the CBI pay databank', *British Journal of Industrial Relations*, 23, 339–57.

Gregory, M., Lobban, P. and Thomson, A. (1987). 'Pay settlements in manufacturing industry, 1979–84', *Oxford Bulletin of Economics and Statistics*, 49, 129–50.

Greve, J. (1990). *Homelessness in Britain*. York, Joseph Rowntree Foundation.

Griffiths, R. (1983). *Report of the NHS Management Enquiry*. London, Department of Health and Social Security (DHSS).

Griffiths, R. (1991). *Seven Years of Progression in General Management in the NHS*. Management Lecture No. 3. London, Audit Commission.

Grubb, M. (1990). *Energy Policies and the Greenhouse Effect Volume 1*. Aldershot, Royal Institute of International Affairs/Dartmouth.

Hahn, F. (1988). 'On market economics', in R. Skidelsky (ed.) *Thatcherism*. Oxford, Basil Blackwell, pp. 107–24.

Haigh, N. (1986). 'Devolved responsibility and centralisation: effects of EEC environmental policy', *Public Administration*, 64, 197–207.

Ham, C. and Hill, M. (1984). *The Policy Process in the Modern Capitalist State*. Brighton, Wheatsheaf Books.

Hamer, M. (1987). *Wheels Within Wheels*, 2nd edn. London, Routledge & Kegan Paul.

Hamnett, C. (1984). 'Housing the two nations', *Urban Studies*, 21, 389–400.

Hamnett, C. (1987). 'Conservative Government housing policy 1979–85', in W. Van Vliet (ed.) *Housing Markets and Policies Under Fiscal Austerity*. Westport, Greenwood Press, pp. 203–20.

Harloe, M. and Paris, C. (1984). 'The decollectivisation of consumption', in I. Szelenyi (ed.) *Cities in Recession*. Beverly Hills, Sage, pp. 70–98.

Harrison, S. (1988). *Managing the National Health Service: Shifting the Frontier?* London, Chapman & Hall.

Harrison, S. *et al.* (1989a). *General Management in the National Health Service*. Nuffield Reports No. 2, Nuffield Institute for Health Services Studies, University of Leeds.

Harrison, S. *et al.* (1989b). 'General management and medical autonomy in the national health service', *Health Services Management Research*, 2(1), 38–46.

Harrison, S., Hunter, D.J. and Pollitt, C. (1990). *The Politics of British Health Policy*. London, Unwin Hyman.

Harrop, J. (1989). *The Political Economy of Integration in the European Community*. Aldershot, Edward Elgar.

Hayek, F. (1944). *The Road to Serfdom*. Chicago, University of Chicago Press.

Haywood, S. and Alaszewski, A. (1980). *Crisis in the Health Service*. London, Croom Helm.

Hebbert, M. and Travers, T. (eds) (1988). *The London Government Handbook*. London, Cassell.

Hill, C. (1983). 'Britain: a convenient schizophrenia', in C. Hill (ed.) *National Policies and European Political Cooperation.* London, Allen & Unwin for Royal Institute of International Affairs, pp. 19–33.

Hill, M. (1982). 'The role of the British Alkali and Clean Air Inspectorate in air pollution control', *Policy Studies Journal*, 11, 165–74.

Hill, M., Aaronovitch, S. and Baldock, D. (1989). 'Non-decision making in pollution control in Britain: nitrate pollution, the EEC drinking water directive and agriculture', *Policy and Politics*, 17, 227–40.

Hills, J. (ed.) (1990). *The State of Welfare.* Oxford, Clarendon Press.

Hills, J. (1991). *Unravelling Housing Finance.* Oxford, Oxford University Press.

Hills, J. and Mullings, B. (1990). 'Housing: a decent home for all at a price within their means', in J. Hills (ed.) *The State of Welfare.* London, Clarendon Press, pp. 135–205.

Hjern, B. and Hull, C. (1982). 'Implementation research as empirical constitutionalism', *European Journal of Political Research*, 10, 105–16.

HMSO (Her Majesty's Stationery Office) (1976). *Report of the Committee of Inquiry into Local Government Finance*, Cmnd 6453. London, HMSO.

HMSO (1977). *Local Government Finance*, Cmnd 6813. London, HMSO.

HMSO (1981). *Alternatives to the Domestic Rate*, Cmnd 8449. London, HMSO.

HMSO (1983a). *Rates*, Cmnd 9008. London, HMSO.

HMSO (1983b). *Streamlining the Cities*, Cmnd 9714. London, HMSO.

HMSO (1984). 'Europe – the future', *Journal of Common Market Studies*, 23(1), 74–81.

HMSO (1986). *Paying for Local Government*, Cmnd 9714. London, HMSO.

HM Treasury (1984). *The Next Ten Years: Public Expenditure and Taxation into the 1990s*, Cmnd 9189. London, HMSO.

HM Treasury (1990a). *The Government's Expenditure Plans 1990–91 and 1992–93*, Cm 1003. London, HMSO.

HM Treasury (1990b). *The Government's Expenditure Plans 1990–91 to 1992–93 Department of Social Security*, Cm 1014. London, HMSO, ch. 14.

Hogwood, B. (1987). *From Crisis to Complacency.* Oxford, Oxford University Press.

Hogwood, B. and Gunn, L. (1984). *Policy Analysis for the Real World.* Oxford, Oxford University Press.

Holmans, A.E. (1987). *Housing Policy in Britain.* London, Croom Helm.

Holmans, A.E. (1991). 'The 1977 National Housing Policy review in retrospect', *Housing Studies*, 6, 206–19.

Holmes, M. (1985). *The First Thatcher Government, 1979–83.* Brighton, Wheatsheaf.

House of Commons, Social Services Committee (1980). *The Government's White Papers on Public Expenditure: The Social Services.* Third Report, Session 1979–80, HC 702. London, HMSO.

House of Commons, Committee of Public Accounts (1981). *Financial Control and Accountability in the National Health Service.* Seventeenth Report, Session 1980–81, HC 255. London, HMSO.

House of Commons, Social Services Committee (1986). *Public Expenditure on the Social Services.* Fourth Report, Session 1985–86, HC 387. London, HMSO.

House of Commons, Social Services Committee (1988). *Public Expenditure on Social Services.* Sixth Report, Session 1987–88, HC 687. London, HMSO.

House of Commons (1990). *National Insurance Fund Long Term Financial Estimates: Report of the Government Actuary*, HC 582. London, HMSO.

House of Commons, Health Committee (1991a). *Public Expenditure on Health Matters: Memorandum Received from the Department of Health*. Session 1990–91, HC 408. London, HMSO.

House of Commons, Health Committee (1991b). 'Minutes of evidence', *Public Expenditure on Health and Personal Social Services*. Session 1990–91. London, HMSO.

House of Commons, Social Security Committee (1991c). 'Minutes of evidence', *The Financing of Private Residential and Nursing Home Fees*. Session 1990–91, HC 421–iii. London, HMSO.

House of Commons, Health Committee (1991d). 'Minutes of evidence', *Public Expenditure on Health and Social Services*. Session 1990–91, HC 229–ii. London, HMSO.

House of Lords, Select Committee on the European Communities (1983). 'Minutes of evidence', *The 1983–84 Farm Price Proposals*, HL 82–11. London, HMSO.

House of Lords, Select Committee on the European Communities (1984a). *The 1984–85 Farm Price Proposals*, HL 153–1. London, HMSO.

House of Lords, Select Committee on the European Communities (1984b). 'Minutes of evidence', *The 1984–85 Farm Price Proposals*, HL 153–11. London, HMSO.

House of Lords, Select Committee on the European Communities (1985a). *Fontainebleau and After: Decisions on the Future of Financing the Community*, HL 66. London, HMSO.

House of Lords, Select Committee on the European Communities (1985b). *The 1985–86 Farm Price Proposals*, HL 112. London, HMSO.

House of Lords, Select Committee on the European Communities (1986). *1986–87 Farm Price Policy*, HL 107. London, HMSO.

House of Lords, Select Committee on the European Communities (1988). *Farm Price Review 1988–89*, HL 83. London, HMSO.

House of Lords, Select Committee on the European Communities (1989). *Farm Price Proposals 1989–90*, HL 34. London, HMSO.

House of Lords, Select Committee on the European Communities (1990). *Farm Price Proposals 1990–91*, HL 34. London, HMSO.

Howarth, R. (1985). *Farming for Farmers*. London, Institute of Economic Affairs.

Howe, G. *et al.* (1977). *The Right Approach to the Economy*. London, Conservative Party Policy Document.

Howe, G. (1984). 'The future of the European Community: Britain's approach to the negotiations', *International Affairs*, 60(2), 187–92.

Huhne, C. (1986). 'Brussels heads for a budget crisis', *The Guardian*, 4 December.

Ingram, P. and Cahill, J. (1989). 'Pay determination in private manufacturing', *Employment Gazette*, June, 281–5.

Institute of Fiscal Studies (1990). *Low Income Families 1979–83*. Mimeo.

Institute of Health Service Management (1988). *Working Party on Alternative Delivery and Funding of Health Services, Final Report*. London, Institute Health Service Management.

Jackman, R. (1982). 'Does the Government need to control the total of local government spending?', *Local Government Studies*, 8(3), 75–90.

Jackson, P.M. (ed.) (1981). *Government Policy Initiatives 1979/80: Some Case Studies in Public Administration*. London, Royal Institute of Public Administration.

Jackson, P.M. (1985a). 'Perspectives on practical monetarism', in P.M. Jackson (ed.) *Implementing Government Policy Initiatives: The Thatcher Administration, 1979–83*. London, Royal Institute of Public Administration, pp. 33–67.

Jackson, P.M. (ed.) (1985b). *Implementing Government Policy Initiatives: The Thatcher Administration, 1979–83*. London, Royal Institution of Public Administration.

Jackson, P.M. (1990a). 'Public sector deficits and the money supply', in T. Bandyo-padhyay and S. Ghatak (eds) *Current Issues in Monetary Economics*. London, Harvester Wheatsheaf, pp. 113–41.

Jackson, P.M. (1990b). *The Reform of Local Government Finance in Scotland*. London, Chartered Institute of Public Finance and Accountants.

James, S. (1990). 'A streamlined city: the broken pattern of London government', *Public Administration*, 68, 493–504.

Jenkin, P. (1979a). 'Jenkin on cuts', *Social Work Today*, 11(9), 10.

Jenkin, P. (1979b). *Speech to Personal Social Services Conference*, 21 November.

Jenkins, P. (1988). *Mrs Thatcher's Revolution*. London, Cape.

Jessop, B. *et al.* (1988). *Thatcherism*. Cambridge, Polity Press.

Jessop, B., Bennett, K. and Bromley, S. (1990). 'Farewell to Thatcherism?', *New Left Review*, 179, January/February, 81–102.

Johnson, C. (1986). 'Britain and the European Monetary System', *The World Today*, 42 (10), 174–6.

Johnston, K. (1987). *Into the Void*. London, Corgi.

Jones, G. and Stewart, J. (1983). *The Case for Local Government*, London, Allen & Unwin.

Joshi, H. (1989). 'The changing form of women's economic dependency', in H. Joshi (ed.) *The Changing Population of Britain*. Oxford, Basil Blackwell, pp. 157–76.

Jowell, R., Witherspoon, S. and Brook, L. (eds) (1990). *British Social Attitudes. The 7th Report*. Aldershot, Gower.

Judge, D. (1986). 'The British Government, European union and EC institutional reform', *The Political Quarterly*, 57, 321–8.

Kaldor, N. (1980). 'Evidence presented to Treasury and Civil Service Committee', *Memoranda on Monetary Policy*, HC 720. London, HMSO.

Kavanagh, D. (1987). *Thatcherism and British Politics*. Oxford, Oxford University Press.

Kavanagh, D. and Seldon, A. (eds) (1989). *The Thatcher Effect*. Oxford, Oxford University Press.

Keliher, L. (1990). 'Core executive decision making on high technology issues: the case of the Alvey Report', *Public Administration*, 68, 61–82.

Kelly, J. (1987). *Labour and the Unions*. London, Verso.

Kemp, P.A. (1988). *The Future of Private Renting*. Salford, University of Salford.

Kemp, P.A. (1989). 'The demunicipalisation of rented housing', in M. Brenton and C. Ungerson (eds) *Social Policy Review 1988–89*. London, Longman, pp. 46–66.

Kemp, P.A. (1990). 'Shifting the balance between State and market: the reprivatisation of rented housing', *Environment and Planning A*, 22, 793–810.

Kemp, P.A. (1991). 'From solution to problem? Council housing and the development of national housing policy', in S. Lowe and D. Hughes (eds) *A New Century of Social Housing*. Leicester, Leicester University Press, pp. 44–61.

King, A. (1975). 'Overload: problems of governing in the 1970s', *Political Studies*, xxiii, 289–96.

King, A. (1985). 'Margaret Thatcher: the style of a prime minister', in A. King (ed.) *The British Prime Minister*, 2nd edn. London, Macmillan, pp. 96–140.

King A. (1988). 'Margaret Thatcher as a political leader', in R. Skidelsky (ed.) *Thatcherism*. London, Chatto & Windus, pp. 51–64.

King, D.S. (1987). *The New Right: Politics, Markets and Citizenship*. London, Macmillan.

King's Fund Institute (1988). *Health Finance: Assessing the Options*. London, King's Fund Institute.

King's Fund Institute (1989). *Efficiency in the National Health Service*, Occasional Paper 2. London, King's Fund Institute.

Klein, R.E. (1981). 'The Health Service', in P.M. Jackson (ed.) *Government Policy Initiatives, 1979–81*. London, Royal Institute of Public Administration, pp. 161–80.

Klein, R.E. (1983). *The Politics of the National Health Service*. London, Longman.

Klein, R.E. (1985). 'Health policy 1979–83: the retreat from ideology?' in P.M. Jackson (ed.) *Implementing Government Policy Initiatives: The Thatcher Administration 1979–83*. London, Royal Institute of Public Admnistration, pp. 189–207.

Klein, R.E. (1989). *The Politics of the National Health Service*, 2nd edn. London, Longman.

Labour Party (1958). *Prosper the Plough*. London, Labour Party.

Laing, W. (1990). *Review of Private Health Care 1990*. London, Laing & Buisson.

Lawson, N. (1985). *Britain's Economy – A Mid Term Report*. London, Conservative Political Centre.

Layard, R. and Nickell, S. (1986). 'Unemployment in Britain', *Economica*, 53, 121–70.

Layard, R. and Nickell, S. (1989). 'The Thatcher miracle?', *American Economic Review* (papers and proceedings), 79(2), 215–19.

Leach, S. and Davis, H. (1990). 'Introduction', *Local Government Studies*, 16(3), 1–11.

Lean, G. (1984). 'Thatcher orders U-turn for farming', *Observer*, 14 October.

Leggett, J. (1990). *Global Warming: The Greenpeace Report*. Oxford, Oxford University Press.

Le Grand, J. (1990). 'The state of welfare', in J. Hills (ed.) *The State of Welfare*. Oxford, Clarendon Press, pp. 338–62.

Le Grand, J., Winter, D. and Woolley, F. (1990). 'The National Health Service', in J. Hills (ed.) *The State of Welfare*. Oxford, Clarendon Press, pp. 88–134.

Levy, R. (1990). 'That obscure object of desire: budgetary control in the European Community', *Public Administration*, 68, 191–206.

Lindblom, C.E. (1988). *Democracy and the Market System*. Oslo, Norwegian University Press.

Lipsky, M. (1978). 'The assault on human services: street level bureaucrats, accountability and the fiscal crisis', in S. Greer, D. Hedlund and J.L. Gibson (eds) *Accountability in Urban Society*. London, Sage, pp. 15–38.

Longstreth, F. (1988). 'From corporatism to dualism? Thatcherism and the climacteric of British trade unions in the 1980s', *Political Studies*, xxxvi, 413–32.

Loughlin, M. (1986). *Local Government in the Modern State*. London, Sweet & Maxwell.

Lovins, A. (1990). 'The role of energy efficiency', in J. Leggett (ed.) *Global Warming*. Oxford, Oxford University Press, pp. 193–223.

Lowe, P. (1983). 'A question of bias', *Town and Country Planning Review*, May, 132–4.

Lowe, P. *et al.* (1986). *Countryside Conflicts*. London, Gower.

Lowe, P. and Flynn, A. (1989). 'Environmental politics and policy in the '80s', in J. Mohan (ed.) *The Political Geography of Contemporary Britain*. London, Macmillan, pp. 225–79.

Lowe, P. and Goyder, J. (1983). *Environmental Groups in Politics*. London, George Allen & Unwin.

Lowe, S. and Watson, S. (1989). *Equity Withdrawal from the Housing Market 1982–88*, Findings No. 5. York, Joseph Rowntree Foundation.

McConnell, S. and Takla, L. (1990). *Mrs Thatcher's Trade Union Legislation: Has it Reduced Strikes?* London, Centre for Labour Economics, LSE, Discussion Paper 374, January.

McCormick, J. (1991). *British Politics and the Environment.* London, Earthscan.

McIlroy, J. (1988). *Trade Unions in Britain Today.* Manchester, Manchester University Press.

McInnes, J. (1987). *Thatcherism at Work: Industrial Relations and Economic Change.* Milton Keynes, Open University Press.

McKeown, T. (1976). *The Role of Medicine: Dream, Mirage or Nemesis?* Oxford, Nuffield Provincial Hospitals Trusts.

Maclennan, D. and Gibb, K. (1990). 'Housing finance and subsidies in Britain after a decade of Thatcherism', *Urban Studies*, 27, 905–18.

Maclennan, D., Gibb, K. and More, A. (1991). *Fairer Subsidies, Faster Growth.* York, Joseph Rowntree Foundation.

Malpass, P. (1990). *Reshaping Housing Policy.* London, Routledge.

Malpass, P. and Murie, A. (1990). *Housing Policy and Practice,* 3rd edn. London, Macmillan.

March, J.G. (1984). 'How we talk and how we act: administrative theory and administrative life', in T.J. Sergiovanni and J.E. Corbally (eds) *Leadership and Organization Culture.* Urbana, Ill, University of Illinois Press, pp. 18–35.

Marquand, D. (1988). 'The paradoxes of Thatcherism', in R. Skidelsky (ed.) *Thatcherism.* Oxford, Basil Blackwell, pp. 159–72.

Marsh, D. (ed.) (1983). *Pressure Politics.* London, Junction Books.

Marsh, D. (1990). 'Public opinion, trade unions and Mrs Thatcher', *British Journal of Industrial Relations*, 28, 57–65.

Marsh, D. (1991). 'Privatisation under Mrs Thatcher', *Public Administration*, 69, 459–80.

Marsh, D. (1992). *The New Politics of British Trade Unions: Union Power and the Thatcher Legacy.* Basingstoke, Macmillan.

Marsh, D. and Rhodes, R.A.W. (1989). 'Implementing Thatcherism: a policy perspective'. *Essex Papers in Politics and Government,* No. 62.

Marsh, D. and Rhodes, R.A.W. (1992). *Policy Networks in British Government.* Oxford, Oxford University Press, in press.

Marsh, D. and Tant, T. (1989). 'There is no alternative: Mrs Thatcher and the British political tradition', *Essex Paper in Politics and Government,* no. 69.

Marsh, J. (1979). 'UK attitudes to CAP', in M. Tracy and I. Hodac (eds) *Prospects for Agriculture in the European Community.* Bruges, De Temple/Templehoff, pp. 364–70.

Martin, C. and Roberts, C. (1984). *Women and Employment: A Lifetime Perspective.* London: HMSO.

Matthews, K. and Minford, P. (1987). 'Mrs Thatcher's economic policies 1979–1987', *Economic Policy*, 5, 57–102.

Maynard, G. (1988). *The Economy Under Mrs Thatcher.* Oxford, Basil Blackwell.

Mazmanian, D. and Sabatier, P. (1989). *Implementation and Public Policy*, 2nd edn. Lanham, University Press of America.

Meadows, W.J. (1981). 'Local Government', in P. Jackson (ed.) *Government Policy Initiatives 1979–80: Some Case Studies in Public Administration.* London, Royal Institute of Public Administration, pp. 42–62.

Merrett, S. (1979). *State Housing in Britain.* London, Routledge & Kegan Paul.

Merrett, S. with Gray, F. (1982). *Owner-Occupation in Britain.* London, Routledge & Kegan Paul.

Metcalf, D. (1989). 'Water notes dry up: the impact of the Donovan reform proposals and Thatcherism at work on labour productivity in British manufacturing industry', *British Journal of Industrial Relations,* 27, 1–31.

Metcalf, D. (1990a). *Labour Legislation 1980–1990, Philosophy and Impact,* Working Paper No 12. London, Department of Industrial Relations, LSE, University of London.

Metcalf, D. (1990b). 'Union presence and labour productivity in British manufacturing industry. A reply to Nolan and Marginson', *British Journal of Industrial Relations,* 28, 249–66.

Metcalf, D. (1990c). 'Movement in motion', *Marxism Today,* September, 32–5.

Millward, N. and Stevens, M. (1986). *British Workplace Industrial Relations 1980–1984.* Aldershot, Gower.

Milne, R. (1989). 'British power stations find it hard to come clean', *The New Scientist,* 23, 3.

Minford, P. (1980). 'Evidence presented to Treasury and Civil Service Committee', *Memorandum on Monetary Policy,* HC 720. London, HMSO.

Minford, P. (1988). 'Mrs Thatcher's economic reform programme', in R. Skidelsky (ed.) *Thatcherism.* Oxford, Basil Blackwell, p. 93–106.

Minogue, K. and Biddiss, M. (eds) (1987). *Thatcherism: Personality and Politics.* London, Macmillan.

Ministry of Agriculture Fisheries and Food (1979). *Farming and the Nation,* Cmnd 7458. London, HMSO.

Mitchell, N. (1987). 'Changing pressure group politics: the case of the TUC, 1976–1984', *British Journal of Political Science,* 17, pp. 509–17.

Mohan, J. (ed.) (1989). *The Political Geography of Contemporary Britain.* London, Macmillan.

Moran, M. (1979). 'The Conservative Party and the trade unions since 1974', *Political Studies,* xxvii, 38–53.

Moyser, H.W. and Josling, T.E. (1990). *Agricultural Policy Reform.* Ames, Iowa State University Press.

Muellbauer, J. (1986). 'Productivity and competitiveness in British manufacturing', *Oxford Review of Economic Policy,* 2 (3), Autumn, 1–25.

Muellbauer, J. (1990). *The Great British Housing Disaster.* London, Institute for Public Policy Research.

Murie, A. (1985). 'The nationalization of housing policy', in M. Loughlin, M.D. Gelfand and K. Young (eds) *Half-a-Century of Municipal Decline 1935–1985.* London, Allen & Unwin, pp. 187–201.

Murray, C. (1990). *The Emerging British Underclass.* London, IEA Health and Welfare Unit.

National Association of Health Authorities (1989). *The National Health Services Handbook,* 4th edn. London, Macmillan.

National Audit Office (1986). *Value for Money. Developments in the National Health Service.* London, HMSO.

National Audit Office (1987). *Competitive Tendering for Support Services in the National Health Service.* London, HMSO.

National Audit Office (1990). *The Elderly: Information Requirements for Supporting the Elderly and Implications of Personal Pensions for the National Insurance Fund,* HC 55. London, HMSO.

National Consumer Council (1988). *Consumer and Agricultural Policy.* London, HMSO.

Newell, A. and Symons, J. (1987). 'Corporatism, laissez-faire and the rise in unemployment', *European Economic Review*, 31, 567–614.

Nickell, S. and Wadhwani, S. (1990). 'Insider forces and wage determination', *Economic Journal*, 100, 496–509.

Nolan, P. and Marginson, P. (1990). 'Skating on thin ice? David Metcalf on trade unions and productivity', *British Journal of Industrial Relations*, 28, 227–47.

Norton, P. (1990). ' "The lady's not for turning": but what about the rest of the Party? Margaret Thatcher and the Conservative Party 1979–89'. Paper delivered at the Annual Meeting of the American Political Science Association, Atlanta, CA.

Odling-Smee, J. (1989). 'Assessment', in *UK Renaissance: Miracle or Mirage?* London, Shearson Lehman Hutton, pp. 26–8.

O'Leary, B. (1987). 'Why was the GLC abolished?', *International Journal of Urban and Regional Research*, 11, 193–217.

O'Riordan, T. (1988). 'The politics of environmental regulation in Britain', *Environment*, 30, 5–8 and 39–44.

O'Riordan, T. (1991). 'Stability and transformation in environmental government', *The Political Quarterly*, 62, 167–85.

O'Riordan, T., Kemp, R. and Purdue, M. (1988). *Sizewell B.* London, Macmillan.

O'Riordan, T. and Weale, A. (1989). 'Administrative reorganisation and policy change: The case of Her Majesty's Inspectorate of Pollution', *Public Administration*, 67, 227–95.

Paehlke, R. (1989). *Environmentalism and the Future of Progressive Politics.* New Haven, Yale University Press.

Pearce, D., Markandya, A. and Barbier, E. (1989). *Blueprints for a Green Economy.* London, Earthscan.

Pearce, F. (1986). 'Dirty water under the bridge', in E. Goldsmith and N. Hilyard (eds) *Green Britain or Industrial Wasteland.* Cambridge, Polity, 231–6.

Pendleton, A. (1991). 'Workplace Industrial Relations in a Public Corporation: Recent Developments in British Rail', University of Bradford Management Centre. Mimeo.

Peterson, J. (1989). 'Eureka and the symbolic politics of high technology', *Politics*, 9(1), 8–13.

Pettigrew, A., McKee, L. and Ferlie, E. (1989). 'Managing strategic service change in the NHS', *Health Service Management Research*, 2(1), 20–31.

Pimlott, B. (1989). 'Is the "postwar consensus" a myth?', *Contemporary Record*, 2(6), 12–14.

Pinder, J. (1985). 'Pragmatikos and federalis: reflections on a conference', *Government and Opposition*, 20, 473–87.

Pinder, J. (1989). 'The European Community and the Gaullist fallacy', *World Today*, 45, 55–6.

Plaskitt, J. (1981). 'The House of Lords and legislative harmonisation in the European Community', *Public Administration*, 59, 203–14.

Pollitt, C.J. *et al.* (1988). 'The reluctant managers: clinicians and budgets in the National Health Service', *Financial Accountancy and Management*, 4, 213–33.

Pollitt, C.J. *et al.* (1991). 'General management in the NHS: the initial impact 1983–88', *Public Administration*, 69, 61–84.

Pressman, J. and Wildavsky, A. (1984). *Implementation*, 3rd edn. Berkeley, University of California Press.

Rallings, C. and Thrasher, M. (1991). 'The community charge and the 1990 local elections', *Parliamentary Affairs*, 44, 172–84.

Regional Chairmen (1976). *Enquiring into the Working of the DHSS in Relation to Regional Health Authorities*. London, DHSS.

Rhodes, R.A.W. (1984). 'Continuity and change in British central–local relations: "the Conservative threat"', 1979–83', *British Journal of Political Science*, 14, 311–33.

Rhodes, R.A.W. (1986). *The National World of Local Government*. London, Allen & Unwin.

Rhodes, R.A.W. (1988). *Beyond Westminster and Whitehall*. London, Unwin Hyman.

Rhodes, R.A.W. (1990). 'Policy networks: a British perspective', *Journal of Theoretical Politics*, 2, 293–317.

Rhodes, R.A.W. (1991). 'Now nobody understands the system: the changing face of local government', in P. Norton (ed.) *New Directions in British Politics*. Aldershot, Edward Elgar, 83–112.

Rhodes, R.A.W. *et al.* (1992). 'Implementing Thatcherite policies: an annotated bibliography', *Essex Papers in Politics and Government*, forthcoming.

Rhodes, R.A.W., and Marsh, D. (1992). 'New directions in the study of policy networks', *European Journal of Political Research*, 21, 181–205.

Riddell, P. (1983). *The Thatcher Government*. Oxford, Martin Robertson.

Riddell, P. (1989). *The Thatcher Decade*. Oxford, Blackwell.

Ridge, M. and Smith, S. (1990). 'Local government finance: the 1990 reforms', *IFS Commentary*, No. 22. London, Institute for Fiscal Studies.

Ridley, N. (1988). 'HAs set for leading role – Ridley', *Housing Associations Weekly*, 24 June, 1 and 6.

Roberts, B. (1989). 'Trade unions', in D. Kavanagh and A. Seldon (eds) *The Thatcher Effect*. Oxford, Clarendon Press, pp. 64–79.

Royal Commission on the National Health Service (1979). *Report*, Cmnd 7615. London, HMSO.

Rutherford, M. (1981). *Can We Save the Common Market?*. Oxford, Basil Blackwell.

Sabatier, P. (1986a). 'Top-down and bottom-up approaches to implementation research', *Journal of Public Policy*, 6, 21–48.

Sabatier, P. (1986b). 'What can we learn from implementation research?', in F.X. Kaufman, G. Majone and V. Ostrom (eds) *Guidance, Control and Evaluation in the Public Sector*. Berlin and New York, de Gruyter, pp. 313–25.

Saunders, P. (1990). *A Nation of Home Owners*. London, Unwin Hyman.

Savage, S. and Robins, L. (eds) (1990). *Public Policy Under Thatcher*. London, Macmillan.

Secretary of State for Health (1991). *The Health of the Nation*, Cm 1523. London, HMSO.

Secretary of State for Health, Northern Ireland, Wales and Scotland (1989). *Working for Patients*, Cm 555. London, HMSO.

Seifert, R. (1989). 'Industrial relations in the school sector', in R. Mailly *et al. Industrial Relations in the Public Services*. London, Routledge, pp. 199–258.

Seldon, A. (1990). 'The Cabinet office and coordination, 1979–87', *Public Administration*, 68, 103–21.

Sharp, M. (1989). 'The community and the new technologies', in J. Lodge (ed.) *The European Community and the Challenge of the Future*. London, Pinter, pp. 202–20.

Shoard, M. (1987). *This Land is Our Land: The Struggle for Britain's Countryside*. London, Collins.

Shoard, M. (1990). 'Cutting the cost of countryside protection', *The Times*, 21 August.

Sieghart, P. (1979). *The Big Public Enquiry*. London, Council for Science and Society.

Skelcher, C. and Leach, S. (1990). 'Resource choice and the abolition process', *Local Government Studies*, 16, 33–46.

Skidelsky, R. (ed.) (1988). *Thatcherism*. London, Chatto & Windus.

Small, N. (1989). *Politics in the National Health Service*. Milton Keynes, Open University Press.

Smith, M. (1988). 'Britain and the United States: beyond the "special relationship"?', in P. Byrd (ed.) *British Foreign Policy Under Thatcher*. Oxford, Philip Allan, pp. 8–34.

Smith, M.J. (1990). *The Politics of Agricultural Support in Britain: The Development of Agricultural Policy Community*. Aldershot, Dartmouth.

Smith, M.J. (1991). 'From policy community to issue network: Salmonella in eggs and the new politics of food', *Public Administration*, 69, 235–55.

Smith, M.J. (1992). 'The agricultural policy community: maintaining a closed community', in R.A.W. Rhodes and D. Marsh (eds) *Policy Networks in British Government*. Oxford, Oxford University Press, forthcoming.

Smith, S. (1991). 'Distributional issues in local taxation', *The Economic Journal*, 101, 585–99.

Smith-Garvine, S. and Bennett, S. (1990). *Index of Percentage Utilisation of Labour No. 55*. Birmingham, University of Aston Business School, pp. 4–16.

Social Services Committee (1989). *Ninth Report: Social Security Changes Implementation in April 1988*, HC 437–1. London, HMSO.

Spencer, P. (1989). 'The UK productivity renaissance', in *UK Economic Renaissance: Miracle or Mirage?* London, Shearson Lehman Hutton, pp. 1–15.

Steel, D. and Heald, D. (eds) (1984). *Privatizing Public Enterprise*. London, Royal Institute of Public Administration.

Stewart, J. and Stoker, G. (1989a). 'Introduction', in J. Stewart and G. Stoker (eds) *The Future of Local Government*. London, Macmillan, pp. 1–5.

Stewart, J. and Stoker, G. (eds) (1989b). *The Future of Local Government*. London, Macmillan.

Taylor, A. (1987). *Trade Unions and Politics*. London, Macmillan.

Taylor, P. (1989). 'The new dynamics of EC integration in the 1980s', in J. Lodge (ed.) *The European Community and the Challenge of the Future*. London. Pinter, pp. 3–25.

Taylor-Gooby, P. (1990). 'Social welfare: the unkindest cuts', in R. Jowell, S. Witherspoon and L. Brook (eds) *British Social Attitudes. The 7th Report*. Aldershot, Gower, pp. 1–20.

Teague, P. (1989). *The European Community: The Social Dimension*. London, Kogan Page, Cranfield School of Management Monograph 4.

Thomas, H. (1984). 'Looking hard and fast for the sane and the serious', *The Guardian*, 13 November.

Thornton, R. (1990). *The New Homeless*. London, SHAC.

Travers, T. (1986). *The Politics of Local Government Finance*. London, Allen & Unwin.

Treasury and Civil Service Select Committee (1988). *European Community Finance*, HC 358. London, HMSO.

Tuchman-Matthews, J. (ed.) (1991). *Preserving the Global Environment: The Challenge of Shared Leadership*. New York, Norton.

Tugendhat, C. and Wallace, W. (1988). *Options for British Foreign Policy in the 1990s*. London, Routledge & Kegan Paul for the Royal Institute of International Affairs.

Twitchett, C.C. (ed.) (1981). *Harmonisation in the EEC*. London, Macmillan.

Undy, R. and Martin, R. (1984). *Ballots and Trade Union Democracy*. Oxford, Blackwell.

United Kingdom Government (1986). *Diverting Land from Cereals*. Sn 26731/1/86, Rev 1 (Agri). Mimeo.

Vines, D. (1989). 'Is the "Thatcher Experiment" still on course?', *Royal Bank of Scotland Review*, no. 149, 3–14.

Vogel, D. (1986). *National Styles of Regulation: Environmental Policing in Great Britain and the United States*. Ithaca, NY, Cornell University Press.

Waldegrave, W. (1987). *Some Reflections on Conservative Housing Policy*. London, Conservative New Services.

Wallace, H. (1986). 'The British presidency of the European Community's Council of Ministers: the opportunity to persuade', *International Affairs*, 62, 583–99.

Wallace, W. (1984). *Britain's Bilateral Links Within Western Europe*, Chatham House Paper No. 23. London, Routledge & Kegan Paul, for Royal Institute of International Affairs.

Wallace, W. (1986). 'What price interdependence? Sovereignty and interdependence in British politics', *International Affairs*, 62, 367–89.

Wallace, H. and Wallace, W. (1990). 'Strong State or weak State in foreign policy? The contradictions of Conservative liberalism, 1979–87', *Public Administration*, 68, 83–101.

Walters, A. (1986). *Britain's Economic Renaissance, Mrs Thatcher's Reforms 1979–84*. Oxford, Oxford University Press.

Ward, H. with Samways, D. and Benton, T. (1990). 'Environmental politics and policy', in P. Dunleavy *et al.* (eds) *Developments in British Politics 3*. London, Macmillan, pp. 221–45.

Webb, A. and Wistow, G. (1981), *Whither State Welfare?* London, Royal Institute of Public Administration.

Webb, A., Wistow, G. and Hardy, B. (1986). *Structuring Local Policy Environments: Central Local Relationships in the Health and Personal Social Services*. Loughborough, Centre for Research in Social Policy.

Wedderburn, Lord (1985). 'The new policies in industrial relations law', in P. Fosh and C. Littler (eds) *Industrial Relations and the Law in the 1980s*. Aldershot, Gower, pp. 22–65.

Weekes, B. *et al.* (1975). *Industrial Relations and the Limits of the Law*. Oxford, Blackwell.

Wells, J. (1989). 'The economy after ten years: stronger or weaker?', *Economics*, Winter, 151–7.

Whitehead, C. (1983). 'Housing under the Conservatives', *Public Money*, June, 15–61.

Whitelegg, J. (1989). 'Transport policy: off the rails', in Mohan, J. (ed.) *The Political Geography of Contemporary Britain*. London, Macmillan, pp. 187–207.

Williams, R. (1985). 'The energy policies of the 1979–83 Conservative Government', in P. Jackson (ed.) *Implementing Policy Initiatives*. London, Royal Institute of Public Administration, pp. 261–85.

Willmott, P. and Murie, A. (1988). *Polarisation and Social Housing*. London, Policy Studies Institute.

Wilson, R. (1985). 'Westminster and Brussels: the relationship of parliament to the EEC', *Public Administration*, 63 (2), 235–40.

Wistow, G. (1986). 'Increasing private provision of social care: implications for policy', in R. Lewis *et al. Care and Control: Social Services and the Private Sector*. London, Policy Studies Institute, pp. 7–20.

Wistow, G. (1992). 'The Health Service policy community: professionals pre-eminent or under challenge?', in D. Marsh and R.A.W. Rhodes (eds) *Policy Networks in British Government*. Oxford, Oxford University Press, forthcoming.

Wistow, G. and Henwood, M. (1989). 'Planning in a mixed economy', in R. Parry (ed.) *Privatisation*. London, Jessica Kingsley.

Wren-Lewis, S. (1989). 'UK manufacturing productivity: an international perspective', in *UK Economic Renaissance: Miracle or Mirage?* London, Shearson Lehman Hutton, pp. 16–25.

Young, H. (1989). *One of Us*. London, Macmillan.

Young, H. and Sloman, A. (1986). *The Thatcher Phenomenon*. London, BBC Books.

Young, K. (1990). 'Living under threat', in R. Jowell, S. Witherspoon and L. Brook (eds) *British Social Attitudes. The 7th Report*. Aldershot, Gower, pp. 77–108.

Young, O. (1989). *International Cooperation: Building Regimes for Natural Resources and the Environment*. Ithaca, NY, Cornell University Press.

Name index

Subject index